No Problem Here

A practical approach to education and "race" in white schools

Chris Gaine

Hutchinson
London Sydney Melbourne Auckland Johannesburg

Hutchinson Education

An imprint of Century Hutchinson Ltd

62-65 Chandos Place, London WC2N 4NW

Century Hutchinson Australia Pty Ltd
P O Box 496, 16-22 Church Street, Hawthorn,
Victoria 3122, Australia

Century Hutchinson New Zealand Ltd
P O Box 40-086, Glenfield, Auckland 10,
New Zealand

Century Hutchinson South Africa (Pty) Ltd
P O Box 337, Berglvei 2012, South Africa

First published 1987
Reprinted with revisions 1988

Set in 10/12pt Baskerville Roman

Printed and bound in Great Britain by
Richard Clay Ltd, Bungay, Suffolk

British Library Cataloguing in Publication Data

Gaine, Chris
No problem here: a practical approach to education and race in white
schools.
1.   Race relations in school management—Great Britain
I.   Title
370.19'342'0941   LC212.5

ISBN 0 09 172971 8

Contents

For Adam and Luke

Preface

There is inevitably something autobiographical about this book. I was convinced of what I wrote in chapter 1 many years before I wrote it, and it was trying to act upon that conviction in my own school which led me into wider policy development, and with initial and in-service training. There is an irony in the biographical element too: what at one time made me move schools is now publishable. In looking for signs of hope I could view this change with optimism, but the pace of change and the resistance to it in some places is not always encouraging.

There must always be too many people to thank individually in the development of any book, but several deserve special mention. Sincere thanks to the many pupils at Hreod Burna school, Swindon, who showed me that the effort was worthwhile; to Christine Greenwood, who lived with the struggles behind my work in school; to Clive Norris, for his resilient dedication to anti-racism; to Cristina Bennett, the best teacher I shall ever work with; to Caroline Beatty, a touchstone over many things; and to Ann Miller, who had constant faith in my ability to write the book and in its value.

Individual chapters relied on helpful comments from several people; Chris Mullard, Richard Hatcher and Robin Richardson in chapter 2; Cristina Bennett in chapters 3 and 4; Caroline Beatty, Liz Gerschel and John Twitchin in chapter 5; John Fisher in chapter 7; and Ann Miller and John Naysmith in chapter 9. They all may well disagree with the end results.

Chris Gaine
January 1987

Part One
Principles...What's the Issue?

1 "There aren't many of them here so there isn't a problem"

Eleven years ago I began teaching in the integrated humanities department of an 11−18 comprehensive which would now be called "progressive", situated in an almost entirely white area. It was taken for granted by the department that unfavourable stereotypes of other cultures should not be presented to children, and I am sure all my colleagues would have expressed disapproval of racist remarks. We might be more sophisticated today: a second year unit on India which I produced contains items I would no longer use, and our fifth year material on development/underdevelopment must have told many pupils that (black) people in poor countries are "thick". That aside, however, and given that we were learning, we were quite consciously trying to create a non-Eurocentric curriculum.

In my second year of teaching I was at a meeting set up by our local Council for Racial Equality, listening to a speaker talking about education. It is something of an injustice to the speaker, although not a major one, to summarize his message as "present other cultures favourably in school and kids will be more appreciative of the value of others' cultures, and this will diminish racism". This is a familiar stance today, as it was then in some areas, but not usually in white ones, and would generally be referred to as "multiculturalism". It struck me forcibly then that I already knew it did not work. It may have a part to play, but to hope that by some process of osmosis, ideas about cultural relativity or knowledge about Ramadan will transform the views on "race" of many white schoolchildren is to hope for far too much. This latter stance might be referred to today as an anti-racist one, but these labels will be considered at length in the next chapter.

For the moment, however, since some people reading this will not be convinced that there is anything particularly amiss with the racial attitudes of white schoolchildren, I want to try and demonstrate something of the attitudes about "race" of what I take to be typical white teenagers in largely or entirely white areas. It is these attitudes which must be our starting point and not, as the title of this chapter suggests, the presence or proportion of minority ethnic groups in our schools.

White teenagers' attitudes

I would point initially to the first chapter of Robert Jeffcoate's book *Positive Image*.[1]* He outlines the experience of some primary and nursery headteachers of schools with small minorities of mostly Indian and Pakistani children. They began by doubting the research evidence on racial attitudes in young children presented to them by Jeffcoate, or at least denying its validity in their own schools. The account is worth reading in full, but briefly he gets them to play the Balloon Game with their pupils, which consists of them imagining they are cast adrift in a balloon and it lands somewhere they would not like, and now write on . . . . They also tried other things, more appropriate to different ages, and although there was a complex range of attitudes shown by the children, many of the heads would, I imagine, echo the sentiment Jeffcoate quotes:

As the result of observation and some research I became aware that prejudice did exist among the children in my school. I should have said quite firmly before my participation in the project that this was not so.[2]

  Looking at a different age range, in the BBC series "Multicultural Education"[3] Gus Horsepool, who works a lot with young people in discussions about "race", speaks of the Jekyll and Hyde transformation that comes over "nice ordinary young people" once trust has been established and the discussion turns to "race". I have no doubt that, like Jeffcoate's group, many of their teachers would not believe it.

  That is all very well, but it would not convince me unless I already suspected it to be true, so I have to suggest that anyone in doubt should try testing their pupils' racial attitudes themselves before they read any further. Perhaps everyone should do this, because attitudes vary from year to year and between classes in the same school, and it would hardly seem wise to embark on the reorientation towards the issue of "race" in white schools which is the concern of this book without testing the market. With secondary age pupils one will probably not have to resort to much subterfuge to get some interesting results. These extracts are from a class of 12 year olds simply asked to write about "Britain's problems".

* Superior figures refer to the References at the end of each chapter.

I think that human population is a problem. It's a problem all over the world because there are so many immigrants in the different countries, and many of them get over-populated. In Britain there is at least 40% black and Pakistani people. This means that 40% white people will be out of jobs. If Britain only let about 10% immigrants [crossed out] black and Pakistani people in to the country then they would be able to keep the population down to a minimum. I think that different countries should keep their own people there except for holidays and only a certain percent may enter of leave the country at that time of year.

Over the last few years the human population has been slowly increasing with all these foreign people coming over. This is beginning to cause a problem. At night and day you get fighting between the blacks and whites, there is the National Front, people getting dirty and smelly homes as well as people getting bad jobs. What should be done about this is to send the blacks and other foreign people back to where they came from, only let them come over here for holidays.

Not all the class wrote about "race", and these date back to 1979, when immigration was more of a conscious issue. In 1981 it was the "riots". I received the following extracts in 1984, having simply asked the class of 13 year olds to write about "black and coloured people in Britain". (At this stage it is probably worth anticipating a point about terminology. I usually find that in white areas "black" is considered not quite nice as an adjective; since I nevertheless use it I am often taken to mean Afro-Caribbean people, so if I say "black or coloured" in a preliminary exercise like this I am fairly sure of being understood.)[4]

The entirely mixed ability class is divided almost equally in their views, though the majority express feelings which are predominantly negative, and these are the ones printed here, along with an example of a "positive" or anti-racist viewpoint. I would hesitate to quantify this further, but in terms of teachers' usual notions of "ability" there is no obvious correlation with the kind of viewpoint expressed. Few are neutral or non-committal, they all seem to have the idea that the topic is one you have an opinion about, and quite a strong opinion. Jobs are frequently mentioned, as is language and religion. The majority are unable to distinguish between Pakistanis (nearly always Muslims), and Indians (in their town nearly always Sikhs). The mixture of attitudes is often striking, for example an apparent acceptance followed by a vehement denial of religious freedom.

Caroline: A large percentage of British people resent the presence of black and coloured people. Their view is perhaps justified. Britain's economic problems are far from new, and these people add to the unemployment and housing problems. Racism is responsible for much of the fighting and disruption which this country suffers from. Although they have a right if they are permitted to live in this country it causes trouble and violence. They should try and organise their own countries so they can live happy lives with people of their own race. I do not see that it should be the British problem to cope with the needs of foreigners. Although they may resent whites being in their country, that is, South Africa, if they were an organised, civilised race they would take steps to take over and seriously rearrange the way their country is run. I therefore feel that black and coloured people should be restricted in the places that they live. Many Pakistanis have also come to Britain. This causes the same troubles as coloured or black people. Their country is not as threatening to Britain as the Russians or Japanese as politically they keep very much within themselves. I still feel that they should not be allowed in this country as it causes many racial problems, and much friction. They do not fit in well with the British race, and I think they would do far better to stay in their own country and live the Pakistani way of life.

Tracy: I think some of the white people don't like the coloured people then they get causing trouble. The coloured people shouldn't be allowed into Britain, they have their own place and they cause trouble when they are here. The coloured people wouldn't like it if us white people went over there to live. I think Pakistanis are horrible people.

As with several later examples there seems to be a complete ignorance about colonial history, perhaps not surprising in 13 year olds, yet many schools are unlikely to fill in these gaps. The solution of racial conflict by the removal of the victims is a depressingly common proposal by youngsters.

Chris: Black people shouldn't be allowed to live in Britain. Our country lets these people in too easy. In Africa, they make a big fuss if any people want to live in the south of Africa. If they stop other people living in their country then we should do the same. It is alright if they visit the country but they cannot live here. Already a lot of black people are in Britain today. Soon they are going to over-run the country.

The geographical and political confusion is self-evident. I do not know exactly what Chris is implying in his reference to southern Africa, nor the logic of applying this to all black people, though Caroline does something similar. These three are more unambiguously hostile than any others, and more factually misinformed. Specifically, their education has failed them so far on the following points:

1   Black people are neither responsible for employment nor housing problems in Britain.
2   The removal of the targets of a society's racism begs a few questions, one of which is about the historical pedigree of such a solution.
3   Immigration did not have a simple genesis in "coping with the needs of foreigners".
4   South African people die daily trying to "seriously rearrange the way their country is run".
5   South Africa is not the only country in the world where black people live.
6   The kind of limits and restrictions on entry favoured by these children have been in force for twenty years.
7   There is no possibility in numerical terms of black people over-running the British Isles.

I use the word "misinformed" rather than "ignorant", since these are not random, chance misconceptions held by the pupils. As the following extracts show, and those in chapters 3 and 4, they are patterned, they are informed of the things they believe, but they are wrong. Thus a much more important point than number 7 is not the real numbers but where their ideas about numbers come from, and why they matter.

  Most of the rest of the pupils combine good intentions with confused bigotry.

Adam: Really, I don't mind black people in Britain as most don't hurt us in any way. Though some people are a bit prejudiced I don't mind them over here as long as there isn't many of them. If anything it's the black race that really get the pounding as some aren't allowed in pubs or to join in some activities. So, as long as there is a certain amount of them I think white people will always rule this country. Though there is a danger of black people having families and the children, because of growing up in England, will stay.

Amanda: I think having black and coloured people in Britain is fantastic. I think we should mix together. I mean, they've got as much right as we have. They are not for Britons to whip and slap. They're very good workers, good doctors. English people haven't got the brains and patience to do much hard work. The only thing I don't want to see is them taking over the country, just to be friends to it. And I want Britons to be friends towards them. What's the matter with Pakistanis, they're all right, they're no different from us except their religion. I don't mind but why don't they go back to their own country?

It is difficult to equate the contradiction of the last sentence in each of these with the main sentiments expressed, which at least demonstrate some awareness of racism. It cannot be the Asian/Black distinction mentioned below since Amanda mentions doctors earlier. Perhaps they begin by writing what they expect teacher to want, then give in to what they really want to say, or perhaps the brief period of thinking and writing reminded them of the scale of our difficulties and so they dived for the simple solution, "send 'em back" ...or sterilise them?

Gary: I think black and coloured and white should be treated all the same as we are all human beings. But what I don't agree with is the people who come over here because of troubles in their country and come along and think they can live the same as they did over there, keeping their religion on, silly things like that, what sort of meat they eat and other such things. If they are going to live in our country they must live our way, if we went over there and asked for wine I'm sure they wouldn't change their ways so we could have it.

Here we have a generalized moral position to begin with, starkly contrasting with the unequal treatment with regard to religious freedom which he then recommends. The equation of Saudi Islamic laws on alcohol with those of all black countries is common, as is the idea that most blacks in Britain are refugees.

Simon: I think that in a way black people should not be allowed in our country, just because they've been kicked out or thrown out of their country. But I don't see we should get such a vast number living in Britain. Why couldn't they be sent to other countries? People who get onto the blacks and coloureds shouldn't really, because they're only human like us and they should be able to live in a country with no trouble. But when they start trouble I think they should be punished just like us.

Again we have here a mixture of benevolence and apparent goodwill, with clear support for repatriation. There is also a confusion of immigrants and their descendants with refugees, presumably a confusion left over from the Vietnamese boat people. In this piece, as with a later one, there is the idea gleaned from somewhere that black people resent being punished, that they get away with things whites would not. None of this can conceivably be first-hand experience.

A common distinction between and preference for Afro-Caribbeans rather than Asians is evident in the following quotations. The usual explanation for this is that it has something to do with class, and the hostility is certainly often expressed in terms of, for example, "taking over shops". Almost as often, however, what is expressed is resentment at the perceived cultural distance.

Neil: I think black people and coloured people are taking over jobs. The Pakistanis wear turbans for a religion and bang their heads against a big wall and kiss the wall, and they smell.

Lorraine: I think black people should be allowed in Britain. Most of them are friendly and well mannered, but Indians I think should go back to their own country. They smell and they take our jobs and houses. If there wasn't so many Indians then there wouldn't be so many people out of work. Most Indians think they own the place. They were brought over here as people to work in the railways but then they started up their own businesses and took over. Blacks don't smell and there aren't so many of them. I've got a lot of black friends and I get on really well. But Indians are so big headed it makes me feel sick. Pakistanis should be banned altogether from this country.

Kara: Black and coloured people are equal to white and any other colour. It doesn't matter what colour you are so long as you are a good kind person. I'm glad Britain accepts any person(s) that are any colour. I am certainly not prejudiced and love the common fact that the colour of the skin has nothing to do with the heart. Although we do get thrown back when the question is asked about a black man or lady wanting to marry a white man or lady. Will God accept this? My views on black and coloured people in Britain are perfectly normal. Love is the greatest thing since Moses parted the sea. Also comparing the church [Christian] to the black church [gospel] I prefer the gospel church. Any colour does not matter, it's your personality that counts. Pakistanis are the same as anybody although they don't tend to be social with anyone else they stick to their own language, so I think if they're gonna be like that they can go back to their own country. I don't mind the colour but when it comes to the religion I will rule that out, all this babble and boys having to grow long hair, heads in turbans and hankies. What a load of rubbish.

Neil: Many people are against coloureds and also against blacks. There is a lot of people who would like to see coloureds and blacks chucked out of this country. They always stir up too much trouble and then don't like being punished for it. Every coloured person likes and wants everyone to give them what they want when they want it. The Pakistanis always wear turbans. The reasons for this is their religion. The Pakis have a very strong religion. Most of them are friendly but you get the odd few that are violent. They also do not get married normally because marriages are all arranged. Also they are pigs.

John: The black people came over to our country to get jobs when it is hard for the white people to get jobs. They come here and take our jobs so we can't get none. I reckon that they should get back to their country and stay there. And the Chinese should go back as well. The Pakistanis take over all our shops, they try to even scrounge money to stay open on Sundays. All Pakistanis do that and when you walk in their shop they smell of curry.

Michael: I think the black people should live in a society where they won't be talked about as not a human species. Even though I call blacks names they can take the mouth. They take over most of the shops and usually they smell of some sort. In a road near here you go in their shop and you can't even understand them. They don't go around calling us names. Pakistanis are taking over the population. When the school bus comes we have a Pakistani driver that wears a turban. We have a Pakistani doctor who does our BCGs. I think they should get out of the country unless they were born here.

One can sense here that Neil begins to write in the sort of reasonable way he thinks is expected of him, and then warms to his task. The word "intolerance" comes most strongly to mind on reading these, and suggests two further points which these pupils need educating about, namely:

1   Cultural difference does not have to signify inferiority, a nuisance, or a threat.
2   Pakistanis do not generally wear turbans, and to confuse religions and backgrounds so completely is to be insulting.

Here is a different kind of comment:

Simon: I think black and coloured people are all right in this country. I
  think that the white people started the Brixton riots. I would like to see the
  government ban the National Front. I would like coloured and white people
  to live in peace.

But Simon's comments are unique in the class.

The class were also asked to write about other things, so the writing
was disguised as a general current affairs lesson. They also wrote on
football hooligans, whom they all condemned, the Russians, about
whom they had mixed feelings, and Mrs Thatcher. In another book
their feelings about Thatcher would make an interesting study. With
only two exceptions they were uncomplimentary to say the least.
Perhaps they do not know her views on immigration?

The school these children attend is a large comprehensive with
perhaps 2 per cent of the pupils being black. The catchment area is a
truly comprehensive one otherwise.[5] Pupils are misinformed and
intolerant about many things, but my thesis here is simply that they
are not just misinformed but dangerously so. If anyone means it when
they say that Britain is a multicultural society then these comments —
highly typical of white British children — have to be taken as giving
clear imperatives for the curriculum.

At about the same time as much of the work in this book the
Rampton (later Swann) Committee was in operation. It provides
some compelling evidence from different LEAs about the racial
attitudes of white children:

[A]... major conclusion which we feel must regrettably be drawn from the
findings of this project, is in relation to the widespread existence of racism,
whether unintentional and "latent", or overt and aggressive, in the schools
visited.... The project revealed widespread evidence of racism in all the areas
covered, ranging from unintentional racism and patronising and stereotyped
ideas about ethnic minority groups combined with an appalling ignorance of
their cultural backgrounds and life styles and of the facts of race and
immigration, to extremes of overt racial hatred and "National Front" style
attitudes....[6]

Not to do something about this, Swann argues, "constitutes a
fundamental mis-education".

Teachers' reactions

Of course there are much less effective and much more misleading ways of trying to gather this kind of data. Robin Richardson cites the following example witnessed by him, a gruesome one in more ways than one.

"Now," he said, "do we have any racial discrimination in Brackenhead? Do we? Who can tell me? Jane?"

[The scene was a secondary school classroom which I happened to visit recently. I shall recount the episode faithfully, though also, I must admit, selectively. It went as follows:]

"...Jane? Come on Jane, you heard the question, do we have any racial discrimination in Brackenhead?"
"Yes sir".
"Have we Jane? Have we really?"
"No sir".
"You're quite right, Jane, good, we have no racial discrimination in...."
"Sir".
"Come on Jane, what is it?"
"Sir there's this Pakkie grocer near us, and last Saturday night someone threw a brick through his window."
"Oh, I see, well, tell me Jane, er, what sort of a person would do that?"
"Dunno sir."
"Jane, would you say that it was a very nasty, mean-minded, prejudiced sort of a person?"
"Yes sir."
"Good, Jane, yes you're quite right."

After the lesson I went with the teacher to the staffroom.

"We've just had", he said to a colleague, "a really good discussion about race relations."[7]

Before the reader goes off to try and get responses like those of my 13 year olds for her- or himself I would like to issue the warning that even with such findings many colleagues in the same school, teaching the same children, simply will not believe that significant levels of hostility exist. This seems to me to be for one or a combination of four reasons.

First, colleagues may not have examined their own assumptions and preconceptions about race, immigration, and prejudice, so the things pupils say may simply not grate on their ears the way they would on others'. For those who do not consider this issue important, pupils' attitudes are simply part of the background noise, they do not register.

Second, teachers are generally aware that this can be an explosive issue and not an easy one to handle in a classroom, or fear that to do so "will make things worse". An HMI document based on meetings held in five LEAs found that

...there was general agreement that race relations in schools were a matter of considerable concern, and that there was a need to respond to this concern.

It also found that teachers often ignore things because "racism is difficult and sensitive territory".[8] Some will argue (with politicians', LEA, governors', head's and parental support in many cases) that it is no business of the school to go into controversial matters of this sort. I will take up this argument later in this chapter, and offer practical pathways through it in chapters 3 and 4. Meanwhile, it is worth noting that some of those most anxious about opening this particular Pandora's Box would rather it was not there at all, so they deny its existence or its rightful place in school.

Third, teachers are usually telling the truth when they say they have never heard children expressing racist attitudes. Particularly in white schools it does not tend to arise as a public issue in chemistry, or typing. We can note here the curious phenomenon of *Grange Hill*, not its "race" content specifically but the fact that children seem to like it while teachers seldom see it as anything but an annoying travesty of school life. So it is, from the teachers' point of view, but for large numbers of children school is the backdrop against which they act out the important things in their lives, friendships, group values and so on. The important things happen between lessons in *Grange Hill* and in real schools, and we teachers are seldom privy to this world.

Fourth, teachers in white areas often point to the small numbers of black children in the school as indications that there is "no problem". "Jasvir is very well integrated", "Carol was elected class representative", "Balvinder's best friend is a white girl" and so on. In fact this is entirely beside the point. Children (and adults) are easily capable of having positive feelings about individuals they know, but simultaneously holding generalized negative attitudes about the group that person belongs to. Individual black children are frequently told, "Oh you're alright, it's all the others...." One of the girls mentioned above, a model to white teachers' eyes of integration and a living demonstration of the racial harmony in the school, had this to say about her time there:

On quite a few, a number of occasions I did have quite a lot of difficulties, I only wish I didn't have them... but it was mainly in the corridors, you know when there weren't any teachers around, when we weren't under supervision at all, or in classrooms when the teacher arrived late perhaps, and you'd often get called a Paki, or "what are you doing in this country" or "why don't you go back where you came from?" Most of the time it was kids who did know me; and I had friends, I had a lot of friends in that school, they never, sort of, did anything to me at all, they didn't even look at me as an Indian. But it was mostly the sort of kids who were ignorant, if I could put it like that.... On the whole I think it happened at least three times a month, a weekly event. It happened in school a lot, but on the streets it happened twice as much.... Before the teacher arrived sometimes you'd get asked "What does your father do? Oh, my father does such and such. Is it true that black people were slaves? Oh, you're supposed to be my slave, you're supposed to be my nanny, go and get me this, go and get me that." And it was often like, "Go and nick some paper from the teacher's drawer, you have to do it, you'd probably be best at it." It was that kind of stuff. This was mostly when I was 15 or 16.... I did confide in one teacher... but she just said to me that oh, maybe it doesn't happen too much, when it happens again you just let me know. You know, it's all very well for the teacher to say "well she seems okay", but seems and being are two different things. Obviously there is not going to be that overt racism when the teachers are around, the kids are obviously going to be a lot more under control... but it isn't like that at all.... I resent the fact of being called a Paki in as much as I wouldn't call someone fatty or skinny, or four-eyes. Paki to me is an insult as much as "curry muncher" is, what if I didn't like curry? Curry muncher, black blob, smelly, you stink of garlic.... What I don't understand is when people say to me "Oh, you're okay, because you're very westernised, it's just the rest." Well I do happen to be a very big part of the rest. This is very insulting.[9]

All of these reasons are important factors in people's resistance to the idea that "race" has much to do with education for whites. Teachers' anxiety about controversy, their often genuine unawareness of pupils' attitudes, the apparent "integration" of the few black pupils, can all collude with of our own unexamined prejudices to produce a pernicious conspiracy of inaction.

Prejudice and racism

The issue as posed so far is one of attitudes, and even if one's colleagues do believe that the kind of attitudes revealed above exist in the school a common response is "Well, yes, but it works both ways doesn't it, I mean they're prejudiced against us as well aren't they?" This is to misunderstand the distinction between racism and racial prejudice, and since it is racism that I think we should be tackling in our schools I should begin to distinguish between the two. Black people can be prejudiced against whites just as easily as the other way round, and many whites would feel that this prejudice is more openly displayed towards them than any they express themselves. A key difference, however, is that these psychologically equivalent "prejudices" have different causes and different effects. The latter has its origin in our colonial past, our subjection and domination of black people, and the beliefs which evolved to justify and legitimate this. Some of these beliefs are still common currency, and the currency remains valid because it is easily converted into today's coinage of declining Britain, structural unemployment, massive economic uncertainty and the conscious and unconscious quest for a plausible "cause". The former, black prejudice against whites, has its origin in a generalized suspicion of whites brought about by patterns of systematic discrimination in employment, housing, immigration law, policing, media representation and the provision of services of all kinds, experienced by black people in Britain over the past 35 years, and colonial subjection for two centuries prior to that.[10]

So much for causes. The effects of black and white prejudice are even less equal, because black people on the whole do not have the power to disadvantage whites. Although this is partly a matter of relative numbers, it is mostly because of the economic and political positions held by white people and those held by black people. The usual formula here is that racial prejudice plus power is racism; therefore although a black African state could be racist towards whites living there, black people in Britain cannot be racist since, on the whole, they have not the power to put their prejudices into practice. It is not simply numbers, of course — blacks outnumber whites many times over in South Africa but given the distribution of power there I cannot see black people being "racist" in any useful sense of the term (but prejudiced, certainly). Similarly, in areas of Southall black people outnumber whites, but they do not control the media, the police, the schools or anything else apart from some local employment opportunities. This understanding of racism will be returned to and developed, but it serves for the present to answer the "They're just as bad as us" argument.

To return to our pupils, however, I am offering evidence that because of the short and long term effects of the attitudes and beliefs of typical white pupils, their beliefs can be called racist. Our education system claims to deplore this. Further, I have said that this is not a matter of "ignorance" but one of misinformation, and a consequent attempt by teenagers to make sense of the world. The problem is greater than "understanding other cultures" because teenagers are less troubled by whether Sikh customs are "funny" or not than by the threat they think black people pose, for example: "There are too many here", "Why are they here anyway?" "They take our jobs (and live on social security)", "They mug us", "They're always fighting the police", "They're taking over all the shops." These things are said and believed, in my experience, by the majority of teenagers. It is against this kind of backdrop that they are dismissive or hostile about aspects of minority cultures (though I am not for a moment underestimating the effect of our cultural heritage, general ethnocentrism, textbook portrayal of black people, media representation, and the rest). It is also worth noting recent evidence from Cochrane and Billig[11] that about 30 per cent of white 16 year olds at school gave the National Front or the British Movement as their first choice political party, on the sole basis of their policies of forcible "repatriation" of black people.

It is not surprising that teenagers think that way. Hartmann and Husband demonstrated long ago[12] that the dominant message carried by the national dailies about "race" was that blacks = immigration = large numbers = a problem. Perhaps the Nationality Act has put an end to that particular paranoia, although judging from recent immigration appeals this seems doubtful,[13] indeed it is far more likely to have further legitimized the message earlier carried by the popular press. An illustration of how sensitized people are to media coverage of anything to do with immigration, is that two years after the arrival of at most 16,000 Vietnamese, my pupils listed them as one of the largest immigrant groups in Britain. The dominant image in the national press and TV has now shifted, it would seem, to black people as having problems and causing problems; it is now an image of conflict.

There is no need to be a Marxist or even left-wing to locate the teenage anxieties outlined above in the material conditions of the late

1970s and the 1980s (and beyond, of course). The real condition of millions of teenagers is that they are scared, and whatever their bravado about the dole or lack of "realism" about career hopes they are scared of the future they see before them. This is an old cliché, it goes back to explanations of the Germans' alacrity at taking anti-semitism on board, but unless it is actually faced as a reality in teenagers' worlds — though not necessarily in their awareness — I do not believe that teaching about "race" is going to touch secondary pupils at all.

Anna Sullivan says this of young National Front activists she talks with in London:

a) they are extremely politicised;

b) they hated teachers and bosses;

c) they were alienated from the trade union movement and the intellectualism and rhetoric of the left; and

d) they believe in revolution where the order of society would change and they would no longer be on the scrapheap. Racism is one of the obvious planks of their politics but not their only objective. Fascism is the extreme expression of racism but these kids did not invent racism.... The only thing that these kids felt they had going for them was they were white and British....[14]

A task for schools?

Most of the teenagers in white areas are by no means as clear about "race" as active members of the young National Front, nor as firm and unshakeable in their views, but what attempt is made to shake them? Making them question their assumptions means we have to teach about the real world, about who they think poses a threat to them, the kind of responses they want to make to those perceived threats, and how they come to perceive them as threats in the first place. It means dealing with some of the unpalatable truths about life in Britain for black people, and thus being critical, which returns us to the point set aside earlier about what a school's business is.

The role of the school ought to be a straightforward matter, since we have it on the authority of the DES that school curricula should on occasion be critical:

[Schools have]... the responsibility of educating the "autonomous citizen", a person able to think and act for herself or himself, to resist exploitation, to innovate and to be vigilant in the defence of liberty.... Curricula give out messages; in any curriculum the selection of subjects and skills that are taught and of the attitudes and activities that are encouraged implies certain political and social assumptions and values, however unconscious. It is not the responsibility of education in this country to give direct ideological support to every aspect of the existing system.... The 1980s may well be years of even greater political and economic tension than the present day.... If so, the greater will be the need for a basic political and economic education for all.... They will need to understand different viewpoints, appreciate conflicting motives, resist tendentious influences, and appraise critically ....[15]

The DES also affirms as one of its purposes of learning in school: "To help pupils to develop personal moral values, respect for religious values, and tolerance of other races, religions, and ways of life."[16] With or without this respectable support it is hard to understand anyone's opposition to the inclusion in the curriculum of the issues of the day. It is also hard to understand why, in eleven years of compulsory schooling, most schools fairly systematically avoid contentious social issues if at all possible. Yet we do. Sex is all right, as are lessons on non-Christianity, prejudice, CND, baby battering and abortion, although these are often only included in peripheral general studies courses (needed, apparently, predominantly by the less able or those going to university), or confined to RE or Education in Personal Relationships. I am not unaware of or unsupportive of the developments in active tutorial work which have come about in the last two or three years, yet the mainstream examined curriculum remains largely untouched by anything contentious unless it happened at least twenty years ago.

   I do not want to do my colleagues an injustice here. I am aware of the battles fought in some schools to replace dry old constitutional history with more modern content and skills-based methods. I know many geographers have slogged away for years for the "third world" element in upper school geography,[17] and I can list other successful moves towards promoting pupils' critical awareness in English, RE, economics, politics and social studies, all achieved with no sacrifice to the standards we have to maintain. These moves are none the less in a minority. For most people, in and out of classrooms, when the place of the humanities subjects is mentioned at all in "core curriculum" discussions they come after the "basics", science, and computing, and depending who is speaking, often after practical/creative subjects too. The specific subjects mentioned tend to be history, geography and RE, and the implied content is "traditional", which suggests that this is not reasoned educational thought at all but an ill-considered reflection of people's own education.

The humanities are a low priority, and controversy a lower one still, and this book is partly to make a case for teaching about "race" in Britain as part of the core curriculum, but more importantly it is to argue for a higher level of awareness on the part of educators about the significance of "race" in people's consciousness. My argument so far can be summarized as follows:

1   Almost all pupils, in almost all parts of the country, have considerable levels of confusion, misunderstanding and ignorance about "race". Many have high levels of prejudice and hostility. (Those who doubt this can test it.)
2   When faced with the consequences of racial hostility people often say the answer, and a better future, lies in education.
3   No-one will ever challenge the states of mind of the pupils unless schools do.
4   Multicultural education as it has been understood may well leave these attitudes untouched.
5   If schools do not take this on board more generations of pupils will leave with their perceptions distorted and hostilities misdirected, and black people will suffer the consequences.
6   The problem of white people's attitudes to black people will not go away, and neither will the trouble which results from it. If this is not tackled in Sussex and Wiltshire and Devon then nothing will change in Brixton, Toxteth, or St Paul's.

If it can be assumed that those reading this book are at least convinced that many white children do have attitudes which could be called racist, I would like to address myself to the problem of what to do about it, or, rather, explore what I have chosen to do about it. Earlier it was asserted that the "celebrating cultural diversity/respect for other ways of life" approach is largely ineffective: as Sivanandan says "To learn about other cultures is not necessarily to learn about the racism of one's own." And while there is a growing number of analyses and critiques of various forms of racial education, there seems to be no theory, still less any body of practice, to inform those working in white areas what these critiques mean in classrooms, or in policy terms for schools and LEAs.

In trying to extend the debate to apply to the "white highlands" I have worked with a particular perspective or understanding of racism, which has partly emerged in this chapter. To be more specific, I have found that I am working with a notion of racism as a set of beliefs and practices which is separable from other beliefs in our society. In other words I have written (and acted) as if racism is not an inevitable part of our society, as if in principle racism could be reduced, even dismantled, without the destruction of capitalism. I cannot profess certainty whether this is true or not. I can (and others will) easily produce arguments suggesting it is not. It was nevertheless the framework within which I was constrained to work as a schoolteacher, and one which has achieved some results in reducing expressions of racism in some pupils and getting the issue more on the agenda in some schools. Events and perspectives may move faster than I was able to, and people can take what they can from my accounts, perhaps preventing the same square wheels being reinvented. Chapter 2 puts the range of views about racial education into context.

References

1   Robert Jeffcoate, *Positive Image*, Readers and Writers/Chameleon, 1979. Described by some as "unfortunately influential" because of its explicit "liberalism", it nevertheless contains some interesting classroom accounts.
2   Ibid., p. 21.
3   The extract is to be found either in the compilation of several programmes, called 'Anglo Saxon Attitudes' or in the programme called 'Education Against Prejudice'. Full details of availability are in chapter 5, note 18.
4   Some reflections on the minefield of terminology can be found in 'What do we call people?', *Multicultural Teaching*, **111** no. 1 (reprinted as Appendix 2).
5   I am indebted to Alan Bolter, then of Hreod Parkway School, Swindon, for these pupils' writings, and of course to the pupils themselves.

  With the help of Chris Barnham of Crawley CRC I have collected some more recent writings. These are the worst from a class of Sussex 12 year olds in 1986:

They should all go because they are taking our jobs.

I don't really mind the Pakistanis living in Britain, they're not too bad but they have a lot of children and they always pray and can be a nuisance.

They are taking all our jobs and not worrying about paying their bills.

They are no different to anyone else apart from a different colour. I think they have stupid religions eg I don't like the way they have to have arranged marriages.... I don't like it when they talk their language at school because I don't understand it.

Pakis...some of them are all right but the others are pigs.

I wish the Pakis would go back to their own country and not stink us out.

I think some of them are trouble, they start violent fights. I think some of them are okay, but I feel sorry for them just because they are coloured.

I can't stand Pakis, they stink like hell and I wish they would f_ off back to Pakistan.

Pakistan. Only two words to say on this subject. Stupid niggers. Smelly Sh_.

6   *Education for All* (The Swann Report), HMSO Cmnd 9453, 1985, p. 236.
7   From *New Internationalist*, 1982.
8   *Race Relations in Schools*, a paper prepared by HM Inspectorate, B1004HI3A (2).
9   With thanks to Balvinder Bharj.
10   The briefest guide to the position of black people in Britain today can be found in *Different Worlds*, Runnymede Trust, 1984. Three publications of the Institute of Race Relations, *Patterns of Racism*, *Roots of Racism* and *How Racism Came to Britain* give some succinct background to my comments here. Full details can be found in the resources appendix.
11   "I'm not National Front Myself but...", *New Society*, 17 May 1984.
12   In *Race as News*, UNESCO, 1976.
13   The Nationality Act and the deportations, harassment and refused appeals which result from it would have been inconceivable twenty years ago. It enshrines in statute measures which only the most right-wing Conservatives dared to propose in the 1960s.
14   From Whose Tomorrow is Tomorrow? in *Schooling and Culture*, Cockpit Gallery, 1984.

15   *The Curriculum 11-16,* DES, 1981.

16   *Better Schools,* DES, 1985, p. 14. (While I may cite this, I would nevertheless question whether "other races" need to be "tolerated".)

17   Though not without the unwelcome attention from Sir Keith Joseph, who said to a geography conference in June 1985 that he regretted the "simple solutions" suggested in some studies of the third world and of inner-city decay.

2 The forms of racial education

At the end of the previous chapter I argued that "multicultural education" as it has usually been understood leaves many of the attitudes and perceptions of white pupils untouched. This suggests that in many ways it also leaves the curriculum untouched. But how has "multicultural education" usually been understood?

At the moment, multicultural education is the term with the most currency to describe anything to do with "race" and education, although it is often used with no great precision. For many people it is part of the wallpaper of educational terms which is pasted on interview rooms and some LEA and publishers' offices. Originally it had a precise meaning, its popularizers wanted it to signify something different from the forms of racial education which preceded it. Today it is used as a catch-all phrase by nearly everyone for any kind of racial education.[1]

The term "multicultural education" is a product of the past ten years. In the last thirty years we have had immigrant education, multiracial education, multi-ethnic education, multicultural education, and the newcomer, the one currently trying to redefine what our concerns ought to be, anti-racist education. This may surprise new readers in this field, who may perhaps assume that these were all the same things and that for various and not very good reasons the names had changed occasionally. They might share the frustration of the administrator at a teacher training college who complained recently that its working party on (what we might call for the present) racial education had only just, after two years, agreed on its own name. Although this process could have been quicker it would be a mistake to see it as a waste of time. Words like "race" matter; whether employed consciously and deliberately (as was presumably the case with the college above), or unthinkingly as is more often the case, an individual or group preference for using "culture", "ethnic" or "race" actually demonstrates the ideological underpinnings of any analysis or proposed action. The agenda to do with "race" has not just changed, it has been a site of struggle; one conception of the issues has not generally abdicated gracefully in favour of a new and younger shaper of our thoughts, despite many cries of "long live the king" the old ones will not lie down. The way we perceive "race" and education, what we identify as "the problem", does indeed shape our thoughts, it is also revealing of how we see society and the processes of social and educational change. Each new name for racial education has been founded upon particular and different understandings of these things, and we shall not understand the changes unless we understand the views of the world which lie behind them.

Immigrant education*

When black pupils began to appear in British schools in the early 1950s there was no explicit policy about their presence. The way they were treated and the generalized practices which grew up to deal with them were the product of Britain's implicit assumptions about immigration. The main assumption was to do with assimilation: "coloured" immigrants' role was to "fit in" to an (assumed) monocultural Britain, to aspire to be "just like us", to settle down and in the course of time to move up the socio-economic scale. Education's task, logically, was to do some of the formal training required for immigrant children to "fit in": this meant English as a second language teaching for those of Asian background and remedial English (at best) for Caribbean pupils whose English was "not up to Standard". Since this view of the world was essentially optimistic (held as it was at a time of industrial and commercial expansion), self-confident (it assumed that everyone saw the present and the future in the same way as the burgeoning white middle class), and liberal (problems will be solved with goodwill and tolerance), it had to hold that "race" relations were, on the whole, good and would present no problems once the blacks had been compensated for their deficiencies. Thus, black children were really white children trying to get in, and once they had been taught to speak and write the language

---

*An important and prolific writer in the analysis of educational policy and practice about "race" is Chris Mullard, of Londons Institute of Education and the University of Amsterdam. Although specific references will be given periodically it would be as well to indicate my reliance on his analysis at the beginning.

(or to do so properly) then the "host community" would have nothing to be intolerant about and any problems about "prejudice" would go away. It was a logical corollary of these ideas that when the proportion of black children became "too high" in any one school (defined in DES circular 7/65 as about one-third) then they should be bused into other schools: if they were the majority they would not be able to assimilate and they might have damaged the chances of the white children.

It also follows that this perspective saw little place in school for the backgrounds and cultures of the black children, nor for their perceptions of how they were treated. It may also be true to say that, although there was some resistance, many "immigrant" parents were sufficiently powerless and imbued with the same ideology to accept this assimilationist model.

Some readers will see nothing wrong with this, and will take exception to the critical nuances built into my description. They would have some sociologists on their side, too, particularly those who theorized about the American immigrant experience.[2] It should also be said that it would be wrong to present this as entirely past history among those working in the field. Indeed, it is still technically the assumption behind most of the direct government funding of racial education. Most specialist multicultural centres and staff around the country are funded by a strange creature known as "Section 11". This refers to a section of the Local Government Act 1966, administered by the Home Office, which allows for provision to meet needs of "immigrant" pupils which are either greater than or different to those of "indigenous" pupils. The rules are interpreted in ways which are quite different from the assumptions implicit in the original act, but as the Association of Advisory Officers for Multicultural Education argues, this kind of language structures thought: one effect of having to use the term "immigrant" in all documentation about Section 11 is partly to be seen in the persistence of the genuine belief that this is what racial education is about.

It has to be said, however, that the assimilationist perspective is not only misguided and indicative of a poor understanding of history, it also involves a good deal of self-deception in some and arrogance in others. To be specific, there are six weaknesses in this perspective.

In the first place, the concept of British culture is built upon sand. It is an interesting exercise to try and outline the parameters of this culture without excluding a great many people who are not post-war black immigrants. I have heard many attempts to do so, and invariably those defining it come up with a class culture, that of the middle class, or part of it. If not, then it tends to be either trivial (fish and chips), or debateable (the quality of the BBC), or at too high a level of generality to exclude anyone (patriotic?).

Second, this perspective demonstrates a poor understanding of history because it pays little attention to what immigrant groups have nearly always done. In brief, they have never assimilated on a cultural level in the way the model proposes. Even where structurally, that is in class terms, an immigrant group has assimilated (and the USA, the usual reference point here in this debate, provides few enough real examples of this), they have not assimilated culturally. This is true for the English, Irish, Poles, Chinese, Dutch, Italians, Jews, Spanish, Greeks, and any other ethnic group one cares to identify in the USA, and indeed it is argued by Gordon that their structural positions do not represent assimilation either.[3] Anyone looking in Britain for large numbers of black people becoming black white people will not find them.

Third, such a debate is unnecessarily theoretical, since if one looks at the actual curriculum even those who staunchly defend the promulgation of British culture cannot defend the status quo. While it is easy to prescribe in general terms "British culture in British schools", in every subject one finds examples where this prescription is broken. There are not many history courses today which do not touch upon the Romans, or the ancient Egyptians, or even colonialism. A good deal of secondary school geography is concerned with the "third world". Foreign languages by definition are not British culture (perhaps learning them badly is). The social context of much of science is shaped by the USA. How many students of art and music (even as teenagers) study only British art and music? Do (or did) home economics classes only study roast beef and mushy peas? All this is not to say that much of our curriculum cannot be made less ethnocentric, but those who defend its present ethnocentrism might first like to justify the study of Tutankhamoun, Bach and Molière.

Fourth, it needs to be said that this perspective has been tried. Perhaps there are those who think we should have persevered for another twenty years, but for twenty years this set of beliefs underpinned much of what was done in racial education and it did not work. It did not work for Afro-Caribbean youth in ways that are written all over unemployment statistics and urban unrest; it did not work for Asians in ways that can be found in the figures for racial attacks and forcible deportations. The demand for mother tongue teaching has not come from assimilated immigrants.

Fifth, we are no longer, for the most part, dealing with "immigrants" in the Britain of the 1980s. It is part of Britain's problem about "race" that it cannot shed this term, it cannot see black people as anything but irredeemably alien, but we cannot go on having "immigrant" education policies for children born and entirely resident in this country.

The final problem with the assimilationist, "immigrant education" perspective, and the most difficult one for us to admit, is that the expectation that black people should assimilate into British culture (even if we could provide a working definition of it) implicitly assumes the superiority of that culture, or at least the greater appropriateness of it in the British Isles. For many people in Britain the phrase "when in Rome..." seems to contain a self-evident truth. Leaving aside the assumption that British culture is so good that we have the right and duty to export it (forcibly if necessary), in the modern world ex-colonial subjects in Britain simply will not accept those assumptions. Whether assimilationists welcome it or not, there are articulate and organized voices resisting assimilation, and after 200 years of colonial cultural hegemony we cannot ignore the voices of ex-colonial subjects now in the metropolis.

It should be clear why many people regard this constellation of assimilationist views as both racist, because they have the effect of making black experiences and perceptions inferior, and inaccurate and misleading, since it reflects an inadequate and inaccurate picture of Britain's present and former place in the world. To promote an educational perspective which is both inaccurate and racist (as well as obviously outdated) is harmful to whites as well as blacks.

Finally, it is worth noting the social context at the time this perspective held greatest sway. Britain was decolonizing, but in a spirit of regret among many and with the overall view that after years of benign stewardship the blacks were "ready" to try and rule themselves. (Advocates of this view can still be found, and there are books which have exposed its ignorance of history and its racism. It would, of course, be remarkable to find a colonial society without such a legitimating set of beliefs.)[4]

Multiracial education

We can next identify a second main form of racial education, "multiracial education". This arose in the mid 1960s as the response of some white teachers and black parents to the racism of immigrant education, and was later accepted by some politicians, notably Roy Jenkins when he was Home Secretary. It is distinguished from the first perspective by its apparent acceptance of some cultural diversity, and it was less explicitly racist. In practical terms it promoted varieties of cultural exclusivity, it promoted a recognition that groups were defined structurally by colour and pressed the expression of this in culture. "Multiracial education" responded to the accumulating data on the self-concept of black children, in itself a powerful indictment of the effects of "immigrant education".[5] In its most "pure" form this was realized in the inclusion of black studies in the curriculum of some schools (although not everyone who can be identified with this phase supported black studies).[6] The focus, of course, was on black children.

Black anger, frustration, and ultimately, resistance in and outside the classroom spurred on teachers and others concerned with multicultural education and studies to introduce Black Studies and other "ethnic-type" subjects into the official curriculum... concern was expressed by black parents and some white teachers about the numbers of children of West Indian origin in schools for the educationally sub-normal, and an increasing amount of money was spent not only on the special needs of these children but on every conceivable — within a framework — activity in multicultural education.[7]

The ideology was one of integration, not assimilation. Black minority groups (Mullard calls them ethnic-class groups) were expected to integrate politically (eventually) with space given for some cultural residues. Recognition was given to the fact that black people were disadvantaged and that some sort of political and educational action had to be taken to provide equal opportunities. Outside the educational sphere it was hoped that for the first time a black middle class was emerging; there were black estate agents, travel agents, small employers. "They were beginning to move up"; it was supposed to be the beginning of the political and economic integration of a group seen as a kind of class defined by ethnicity, an ethnic-class group.

  With Mullard's examination of this perspective we return to the debate touched upon at the end of chapter 1, the "liberal" versus radical analyses of "race" in Britain. Mullard identifies the problem with the liberal perspective as the model of society it presupposes and the place of black people in it. It perceives black peoples as ethnic-class groups and tries to centre the axis of action on ethnicity, on culture, rather than on what he sees as the real, structural axis, race–class groups.[8] The difference is that a "race" is a socially evaluated group defined by biology (colour), whereas an ethnic or cultural group has beliefs, languages, and customs in common.[9] Often, in the current British context, ethnic groups are identified and evaluated primarily by colour, although cultural characteristics are also socially evaluated. But the mistake Mullard wants us to identify is that of thinking "race" is just ethnicity. "Race" is rather, and much more importantly, the outcome of British colonial and post-colonial history, and fundamental to our social order. To paraphrase Mullard more directly, where there is a group of people who materially experience "race" then racial oppression is part of the economic order and "race" groups are formed. "Race" can also be experienced non-materially and this becomes part of the cultural order, for example language and religion, and groups defined by these are ethnic groups. Multiracial education confuses its analysis by thinking of ethnicity as the primary determinant of class, in fact, he argues, "race" is the key. The "integration" it has as its object is on the strict condition that allegiance to the political and economic order is not threatened. As ever, colonial subjects were to have contact with Britain on British terms.

Multiracial education had already been eclipsed by the time Maureen Stone's critical account of it was published in 1981.[10] Mullard argues this is because of its lack of recognition of the importance of the conjunction of 'race' and class. It "provided the space for resistances to be mobilised solely along the cultural axis of ethnicity and ethnic-class groups rather than along the structural axis of 'race' and race-class groups". In other words, "race" is a structural term, black people, whatever their cultural ethnic identities, have a common class relationship to British capitalist society, they are ex-colonial migrant labour.

Although multiracial education recognized the structural inequalities faced by black peoples it did so in terms of ethnic-class groups. Put another way, multiracial education did not see Britain as fundamentally a class society which was founded upon class inequalities, "race"-classes among them. Its object, then, was integration, the rising of an ethnic-class in the economic order, a kind of separate-but-equal position comparable to the one Jews are commonly held to occupy. Mullard says:

In short, political and economic values and beliefs, those on which our society and its major institutions are based, need to be separated from the rest — religious beliefs, cultural customs, and so on. And, as the most important values and beliefs in the sense of their determining the substructural base of our society, they become the ones which must be protected at all costs and to which black pupils and adults must be persuaded to subscribe. By allowing limited diversity in respect of religious beliefs, customs, and even language, it is assumed within the framework of the model that blacks will be more likely to accept than reject outright those which actually shape our society.[11]

In its wider context, it was adhered to by both black and white groups, and was a radical formulation compared both with the racist assumptions of "immigrant education" which preceded it, and the ignoring of structure in the assumptions of "multicultural education" which followed it. It came after the initial immigration needed by Britain's industry was over. The economy was no longer expanding, and if there was a need for black labour it was for skilled labour — hence the development of long-term immigration control and the ideology of a finite ethnic-class group moving upwards in an integrated social order.

It is difficult to make much headway into this thicket of terminology, and I am not aware of anyone else other than Mullard who makes such fine distinctions between ethnic-class and race-class as they operate in practice, nor anyone who sees "multiracial" education as such a distinct form. Indeed, Mullard is the only commentator who takes the various terms as having exact meanings with specific underpinning ideologies. Maureen Stone, as mentioned previously, has written the most detailed critique of "multiracial education" (MRE), although at times she is not writing about quite the same thing as Mullard.[12] Stone criticizes most of the work she found being done in racial education, although not all of it really belonged to this phase, but she does identify some practices and assumptions which clarify what Mullard is describing at a more theoretical level.

Stone sees the main thrust of MRE as trying to compensate for the twin "problems" in black children of cultural deprivation and low self-esteem. Some of the tenets of MRE which she lists are as follows:

1   It will help minority group children to develop pride in their identity and their group.
2   It will encourage white pupils to see their black classmates in a more positive light.

3   It will reduce alienation of minority group children, especially West Indian pupils.

4   By developing new curricula and new teaching methods it extends the concern of the school into the home and the community and thus makes schooling more relevant to groups which are hard to reach.

5   The new curricula will be more successful in motivating minority group pupils and in promoting positive attitudes to school and teachers.

Stone calls these objectives "vague and undefined" and suggests they totally ignore the issues of power and control in the school system. Such liberal notions of multiracial education ignore the structural and class forces at work in our society, and hence in our schools and our conception of the curriculum. She points to the well rehearsed argument that education cannot do other than peddle the dominant culture. Since, therefore, our education system never reflected the culture of the working class, why should it start now with a small section of it? The reality is, she argues, that educationalists have often conceived of education as "leading out" children from their "deprived" or "inadequate" working-class culture into a better one, and this cannot be equated with giving credence and status to black ones.

Stone therefore argues that from the Afro-Caribbean child's point of view schools should leave multiracial education alone, home will see to culture, both because it always has done so in historical conditions far more oppressive than Britain in the 1980s, and because she fears the legitimizing or subtly dominating effect of the colonizing of black cultures by white educationalists, however well meaning. Stone is describing and criticizing what she sees as a special form of education conceived for blacks in the hope that it would be more palatable to them, and in the genuine belief that it would be less racist to do so. What happened, she claims, is that a second-class, marginalized, non-exam curriculum was emerging which would as surely condemn black pupils to disadvantage as the most rigorously ethnocentrist one.

There is much in Stone's analysis that is similar to Mullard's, although it is worth stressing that, as her title says, she is not writing about the totality of education in Britain, but about the education of black children. Her preferred solution to the situation has probably been overtaken by events. Certainly supplementary schools, of which she is very supportive,[13] have spread, as has her dislike of "progressive" methods of teaching (but not for the same reasons). Her conviction that black pupils should be given the same curriculum as whites has been orthodoxy since before her book was published, but this is the standpoint of both the newer lobby in racial education and those who have always resisted any change at all. These are strange bedfellows: one says "leave everything alone" and the other says "change virtually the whole curriculum".Whereas Stone seems remarkably uncritical of what this curriculum has generally been (simply insisting that if black children are going to get on they need geography 'O' level as much as anyone else does, whatever the content of that geography), the views of post-multiracial education are far more critical of what has been offered to all children in the past, but perhaps less critical of the education system's ability to change.

Multicultural education

We move then to multicultural education, currently the dominant form of racial education and the one which gives its name to the surviving remnants of previous forms. This developed not with the expansion of industry of the 1950s nor its contraction in the 1970s, but with its crisis in the late 1970s and 1980s, with a zero labour requirement and the greatly increased use of deportation. In a sense it is "where I came in"; I referred to it at the beginning of the last chapter as the first perspective on "race" and education which I met as a teacher.

Whereas multiracial education was underpinned with an idea of the primacy of class, albeit modified and influenced by ethnicity and culture, multicultural education seems to conceive of society as composed primarily, and most importantly, of cultures. Various assumptions might be made about the comparative and potential equality of cultures, but the idea is of a plural social order. Cultures, according to this model, are generated by several things, often in concert: one of these is class, another is region, another is ethnicity, so we may speak of "northern" culture, or Punjabi culture, and these exist side by side in a plural social order, an order differentiated by culture rather than or at least as much as stratified by class.[14]

Although one common theme of writers holding this perspective is that (black) ethnic cultures are devalued, there is the assumption that in principle this can be changed towards a diversity of equal cultures. Nowhere has this perspective been put more clearly than by the Schools Council. In their explanatory leaflet about the council's initiatives in this field it is stated that there is move in Britain towards

cultural pluralism, which recognises that our society may be positively
enriched by the presence of a variety of cultural patterns... successive British
governments have firmly endorsed a policy of mutual understanding and
respect for individual differences and cultural diversity.... The goal is a plural
society where cultural groups can maintain their own identity, but where
there are sufficient shared experiences and values for social cohesion and
sufficient understanding of each other's culture for stability.[15]

This document recognizes that the goal it identifies has not been
reached, and the reasons it gives for this are revealing of the
underpinning analysis:

assimilation is difficult to achieve for some cultural groups now in Britain.
Many of these groups are loosely referred to as "ethnic minorities".... Skin
colour and language differences make some minority groups visibly and
audibly distinctive; differences in religious belief and practice may reduce
social interaction and intermarriage. Groups which can so easily be identified
and which may seem strange or unfamiliar are an easy prey for prejudice,
hostility and discrimination.[16]

According to the Schools Council, then, the necessity for
multicultural education arises from strangeness, inadequate
recognition and understanding of each other's cultures, and from
"prejudice". Its remedy has been both summed up and mocked by
Gerry Davis's memorable phrase, "the steel band and Diwali"
approach: import some "ethnic" musicians and have some assemblies
for the festivals of non-Christian faiths.
  The Schools Council's perspective is shared by the Swann
Committee, although it uses the term "pluralism". It recommends a
critical perspective at times, and argues that the central curriculum
point, especially in white areas, must be to deal with racism, but it
nevertheless has a fundamentally psychological understanding of
what racism is. (The closest the report gets to closely defining it is in
its second chapter, where it uses it synonomously with "negative
prejudice".) Their view of society is as follows:

We consider that a multi-racial society such as ours would in fact function
most effectively and harmoniously on the basis of pluralism which enables,
expects and encourages members of all ethnic groups, both minority and
majority, to participate fully in shaping the society as a whole within a
framework of commonly accepted values, practices and procedures, whilst

also allowing, and where necessary, assisting the ethnic minority communities in maintaining their distinct ethnic identities within this common framework.[17]

This "celebrating diversity" approach can be argued against on several levels. It is frequently said nowadays that the approach is too weak, naive and liberal, and that racism (only mentioned in passing in the Schools Council document) is the real issue. This point was made at the beginning of chapter 1. It is essential, however, to tease out the variety of positions which lie behind this argument. We might, perhaps, begin with the "weak" anti-racist position, and later contrast it with a "strong" anti-racist position. These terms do not make judgements about the personal strength of feeling of their adherents, the difference is that a "strong" anti-racist position is one influenced by Marxism.

"Weak" anti-racism, or education for racial equality

For those who genuinely espouse it, the key feature of the "weak" position is that it regards racism as an isolatable phenomenon within society, not an inherent part of its structure, and as already indicated this was my own implicit position while doing much of the work described in this book. Thus, although one may see racism as inescapably having its origin in colonialism and capitalism, because of the necessity of imperialism and slavery for economic expansion and the necessity of a set of beliefs to justify and maintain it (although one may trace the continuation of this into this century and argue that the way immigration and nationality has been used is clearly linked to economic forces), one may still regard the phenomenon of racism as an ideology and set of practices which can be analysed and countered separately from the structures of class.

An explicit engagement with this argument is to be found in Robert Jeffcoate's book *Positive Image*. Arguing from a position he himself characterizes as "liberal", he takes exception to Chris Searle's Marxist argument that the fight against racism is part of the struggle for the socialist transformation of society.[18] But he is no believer in "steel band and Diwali", and it is confusing that his and others' weak anti-racist position is still labelled by some as "multiculturalism", although there is no doubt that it does not have a coherent class analysis. It is unhelpful not to separate out this approach because it has recently captured centre stage; the fact that it still comes under radical attack cannot be explained by saying it has a purely cultural focus.

Following Berkshire's policy document Richard Hatcher[19] calls "weak" anti-racism the "education for racial equality" (ERE) perspective, reserving "anti-racist education" for more radical stances, a usage I propose to adopt. (Another term might be "hard" multiculturalism, counterposed with the "softer" cultural diversity approach.) The definition of racism Berkshire gives on the opening page of its policy is as follows:

Racism refers to institutions and routine procedures as well as to the actions of individuals, and to unconscious and unintentional effects as well as to deliberate purposes. It summarises all attitudes, procedures and social patterns whose effect (though not necessarily whose conscious intention) is to create and maintain power, influence and well-being at the expense of Asian and Afro-Caribbean people; and whose further function is simultaneously to limit the latter to the poorest life chances and living conditions, the most menial work, and the greatest likelihood of unemployment and under-employment.[20]

Despite its critical tone it is important to note that the definition, and the rest of the policy, implies that racism can be countered to the benefit of British society as we know it. While the Inner London Education Authority (ILEA) mentions class and gender inequality as well, neither suggests the total restructuring of British society. (Swann, incidentally, explicitly says this is not what it wants.)[21] A concept closely related to the ERE approach is that of "institutional racism", which has been refined in the past two or three years to refer to the network of (sometimes) unexamined assumptions, procedures and practices in British society which have the effect of disadvantaging black people and maintaining white power. It also argues that racism and inequality be addressed more centrally by the school curriculum.

ERE believes that multiculturalism is naive at two levels: the level of theory which argues, as Swann and the Schools Council do, that the "problem" is largely one of unfamiliarity and attitudes; and second, on the level of practice, since it can be argued that as a strategy it simply does not work.

This is above all the case in white areas and partly explains why the "multicultural" conception of racial education has never really caught on outside the cities.[22] It has rather a distant ring in the majority of schools, since there is not much (ethnic) cultural diversity to celebrate. As a topic to have an opinion on teachers may or may not be old-fashioned assimilationists, but the issue hardly has the urgency for tomorrow's lessons that it does in central Birmingham, so it will never provide enough of a motive to touch the curriculum, and it will be a long time before racism appears on the agenda. The "weak" anti-racists suggest, however, that there is the possibility of a short cut being taken through the educational development of the big conurbations. Without the distraction, so to speak, of the black communities and the various understandings of their needs in school we can look directly at the needs of white pupils. People have been right, in a way, to say "it's not an issue here" when the issue is defined as assimilation or cultural diversity; they are even right, to a lesser extent, when they cannot see active discrimination because there are no black people around locally to suffer it.[23] But if the issue is clearly identified as one of white people's beliefs and practices then the curriculum imperatives are the same for East Grinstead as they are for East Ham. The needs of black people have served as a distraction because they have enabled us to pose the problems as black problems — language "deficiency", poor self-image, "disadvantage" — and as long as the problems are defined as ever-more sophisticated ones within black communities (underachievement of young Afro-Caribbeans, young Asians between two cultures, mother tongue maintenance, recognizing Rastafarianism) then white people can postpone looking within white attitudes and institutions.

As I have said, a good deal of this book is implicitly arguing from a "weak" anti-racist stance (ERE) against the kind of multiculturalism which wants to make no mention of racism. The essence of the argument is this: while celebrating cultural diversity and using it as a real resource in teaching is good educational practice, good for everyone's self-esteem, and dictated by a belief in equality, it is rather naive to think that it will counter racism. In chapter 1 the children's writings point to racism, not cultural misunderstanding. The teaching strategies outlined in chapters 3 and 4 try to deal with racism not understanding other cultures. The policy programmes in chapters 6, 7 and 8 are not about celebrating diversity. So ERE would claim to want to give pupils a critical understanding of racism rather than hope for "harmony" through goodwill, and it seeks to rethink structures and practices which diminish life-chances for black people. In practice this means, for instance, positive action on black recruitment, monitoring job appointments and being prepared to act upon the results, and having enforceable sanctions for racists at any level.

"Strong" anti-racism, making the connections with class

Marxist and other radical anti-racists would not disagree with the ERE position that it is rather naive to expect that celebrating diversity will reduce racism, but the key omission in the ERE position for Mullard's kind of analysis is the importance placed upon the societal structures of racism, and hence, class. We have seen Mullard's and Stone's dismissal of multiracial education not as paying too little attention to class but in misunderstanding its nature. Both agree that MRE wanted to deal with class factors, but argue that it was misdirected along the axis of ethnicity. Ethnic-class is what it dealt with, not race-class. Multicultural education, meanwhile, does not really recognize race-class as a factor at all, and ERE, despite its radical tone, does not have class structuring as part of its model of society, so it does not build it into its model of education.

Mullard argues that racism can only be truly understood and combated from a Marxist standpoint and that, therefore, the only true anti-racism is Marxist. In this he would be supported, at least partly, by many on the left who see no separation between racial and other forms of oppression, like those of gender and class. They have different expressions and different power, but broadly speaking they are to the left all of a piece in that they are part of the system of relations which shape and maintain our society. Each one is not an aberration or an unfortunate hangover from the past, they are profitable. Thus the apparent assumption in ERE policies that racism can be dismantled is misconceived because, as Salman Rushdie says,

racism is not a side issue in contemporary Britain, not a peripheral or a minority affair, I believe that Britain is undergoing a critical phase of its post colonial period, and this crisis isn't simply economic or political, it's a crisis of the whole culture, of the society's whole sense of itself, and racism is only the most clearly visible part of the crisis.[24]

To the best of my knowledge Rushdie is not a Marxist, but he is identifying here the cultural expression of the critical place of racism in British capitalism.

It is important to add that, to Mullard, one of the distinctive features of anti-racist education (ARE) is not the classroom practices it recommends but its roots and origins in black people's struggles. It is not solely a set of ideas developing out of older ones, but a force, a black response to white racism. It is actually located structurally, whereas multicultural education was, he argues, a cultural phenomenon. (Others have argued multicultural education had a different genesis, it was a white response to black demands, a way of not facing up to the the real issues.) So unlike multiculturalism, with its rarefied, decontexualized and "microscopic" view, Mullard argues that true anti-racist education is periscopic, because

it is concerned with the production of quite a different kind of consciousness than that with which it is in contest. Unlike multicultural education which seeks to produce a passive consciousness of cultural differences, anti-racist education seeks to produce an active consciousness of structural similarity, inequality and injustice.[25]

This partly provides an answer to those who argue that the concentration upon "race" is a distraction from the class struggle; if in fact the examination of racism is periscopic, if it is, as Rushdie says, "the most visible part of the crisis", then it may be like a brand of lager which reaches parts of our understanding that the others do not reach. Multiculturalism, "without abandoning its descriptive and sociologically facile concept of culture and without discarding its ethnic orientation, is incapable of mounting any kind of attack on institutionalised racism". The Education for Racial Equality stance cannot do so either, and "any such claim that it can is suitable only for the garbage can of empty rhetoric".[26]

So what, then, do "strong" anti-racists do which "weak" anti-racists do not? There is a large degree of overlap and common ground because both believe children should have a critical consciousness about racism and both recognize that structures have to be changed. At the risk of considerable oversimplification I would suggest that in classroom practice ARE is more likely to develop a "left" view of society with racism within it, which might mean much more working-class history, project work on deportation campaigns, examples in maths taken from South African statistics, and the politics of food in Home Economics. (This comparison of approaches is touched upon again in chapters 3 and 4, about my own "anti-racist" teaching.) Outside the classroom an ARE stance would also mean considerable community involvement, for example against the Police Bill, or in campaigns about racial harassment and deportation. Of course, circumstances differ: some teachers who would not accept the overall philosophy of ARE work in schools which have banned police visits, others who would are constrained by what is possible in the shires.

The distinction between ERE and ARE is perhaps more recognizable in a formal and analytic sense than in educational organization or classroom practice. To some extent I have been describing "ideal types", notional pure forms and personal positions which do not exist in reality with such clarity. It is hardly surprising that the formal statements of the ERE position (like Berkshire's above, p.33) do not overtly take a more radical stance, the whole point of radical and neo-Marxist critiques of them ought to be that it would be impossible for them to do so. They are designed to get through political committees. As mentioned in chapter 7, the earliest of the ERE policies, Berkshire's, was passed by a "hung" council, which meant it had to get Conservative votes. Bradford's, indeed, was passed by a Conservative council. The ERE position can be elusive, and usually has to take a stance suggesting that racism is not an inevitable and necessary part of society. But a "weak" anti-racist position is often argued by those holding a stronger one and who dare not say so. These people work in education, generally in or around schools, where with very few exceptions they deem it personally and strategically unwise to be identified as "too extreme". (There is, of course, an argument which says such compromises weaken the struggle and should not be made.) The best example of this is Mullard himself, who was involved in writing both the Berkshire policy and the ILEA's, and who now subjects them to a Marxist critique. As already mentioned, he calls the "weak" position a multicultural one, which is unhelpful as far as clarity is concerned (though it may have strategic advantages.) Hatcher calls it "education for racial equality"; they are talking about the same thing. Thus in this territory many people are in disguise. Marxist anti-racists call themselves multiculturalists, "steel band and Diwali" types wear anti-racist badges, and many people combat injustice without a watertight and coherent social theory. There are other arguments, not entered into here, about the strategies of labelling and the labelling of strategies, but the labels are never "just words".

In a spirited attack on policies like Berkshire's, Flew[27] misses this point entirely. In trying to sound a right-wing alarm at the entry into educational policy-making of some critical stances, he makes the mistake of lumping all anti-racists together as Marxists. The logic of his argument would therefore appear to be that it is not possible to see racism as anything other than bound up with capitalism. An interesting position for a right-wing ideologue.

Education for racial equality, I would argue, is now the defining characteristic of racial education policies, and can be used to distinguish even their most radical forms from their would-be successor, anti-racist education. As I have tried to show, ERE is not Marxist. Although often radically counterposed to views like the Schools Council's and Swann's, ERE is in turn criticized in Marxist terms by Mullard, and also Hatcher, for slightly different reasons.

Hatcher's analysis is similar to Mullard's, at least initially. He notes the extract of Berkshire's policy quoted earlier (p. 33), and continues

This is a concept of equality which accepts the existing hierarchical structure of society. It defines racial equality as proportional distribution of black people throughout the class structure. What it aims at is colour-blind meritocracy.[28]

With Mullard, he argues that since our social structure and racism are inextricably linked, for our society to claim to have such a goal is contradictory.

This brings the debate up to date. As to where it will go in the future it seems to me that Hatcher and Mullard part company on what to do next, in other words what ought to be important parts of the practice of anti-racists in education. The argument hinges largely on the role of the left. Mullard asserts the primacy of the anti-racist struggle while recognizing other alliances and other struggles, whereas Hatcher points out that the landscape in which the struggle will have to take place is already "occupied, guarded and ruled"[29] and that the anti-racist movement on its own will be crushed or co-opted. His consequent criticisms of Mullard and corresponding strategy of linking the anti-racist struggle much more closely to others have yet to be critically engaged within the educational anti-racist movement, though many of its members would disagree with them both that socialism or Marxism has taken out a patent on anti-racism. This will be the location of the argument in the next few years, and we can expect Hatcher's position to be opposed by whites, whether for reasons of liberal non-politicism or out of strategy, and by blacks who fear yet another co-option of their cause.

References

1   Some important exceptions are the DES, who take advice from HMIs in "multiracial education", the ILEA, which has a policy on "multi-ethnic education", and Berkshire, which has a "policy for racial equality", and NAME, until recently the National Association for Multiracial Education. Some of the reason behind this is the unacceptability of the word "racism" to those in a position to practice it, and "multiculturalism" to those trying to fight it.

2   cf. Robert E. Park's "race relations cycle".

3   Milton Gordon, *Assimilation in American Life,* Oxford University Press, 1964. He suggests the concept of "ethclass" to represent the conjunction of class and ethnic relations. The WASPs are on top.

4   See, for instance, the books and other materials listed under history in the appendix.

5   See David Milner's *Children and Race,* Penguin 1975.

6   See The Select Committee on Race and Immigration, *Report on Education* (1973), paras. 102, 103, 104. Quoted by Mullard in J. Tierney (ed.), *Race Migration and Schooling,* Holt 1981, p. 126.

7   Mullard in *Racism in Society and Schools, History, Policy and Practice,* London University Institute of Education, Multicultural Centre, 1980. In this extract he is uncharacteristically imprecise about the term "multicultural".

8   As Mullard puts it: "[it] either makes overtures to the various ethnic or cultural descriptions of the socio-educational order or attempts to reform and account for ethnic and cultural differentiations in terms of structural realities...". *Anti Racist Education, the 3 Os,* NAME 1985, p.12. It was itself a cultural expression of the structural inequalities stemming from "race".

9   C. Gaine, 'What Do We Call People?', *Multicultural Teaching,* **111** no. 1, which included here as an appendix. In this book I always put "race" in inverted commas, to signify that it is not real in the sense that many think it is.

10 Maureen Stone, *The Education of the Black Child in Britain, the Myth of Multiracial Education,* Fontana 1981.

11 Mullard, in Tierney (ed.), *Race Migration and Schooling,* pp. 127-8.

12 Madan Sarup's book, *The Politics of Multiracial Education,* RKP 1986, is actually about what most people call multicultural education, i.e. the dominant practice today. He is not using the

term with the precision Mullard intends or with the same focus as Stone.

13   Up to 12 per cent of Afro-Caribbean children attend them, according to Swann.

14   This social theory underpinning "multicultural education" can be found in Maurice Craft's pamphlet *Education for Diversity*, University of Nottingham 1982. Reprinted in Craft (ed.), *Education and Cultural Pluralism*, Falmer 1984.

15   *Multicultural Education*, Schools Council 1982.

16   ibid., p. 3.

17   *Education for All* (The Swann Report), HMSO, Cmnd 9453, 1985, p. 5.

18   Robert Jeffcoate, *Positive Image*, Writers and Readers/ Chameleon, 1979. Chris Searle, *The World in a Classroom*, Writers and Readers 1977. Jeffcoate argues from a position he himself characterizes as "liberal" that pupils have to be free to choose their ideas for themselves and that it is not the place of teachers to structure the world for them. "Teachers have no business thrusting their cherished ideologies on young and malleable minds; it is for children to determine for themselves where they stand politically and culturally." In a way Jeffcoate's argument is hard to follow, since it would seem from some of his classroom accounts that he wants his pupils to know his own response to at least some forms of racism. What he is really talking about in the above extract is a class perspective, a socialist ideology. Like some other teachers, when the chips are down he is prepared to take a moral stand against racism and seek to persuade children towards a similar standpoint. But anything more "political" is strictly off-limits, it is "indoctrination". In his *Education and Ethnic Minorities* (1984) he seems to retreat from what he actually did in the classroom reported in *Positive Image*, since he explicitly applies the principle quoted above to teaching about "race".

19   Some comments on Mullard's papers for NAME. Richard Hatcher, 1985 (unpublished).

20   *Education for Racial Equality*, Policy Paper 1, Royal County of Berkshire.

21   "We are not... seeking a radically different social structure..." op cit. p. 7.

22   The most well argued attempt to do so can be found in A. Page and K. Thomas, *Multicultural Education and the All-White School*, University of Nottingham 1984.

23 I am not saying here that less "prejudice" exists in white areas, or that it plays no part in keeping white areas *as* white areas.

24 Salman Rushdie, 'The New Empire within Britain,' *New Society*, 9 December 1982.

25 op cit. p. 33.

26 ibid. p. 37.

27 Anthony Flew, *Race, Education, and Revolution*, Centre for Policy Studies 1984.

28 Hatcher, Some comments on Mullard's....

29 ibid.

Part Two
Practice... Teaching about "Race"

3 "Race" in the timetable

When I first walked in I didn't know what to expect, just a sort of play or something. When they first gave out the envelopes and things I thought it was a bit stupid and didn't really see the point of it. At first, when we started playing, I thought it was a big joke, but then, trying to get my pretend wife over and trying to get a job, I began to get a bit impatient and angry because no-one would help us. Every time we wanted something there was always an excuse to stop me, people kept calling me Paki as if colour mattered, and that made me feel angry, not just at them but at myself, 'cos I've done the same sort of thing, not out loud but to myself as I saw a coloured person. The things the people in the drama thing wanted to know had no relevance to me, I didn't realise that that sort of thing actually goes on. I know it was acting and everything was overdone, but if I got angry and annoyed during that short time, only 45 minutes, I wonder how the coloured people feel going through it every minute in every day, it must be humiliating and degrading.

When my pretend wife said "Go over and get a job and send me back the money". I didn't want to leave her, and I didn't want to be on my own, where I didn't know anybody. Then I worked as hard as I could to get the money and then we had to fill in a form, then another form. In the end we bribed the man to let us through.... The next time I see a coloured person I expect I'll pity them, but I don't expect they want pity either, I won't know what to do or say, but I willl pity them inside. I'm really glad I'm not coloured, not because of the colour but because of what they have to go through just in order to live a life, and even that life isn't really pleasant.

Coloured people are always called names like wogs, Pakis, jungle bunnies etc. I don't even understand these names yet I use them.

White people seeem so false and hypocritical to the black people. Coloured people seem so down to earth and real. From watching the film I knew people hurt, but I never knew how much they hurt. I didn't even realise some things went on. I wish I hadn't been brought up in a racist culture then maybe I wouldn't feel so guilty now. When you read things in the paper about fights and things involving black people you don't think about the white people involved and you think "Oh, that doesn't involve me so why should I worry".

I wish I knew a coloured person, I mean, really well, then if I went out with them I could feel I wasn't racist and I didn't care, but that's hypocritical as well, because I would know their colour and I shouldn't care about it.

I would like to write to a coloured person in another school in Britain... but wouldn't the person mind being singled out to write to me just because they are coloured?.... Maybe it will make me feel and react better if I know just how they feel about everything... we think they owe us a lot, but really the way most of them are treated they don't owe us nothing but hate... (Sue, aged 15).

It is one thing to complain that pupils know nothing or too little about "race" in Britain, and quite another to translate this complaint into action in the form of classroom practice. The notes above are reactions from a pupil to a course of study which tried to fill the gap complained of. The opening comments are about a simulation game called "Passport" in which she has been given the role of an Indian trying to enter Britain in the 1960s and trying to get around the discrimination she meets. (The game is explained more fully in the following chapter.) Sue is not entirely typical, but she is indicative of needs and possibilities. More pupils' responses are given later.

There are several ways of trying to get "race" into the curriculum. What follows is an account of a sociology/social studies course with "race" as a large element in it, set up in a school where for various reasons the circumstances were favourable to this strategy. Plainly this was only one solution to the problem of white knowledge and white attitudes, but since it was (and is) a strategy seldom employed, since it actually exists rather than remaining stuck as a prescription, and since in its way it works, it ought to be possible to learn some lessons from it.

However, since part of the purpose of setting this down is so that other teachers can critically evaluate its content and methods, and its applicability in other situations, it seems worth going into some of the background factors which shaped the course.

The school

The school in which the course was developed was a true comprehensive, in that it contained pupils from all classes in about the same proportion as the population as a whole. It served older council estates, including some dumping ground areas, old working-class terraced housing, brand new council and private housing estates, large pre-war semi-detached houses, a 1960s estate of semi-detached houses and bungalows, and a few large detached Edwardian houses. It was a senior high school organized in what is known as the "Leicestershire Plan", namely 11—13 junior highs in the buildings of old secondary moderns, feeding 14—18s in old grammar schools. It had been set up as deliberately innovative in 1969, with a democratic staff-meeting structure, a pupils' representative council which actually decided things, no uniform, and a good deal of mixed ability or at least wide-ability teaching.

The autonomy subject heads enjoyed was surprising, coming as I had from a collaborative integrated faculty, and was the result of the school having no faculty structure but a large number of individual subject "barons". (These were usually well qualified and well paid, one advantage of the Leicestershire Plan, for those in the senior high schools, being that the way points are allocated meant the senior highs were embarrassingly well provided for.) The school had had from the beginning a department of social studies and another of economics, as well as the usual history and geography. Although the sociology option was well established, the two teachers running it both left at the same time. As a new baron, I soon realized that the time was ripe for a "new broom", not least because I realized the quality of the other teacher who had been taken on with me.

The barons' autonomy was limited only by the head, deputy heads, what prospective pupils actually chose to study (from a pool offering 20 subjects at once, at times), and the exam boards. The head was new, and he was clearly expected by some of the governors to move the school in a more traditional direction. On the face of it this may seem like an obstacle in bringing about a curriculum development which many would see as "radical", yet for reasons I have never fully understood the new head gave some staff a lot more space than the liberal one whose school I had just been eased out of (for being too "radical"). Many teachers will know that this is a vital factor. Copies of my course outlines were always given to the head and the academic deputy, who, despite any misgivings they may have had (and I never knew whether they did or not), not only allowed me to get on with it but on occasions defended me from a racist parent and an antedeluvian governor.

Another constraint was the pupils' "choices", and these were mediated to some extent by the staff of the junior high schools. (Few males chose sociology, and although this is a national pattern at any level it was possible to see some causal factors at close quarters. In the case of one of the feeder schools every single boy in the top stream "chose" geography as his humanities subject.) This kind of influence on pupil choice did not necessarily affect the content of our sociology course, but it certainly affected the responses, and one can only make guesses at how much classes which were more mixed would have responded to this particular material. It is an opinion which awaits systematic testing, but I am convinced that girls are easier to teach about "race" than boys. It may be that they really are socialized to relate and empathize more with other people, or it may be that being oppressed themselves they can recognize more easily someone else's oppression. Be that as it may, since these pupils were mostly female, and volunteers for the subject at that, it is an open question whether the strategy employed here would work in other places. Some teachers will certainly want to say that their own bigots are made of sterner stuff than ours were.

Can you do an exam in it?

The exam boards were another problem. This constraint was potentially a major one since virtually everyone in the school was doing exam work, but on the other hand almost all departments ran well established mode 3 schemes, at least at CSE. In principle the mode 3 CSE which we had inherited had space for a "race slot", but since the option was for the top 80 per cent or so taught in mixed groups, whatever was taught had to be applicable to the mode 1 GCE exam to be faced by some of the pupils. AEB mode 1 sociology had some things in its favour, but it seldom had questions on "race". (In recent years such questions had been getting more scarce, perhaps because they tended to be answered so abysmally.)

One answer to the problem of how to put good material about "race" into an 'O' level course was to write one's own and have it accepted by the board, a "mode 3", but as many teachers know GCE boards became progressively less amenable to mode 3 schemes (and their fate has varied in the comparable GCSEs). A solution was found in the JMB "course" called "Integrated Humanities", which was technically a mode 1, but it worked like a mode 3 in that teachers designed and graded the assessment and had considerable control over the course content. Apart from its advantages from the point of view of teaching about "race" it allowed for far less dependence on timed final essays and thus could test for a wider range of useful skills. This course lives on in GCSE: the Northern Examining Association has a GCSE called Integrated Humanities which functions in all respects like the old GCE, without the untidy rigmarole of devising a matching CSE.[1] The association (previously the board) offers fifteen units of which a school has to teach five, or four of the NEA's and one of their own. This might make (as in our case) one unit per term, unless a school really takes integration seriously and weaves the entire five elements into a single cloth.

Having discovered this course and its possibilities, we had little hesitation in switching to it. Since in the school concerned the subject went under the name of "sociology" the subjects chosen from the board's options were mainly sociological, or at least were treated in a sociological way. The first term was called "The Family", followed by "Persecution and Prejudice", "Class and Politics" (our own course), "Education" and "The Mass Media". Put another way, term one actually focused a lot on gender inequality, term two on the inequalities which arise in Britain from "race", and term three on class. The two terms in the fifth year then examined the wider significance of these inequalities in the institutions of education and the media. The board's course outline for the "race" part is reproduced below, though it will be clear from the next chapter that this is not rigid or restricting in practice.

Persecution and prejudice

The study of persecution and prejudice should provide the pupil with some insight into the ubiquitous nature of this field of human behaviour on personal, national and international levels. This theme is more concerned with the recognition of persecution and prejudice than with the prospects of changing attitudes, although it is expected that logical, reasoned arguments would weigh more than unsupported, one-sided opinions of whatever standpoint, in the assessment of students' work.

1   The universality of prejudice
    "Man's inhumanity to man
    Makes countless thousands mourn."
    Xenophobia, segregation, scapegoatism, victimisation, ostracism, bigotry, endogamy, paranoia, stereotyping, snobbery, elitism, etc.

2   The techniques of persecution
    Anti-locution.
    Avoidance.

Discrimination.
Physical Attack.
Massacre/Genocide.

Students should be expected to demonstrate an understanding of this sliding scale of persecution, in part or in total, and to appreciate how one step on it provides a threshold for the next.

3   The study of at least one major area of persecution or prejudiced behaviour at home or abroad; e.g. at least one of the following in the contemporary world or from the recent past:

racial,
political,
religious,
social.

For some people all this treatment of inequality brands myself and my colleague as simply Marxists seeking to indoctrinate children into a left-wing view of the world. Such a view is itself simple, even simple minded, and demonstrates little knowledge of classrooms or pupils in provincial areas of Britain, or as far as "race" is concerned, any knowledge of the varieties of anti-racist views. Some of the diary accounts quoted later from pupils themselves should make it clear that 15 year olds are not easily manipulated, and that the teacher's purpose has more to do with encouraging a critical awareness than with imposing a single interpretative theory. Judging from the DES document quoted in chapter 1, they should approve, and as the Swann Report noted:

political education should... through encouraging pupils to consider how power is exercised and by whom at different levels in our society, how resources are allocated, how policies are determined and implemented, how decisions are taken and how conflicts are resolved, be no more likely to lead them to question and challenge the status quo, other than where this is justified, than to defend and seek to retain it.[2]

Assessing the work of the pupils is difficult, partly because of the requirements of the board and partly because of the complexity of learning about "race". Both of these difficulties have to be welcomed, since they get to grips with something which matters in education.

The assessment as we would normally understand the term has to be based on four criteria determined by the JMB (now NEA). These are

1 Knowledge.
2 The ability to locate and select evidence.
3 The interpretation of evidence and evaluation of argument.
4 The presentation of explanations, ideas and arguments.

These are weighted so that the first counts for more than each of the others, and assessment tasks have to be set so they test these skills. Monitoring and responding to pupils' feelings was dealt with by us in another way, which is outlined at the end of this chapter (see p. 52).

Why bother with exams?

First, though it is worth considering an argument which tends to be put by those involved in active tutorial work and the pastoral curriculum, and/or those seeking to erode the domination of secondary schooling by public examinations. They question whether something which has so much to do with attitude change belongs in the examined curriculum at all. The problem with arguing for its inclusion is that I might be understood as defending the current exam system, and even pressing for its extension. This is not my position. As has already been explained, this course was designed for specific circumstances, partly to have an effect in the area where the decision was in my hands, and partly as an experiment. If I had been made responsible for the pastoral curriculum I would probably have worked in that area instead.

This biographical detail aside, there are other reasons for other schools to follow this route. One reason for dealing with "race" in the mainstream curriculum, the examined curriculum, is that it never is dealt with there. A survey of secondary school curricula in white areas would probably show that "prejudice" is featured somewhere, but whether in years 1–3 or above it is more likely to be in RE than anywhere else, unless the school is in tune with the national growth of overall "pastoral" programmes, in which case it will be found there.

One shortcoming of this placing of "race" or "prejudice" is simply the question of time. Very few secondary schools allow more than an hour a week for RE in years 1–3, and most would be nearer half an hour. Similarly, pastoral/tutorial programmes have relatively small time allocations. To go into any kind of factual detail would therefore require many consecutive weeks, and one look at pastoral programmes or RE clearly indicates the demands already made upon these "slots" (conceivably everything from personal hygiene and

greeting visitors on the one hand to all the world's faiths on the other).
It is likely, I would argue, that when racism is approached at all in this
area of the curriculum it is under heavy constraints to be brief, and,
more subtly, to be centred upon discussions, opinion, and thus
founded upon different sorts of suppositions from "worthwhile"
activities elsewhere in the curriculum.

The point about discussions will be taken up next, but if we look at
the problem of time this increases as one moves up the age range. RE
is more likely to take on current affairs and moral issues than it is
lower down the school, and where time can be spared from talking
about sex a good deal of work might be done on "race". This is
particularly the case where RE has a central and valued place in the
view of both pupils and staff, but this is not a common situation
(though many people would like to think it is). Where RE is a major
examination option, perhaps on a par in numbers with history, then
in principle there is more scope, although when one actually examines
available syllabuses it becomes clear that the real possibilities are
somewhat limited. Pastoral programmes, meanwhile, where they
operate much demarcation from RE, have increasing demands made
to deal with careers, sex (again), and other "older" concerns like
drugs, so that "race" becomes simply one of many "social issues".

With these constraints on time it is easy to understand those
committed and concerned teachers who are anxious about raising
"race" because they wonder if they have the skill and whether they
may, if not create a problem where none existed, perhaps make it
worse. "Stirring the pot" for half an hour, without the time either then
or later to help the contents settle in a way which would be positive
educationally, could certainly make things worse. It has the effect of
raising a vague background problem in many pupils' minds and
bringing it forward, but not enabling any resolution to take place. As
many teachers will know, what happens next is an eruption of opinion
and argument, a dozen separate sub-issues about "race" spring up
(typically South Africa, Chinese takeaways, crash helmets,
immigration, mugging, riots, unemployment, social security, and the
smell of curry). None can be adequately addressed and the class
tumbles out when the bell goes to a mixture of relief and despair on the
part of the teacher. What can she do? Where can she start? Where did
she go wrong? Has she made it worse?

Indeed she has, but it is hardly her fault. The class jokers have had
their role reinforced and they exchange racist jokes for the rest of the
morning; the majority of pupils, who will have had a mixture of

confusions, half truths, anecdotes, and strong feelings about "race" in the first place, will have these agitated a little; the (rare) pupil who stands outside this common pattern will be able to find no other role but silence; and if there happens to be a black child in the class she will just have to be angry all day, or helplessly join in the "joking", or emotionally withdraw, and in any case will wish that Miss had got on with the proper lesson. "Things were all right until you started talking about it."

None of this is a recipe for doing nothing. If the issue of "race" is considered important enough to do at all then presumably people would want it done well, yet to do so in real schools, with real staff, very restricted resources, no timetabled planning time and many other demands is a major task.

As one concerned to bring about changes in secondary education, and no supporter of the public exam system as it is (I am not yet convinced of a profound change in philosophy arising from GCSE), some colleagues would not expect such an emphasis on exam-orientated work. Surely, they ask, the building up of the non-examined curriculum is the way to break the stranglehold of educational labelling? Idealists in one field often see themselves as realists in another, and as far as public exams are concerned it seems to me realistic to expect their continued domination of secondary education, and no decline in society's expectation that schools will have a grading function.

If this is the case then the important work of a school will still be seen as the assessment-orientated work. In the short term, the way to get "race" on to the curriculum agenda is to argue for its inclusion along with the other things schools give priority to. After all, what kind of argument is it which says, in effect, the divine right of biology and home economics as examinable subjects can remain unquestioned, while newer concerns will fight the double battle of recognition and of status. (The battle has to be fought in pupils' minds too; they have little doubt about what "counts" in school.)

To repeat, my argument is not really against the diminution of the importance of exams, it is more to question the usual boundaries of the examined curriculum. It is undeniable that there are considerable affective dimensions in the kind of course being described, but it is a trap to therefore conclude that much of the work cannot be assessed in the same sort of way as other subjects. To do so would be to argue that studying "race" was all or mostly a matter of "discussions", of attitudes and feelings, and hence best dealt with as a matter of opinions. It is not: people's feelings cloud the issues, but there are nevertheless facts and evidence, historical and economic analyses, media biases and geographical distributions, all of which are employed in studying wars, industrial decline, smoking, and many other things which have a toehold in the mainstream curriculum. If we value academic skills we ought to be prepared to apply them to things which are divisive and controversial. To do so is to be really at the sharp end of teaching, and can potentially develop skills of evidence and judgement, separating emotive from factual statements, as well as all the skills of reading, studying, and appropriate language use which schools are rightly expected to impart.

There are nevertheless undoubted problems when pupils' emotions get in the way of their factual judgements, and many would argue that the same is true of teachers. I can offer no simple solution to these problems. My own way of dealing with them is to give them the time they need, which means a willingness to talk a lot with the pupils involved in a way which allows them to speak their minds. Sharing the problem with other staff at various levels, and with parents, can also prevent simplistic charges of bias suddenly arising. They will still arise from time to time, but to seek to eschew affective and political dimensions in "academic" subjects is take the road to irrelevance. A curriculum where the things that count in people's lives are consigned to "pastoral" and things that are drained of everyday relevance are examined would be a fundamentally misguided one.

Monitoring and responding to pupils' feelings

Returning to how the course in question began to take into account the attitudes and feelings of the pupils, the affective dimension referred to earlier, the learning logs quoted in this chapter and chapter 4 were an attempt to be aware of the "informal" process of learning which intertwine with the usual formal appearances. They will perhaps indicate that despite the heavy public exam bias in this course we were under no illusions about the complexities of the task we were involved in.

This method of recording pupil reactions had no necessary connection with the course: the teacher concerned developed the idea of learning logs while in a series of Schools Council workshops called "Learning about Learning". The principle is highly relevant to this course, since it is to get pupils to reflect, in an organized but informal way, on what they have learned or not learned, allowing the teacher to participate in this reflection too.

With classes of thirty, or more in this case, it is impossible in even the most apparently straightforward lesson to be aware of what many of the class are getting out of it. Any good teacher knows how misleading it is to generalize from the pupils who talk the most or from written work which is directly assessed. There is an obvious problem with marking the work in this course, especially the work of those most resistant to the factual content (although surprisingly this has never been a really major hurdle). We need to monitor pupils' responses in some way in order to avoid teacher domination of the acceptable things to express, and to stay in touch with pupils' feelings and reactions, and their needs from the lesson. These logs, therefore, were an attempt to get pupils to write a few of their thoughts to aid their own sense of direction in learning, but also to give the teacher some idea of the way their views differed from hers in respect to what was happening.

Ironically, the constraints of the secondary exam curriculum within which this course was set up prevented the teacher from departing radically from the syllabus as agreed with the exam boards. On the other hand, it did give her some insight into what more of the class were thinking than she would have obtained in the normal way, and to some extent she could orientate the next lesson accordingly.

Learning logs had been employed with the class throughout the previous term, so they were familiar with the purpose and procedure. At the end of some lessons pupils would be simply asked to write something in their logs, something they thought they had learned that day, a question that was unanswered for them, a feeling they wanted to express but had not otherwise had the chance to. No account was taken of spelling or careful sentence structure, or handwriting, so the logs are freed, in theory at least, from some of the usual constraints of pupil-to-teacher writings. It is easy to see when looking at them that at times they become fairly informal notes and comments.

Logs take a large amount of teacher time, and any reader's reflections on them ought to bear that in mind. The more formal marking load generated by this course was enormous — if we had two classes each we would regularly have sixty-four essays apiece to mark, many of them eight sides of A4 or longer. To use learning logs as well is pure extra workload. Of course, it makes one's understanding of the class better and therefore one's teaching ought to be better, but it still takes some of that most scarce of good teachers' possessions, time. Many of the comments the teacher wrote here were off the cuff, quick replies to keep the dialogue open with the pupils and to stimulate them to write again another time. On her part, too, there was no great attempt to be formally grammatical.

As to the comments themselves, those of the pupils should demonstrate to anyone not familiar with such work the tangled and complex task teachers have in guiding any learning, let alone learning clouded by as much emotional fog as this is. The pupils display sympathy and generosity at the same time as intolerance and learned misinformation. One or two also demonstrate considerable resistance.

The class was, as will be obvious, mostly female, the perennial pattern in the social sciences. One girl in the class was "black" in the sense employed in this book, although as some of the comments reveal that this might not be her own description. The teacher had two Indian grandparents, but the class did not know this and it would probably not have occurred to them. The class was a largely mixed ability one, but not entirely so. In accordance with the school's option system approximately the "top 80 per cent of the ability range" could choose sociology as an option for CSE or GCE. As for attitudes when they began the course, there was obviously some self-selection in those who choose to study a course a fifth of which they knew would be about "race".

Lest the level of language competence cast doubt on the ability range represented here, it should be pointed out that the spelling and punctuation have been tidied up to make the comments more easily readable. It is nevertheless surprising how fluent some of the writing is when rewritten in this way, freed from the visual shackles of almost illegible handwriting and often very inaccurate spelling.

The extracts here are from the first two or three weeks of the course. The pupils played the "Passport" game, exchanged some "images of black people and white people" in small groups, had some fairly brief class talking, watched the beginning of the *Enemy Within* tape-slide sequence, watched the TV film *Our People* on immigration, undertook some formal written work, looked briefly at media imagery, watched most of a TV play about the immigration and eventual marriage of a Sikh man in Britain, and undertook some study and formal writing about what we called (over-simply) in the course "Asian Culture".[3]

For reasons of space not all the class's logs have been reprinted, but those which have are given in their entirety. To have selected extracts would not only have disturbed the dialogue where it exists, it would also have diminished the insight into the pupils' awareness afforded by the full versions. In addition, it is important that those unfamiliar with this sort of work in classrooms can read relatively unmediated writings from pupils. Any selection on my part would build in biases and preferences about what I wanted people to read.

Simon: When I arrived I thought it would be a boring lecture by some black person about race relations, then when I got into the room I thought it would be a play by some morons. The game was all right, it was easy to pinch the money from Mr Bolter, he was a sucker. All the white people wouldn't let the black people get a job. All in all it was a good game, it was more like real life than a game. All the blacks couldn't get a job, only if you pinched one, and the same applies to buying a house, you couldn't nick one. I have learned that 43 per cent of the black people are born in England. End of chat, OK?

(You say that this was fairly realistic, can you explain this a bit more?)

No.

Every black person has a lot of difficulty getting in here, we found this out in the reading you done. Since we are in the EEC we have to let in the frogs and all of that lot in, so we stop all of the blackies getting in by putting them into detention centres and questioning them a lot.

(Simon, it appears from what you've written that you're not keen on any foreigners being here, from any countries... can you explain why? And here's something to think about, there are few "pure" British people in this country, most of us came from very mixed backgrounds of different European and Asian countries.)

Us Brits emigrated to find jobs which are scarce in England today. Some people go to Antipodean countries because the climate is better than ours, it's warmer and not so crowded as England like today. It may be cheaper as well.

   We found out that the black people are scared of us more than the NF or the British Movement. They have learned not to be scared of the NF they are scared of the innocent passers by.

(I think you've misunderstood the message being put across in the filmstrip. Groups like the NF show their hatred, black people are frightened of them, but they know to expect hatred from these people. You say blacks are scared of the innocent passer by, this is where you've missed the point really, because people who aren't members of the NF have continually been unkind to blacks it has made them more wary of white people. If you were to meet someone who was tolerant of you one minute then turned on you the next and this happened more than once, wouldn't you begin to suspect all people's motives when they wanted to be friendly?

By the way, I don't know why you drew the Union Jack on the back of this log book, what are you trying to say?

PS. Do you know anything about the National Front, British Movement, Ku Klux Klan?)

Yes, a bit. The NF don't treat them fairly and hate 'em. The Ku Klux Klan is the American version of the NF who wear white hoods and burn crosses on black people's doorsteps.

(Do you know the reasons behind this hatred?)

They don't like them of course.

(Yes, but why?)

I feel that the black Asians should wear what we wear, not a load of rags, which the females do wear. If the 4 per cent of blackies were to leave, the unemployment would go down. So the Pakistanis are getting the jobs that the British would want.

(Aren't you being rather unreasonable saying that people who don't wear the same clothes as you do wear rags? Why do you think it is necessary to criticize other people for not being like you? Can you not accept others? I'm also rather confused by your ideas that black people leaving the country would help the unemployment problem. Are you saying that people in those jobs are preventing "white" people from working? If so, I think you'll soon discover that you aren't quite right in believing this.)

Well, it would not be true to a very fine point, but if they leave, the unemployment will go down. I think that if you were black and you committed a crime you should be deported back to India or where you came from. That would slow down the unemployment and have more places in the prisons.

When that bloke arrived he thought he was dreaming, but only on the train ride. But when he got to the cities he must have been flabbergasted to find hardly any turbans on Asians' heads. He must have had second thoughts about his visit to here and he must have wanted to go back, but his family needed the money.

John: I thought that it was a bit one-sided because it did not show how the whites were mistreated by the blacks, because once the equal rights act was passed the blacks thought they were god, and... [illegible]... is afraid to turn them away because he will get in trouble with the race relations board. And they are scared because the nignogs might write to the newspapers and have all those do-gooders going mad. And it didn't tell you that all the coons coming into Britain go straight into a council house with it fully furnished, and they have hundreds of kids running all over the place. This part gets right up my nose because all you hear is the poor Pakis are being victimized, nothing is said about the British people who were born and bred here and haven't got job or money and a lot have nowhere to live. If we spent as much time and money on our own people it would be a lot better. And it isn't the whites who have race riots and go around mugging people. There was an incident in this school where a boy was going home from football and a black came up to him and hit him for nothing.

(John, your ideas about the black people arriving in Britain and going straight into fully furnished houses don't seem quite correct. Where did you get this information? I can see you feel bad about the fact that there are white British people with no money, no jobs, etc., but this hasn't got anything to do with the numbers of black people in this country. If they weren't here, we'd still have a lot of poverty amongst white people. Hopefully, I'll try and explain this during the course.

PS. You were obviously angry after Thursday's lesson to draw the Union Jack on the cover of the log book, what are you trying to show me by drawing this?)

I think that the blacks are put down, but too much is made of it, because nothing is said about the thing that happens to whites that if anybody takes the mick out of blacks they go mad and call you a racialist, but if they take the mick out of us we just give it back. If they don't like the way they are treated they can go somewhere else where they will be treated better, and stop annoying us. And if they can't afford it let the government pay, I doubt if the British people will mind. This doesn't affect the blacks like Jamaicans and Africans, but this should be done to the Pakis and the Indians.

(Hallo. Why do you think blacks react so quickly when they have the mickey taken out of them? Could it be that they don't like it because it happens too often and it isn't a joke to them? Is it more than taking the mickey? The names some black people are called are insults and shouldn't be used. It would not be right to insult someone every time you spoke to them. You say if they don't like the way they are treated they can go somewhere else, is this realistic? Where? Why? Why do you think this is a possibility? You make a distinction between West Indians and Indians and Pakistanis, why?)

I think it is one sided so far, we have only looked at how the blacks feel. The pink minority groups have only been frowned upon, we learned nothing about how the NF or the Nazi party feel, or even the British party. These are minorities as well and I think we should know what they feel.

(Well John, you're jumping the gun a bit. We will be looking at the "pink minority" groups which you mention and you will get to know what they feel. This will come later on in the course, so be patient! And in the meantime begin to think about where your attitudes have come from and why you hold them, I'd be quite interested in this.)

There has never been a fool proof system to stop illegal immigrants.

(Of course the idea of a fool proof system isn't possible, but think along these lines... why do you think people might bother to enter the country illegally anyway?
PS. When you were playing the "Passport" game did you ever consider illegal immigration as a possibility? Did any other Indian citizens consider it?)

I think the immigration should be the same for all immigrants no matter they are white, black or blue. I don't think we should let people from the common market come in so easily, and definitely not from Arabia, because one minute they hate us and the next they are living here.

(Basically I agree there should be the same immigration laws regardless of colour. But as a member of the EEC we have agreements with the other 11 countries to have unrestricted entry for all citizens so we can't break this agreement. What should happen is that the law should be made more realistic and humane, by limiting numbers if necessary but not treating blacks so differently from whites.)

I think we should come out of the EEC because it has only been trouble since we started. And we would have to have a lot of strangers coming over. The information I had about them coming over to a fully furnished house is first hand experience. Some blacks next door to my Nan got a house fully furnished and for nothing.

(How do you know this? Did you speak to the people?)

If the blacks were not here we still would have some jobs even if it wasn't very many, plus we would save money because they wouldn't get the dole. I have had more experience with the West Indians and I just don't like Indians and Pakistanis.

(Why?)

I accept that some Asians who have been born over here are British. But I would have thought that the wish of the white British people could be considered. Because they don't want any more black people coming into our country, and if there are white people who want more in it is probably a minority. Why should a minority rule a majority?

(In fact, there are very few black people entering Britain today.)

West Indian Culture. The main religion among the West Indians is Christianity, this is because England went over there and converted them. But they do not worship like us, they sing and shout and mainly go daft, but us British we keep serious. The West Indians have the same family system as the English because we taught them what to do and to keep their family down. They have turned to the religion of Rastafari because they say they are being victimized by the white people and their society, so they have made their own to combat the pressure they say they are under.

Mandy: On Friday afternoon I thought we was going to watch a play. I did not have any idea that we was going to play a game. I found the game very interesting apart from me being a Paki, as it was harder for us to get a job and to buy a house. Like when I queued up for a job they wanted to know my name and where I lived but I could not even pronounce my name so I was taken to the policemen and he sent me back to India, so then I had to pay another £400 to get back over to Britain. Playing this game shows that it is harder for Pakis to get a job than what it is for white people. Like they got called names like I got told I stunk of curry and other rude comments like that. I don't really think this is fair to Pakis, like they say go back to your own country and get a job there. So really, playing this game showed me how hard it is for a Paki to get a job as this most probably does happen in this country. You can't just say that black people are bad, as you have got to listen to both sides of the story first. Like when a white boy got beat up by two coloured boys older than him we don't know if the white boy asked for it by calling them names. I can't say that I am prejudiced because I have nothing against blacks. Like there is a coloured girl in the 5th year called... and I think she is really nice, and she gets on with nearly everyone. Some coloureds can be nasty like beating up people for no reason. But I agree with most of the things we have been talking about in this lesson.

(It's interesting you say you aren't prejudiced, but I'm puzzled as to why you use the term "Paki" when describing Asian people. There's more than one black girl in the 5th year, but being in such a minority it must be very difficult to be seen as a person, rather than "one of them". I'm glad you found the game interesting, I'm sure the course will be interesting too.)

When black people come to live in England it is very hard for them to get a job. The people that work in the job centres or when they go for an interview they always turn the black people down and say somebody else has already got the job, which I don't think is fair especially for the black people who was born in England. The workers don't give them a chance to find out what their personalities are like etc. They just take colours to be the same, by creating trouble etc.

(And this is based upon misunderstanding about stereotypes!)

Hi again. It is easy for white people to get into the country than it is coloureds. Before this lesson I didn't have a clue what immigrants meant, so really I have learned a lot from this lesson.

(That's what I like to hear!)

It is interesting to learn about Asian culture, about where they come from and what religion they follow. I think it is also weird the way they dress, what with the turbans and the way they let their beards grow and their hair down their back, but that is their way of dressing, I suppose, they probably find our clothes weird. The thing which I found interesting today which I did not know before was that the Sikh names, with Singh as a middle name for a man and Kaur for a woman.

(I'm glad you found the lesson useful in some ways. It's quite difficult to realize that not all people are exactly the same, but once everyone understands and accepts this things will be a lot easier.)

Caroline (the black girl referred to earlier): I didn't really know what to expect on Friday. I enjoyed what we did though. I think it was quite realistic and I was glad I was English. It may have changed some people's opinions about race and colour because I think when you are being told not to be racists nobody really wants to listen. It was better going through the sort of things the Indian people have to go through. Most people now know what it feels like to be called Pakis and to be insulted when you have a right to be a different race. Some people might just laugh when they are called names, but some people may feel really hurt. It doesn't bother white people as much as coloured people when they are called names.

(A thoughtful response Caroline, your last point is quite important. Why do you think this is the case?)

Most of the points made about black people were negative. Most points made against black people had an answer or explanation for them. Most people now do accept black people but people who don't probably don't know a black person. Not all black people are the same. Their images are exaggerated a lot just to make them look stupid. They try to be accepted into the society but a lot of people won't have them.

(Why won't a lot of people accept them? The answer to this question isn't easy, but it's based on the fact that, as you mentioned earlier, people who say racist things don't know black people, or if they do, they use stereotypes to describe these people rather than describe them in their own right.)

The point about when a black person does something and the rest of the black people seem to be blamed also, and white people don't think about what other white people do is true, I think. I hadn't realized how much it hurts people to be called names, because if I am called names I don't think the person has ever really meant to hurt me. Even if somebody really meant it I don't think I would take it seriously. You can tell if the person is really serious or is just joking. I don't think as many people would call blacks names if they thought it was really going to upset them.

(I'm not so sure. There are some white people who hate black people, but not in an outward way; therefore, the name calling is a way of showing how much the whites hate the blacks. But you're right in saying people call others names without really thinking about it. Perhaps we should all be more aware of what we say in the light of the effects it can have on some people.)

Can't the leaders of the countries where the black immigrants come from do anything about how the immigrants are treated before and after they enter Britain? The people who question the families obviously don't want the families to leave their home country, but why?

(The answer to your first question, Caroline, generally no! Because whether or not they like it, the British officials are considered to be more "high up" and not to be questioned! This does seem very strange, but the British have had quite a strong hold over Asian countries in particular for an extremely long time. And to the second question... the best thing would be for you to see the video again, one lunchtime perhaps, to see if you can come up with your own answers.)

I was surprised that the men Sikhs when they came over to work were so surprised about England and they thought that England would have been such a wonderful place. The women didn't seem to take long to get used to all the different things. I thought that the men would know that if they wanted to come and live in England they would have to do things like cutting their hair and beards, and I felt they shouldn't have been so surprised. I would like to write to somebody but would not know what to write.

These pupils' logs and the course outline itself ought to give some insight into what kind of classroom enterprise is involved, and the next chapter contains a lot more detail about content and method. It may be as well at this point to pose the questions which most commonly arise about the course, particularly from other teachers. These can be summarized as follows;

1   Will I create a problem where none exists?
2   Is it in the exam syllabus?
3   Will my classroom just explode?
4   Do I have the necessary skill?
5   Do I have the necessary knowledge?
6   Is it academic enough?
7   Is it inevitably doctrinaire and biased?
8   Will pupils be negative and hostile because it is "school knowledge"?

9 Are there any books and resources?
10 How will the black pupils feel?
11 Does the course duck the real issues?

I hope I have already demonstrated that a problem exists in the attitudes of many white pupils, and as for exam syllabuses, since race seldom appears, one has to write one's own.[4] The other questions will be recurring themes in the next chapter, and responses, if not answers, will be given at the end of it.

References

1 The Southern Examining Group's humanities course has a fairly flexible assessment scheme, though 30 per cent is by examination, and "Race and Culture" as well as "Prejudice" are in their list of topics from which centres can choose. Neither their sociology nor their social science courses have the potential to study "race" in as much detail as humanities.

 Another option in this respect is the Midland Examining Group's integrated humanities. If successfully piloted it will operate in a very similar way to the NEA's.

NEA:	Joint Matriculation Board, Manchester M15 6EU.
MEG:	E. Midlands Regional Examining Board, Robins Wood House, Robins Wood Rd, Apsley, Nottingham NG8 3NH.
SEG:	Associated Examinations Board, Wellington House, Station Rd, Aldershot, Hants GU11 1BQ.

2 *Education for All*, HMSO, Cmnd 9453, 1985, p. 334.

3 These materials are referred to again in several places and full details are given in the resources appendix.

4   Course outline

Title	Lessons	Method/resources
Introduction	2	"Passport" game
	1	*Enemy Within* tape/slide and discussion groups.
Immigration to Britain	1	Brief quiz about basics of numbers, causes. Discussion
	2	Video *Our People* on immigration. Follow up with *Immigration to Britain* booklet which matches film.
	1	Read leaflet *It's easy getting into Britain*.
	3	Go through booklet *Why they come*, and do map of former colonies. Notes on push and pull factors, with maps of Pakistan and India.
Cultures of minority groups in Britain	2	Class notes on varieties of Afro-Caribbean and Asian cultures
	1	Videos: *Multi-racial Britain* (4x15mins); extract from play (45 mins); *16UP* on Rastas.
	2	Guided project work on aspects of Asian cultures.
Stages of intolerance	1	Explanation and notes on Allport's 5 stages. Guided research project on extent of prejudice and avoidance in everyday life.
	2	
(Prejudice)	1	Videos: *Multiracial Britain* (15mins); *16UP* – Racism. Discussion and questions.
(Discrimination)		Video *Our People* and discussion. Work through backup booklet.
	1	
	1	Booklet on housing, with questions.
	1	Tape/slide *Racism in Britain*, part 2.
(Physical attack)	2	Audio tape about racial attacks, with questions. Various readings.
	1	Video: *Politics of Racial Hatred*.
(Extermination)		Prejudice filmstrip. Various readings.
	1	Interview with NF organizer.

| Stereotyping and prejudice | 2 | Video: *Scene, Why Prejudice?* Tape/slide *Racism in Britain*. Discussion and notes. |

Homework is either continuing/finishing classwork, or writing preparing for assessments.

Assessment

Criterion 1: Knowledge.

Tested by factual recall test on immigration (history, law, campaigns, numbers etc.) and by timed essay on distinctions within "Asian culture".

Criterion 2a: Ability to locate and select evidence.

Tested by projects on Asian cultures and on prejudice.

Criterion 2b: Interpretation of evidence, evaluation of argument.

Tested by structured questions on teenagers' attitudes to marriage or by structured questions on immigration myths.

Criterion 2c: Presentation of explanations, ideas, arguments.

Tested by long essay on Allport's 5 stages.

4 "Race" in the classroom

In the last chapter the context of a course on "race" was given, together with some of the circumstances leading to its birth, and pupils' reactions to it. This chapter will examine the course in more detail, with some explanation and justification of the different sections, and some extracts from pupils' logs.

The "Passport" game

There is much to be said for a dramatic start to any topic, and in the "race" unit this can be provided by the game "Passport".[1] An ordinary classroom is quite adequate for the simulation, provided that it can be rearranged so that most of the desks form a barrier dividing the room in a ratio of 2:1, leaving most of the rest of the floor space free. Ideally the furniture should be arranged in advance. This means that it is possible to announce that it is 1960, that they are being given new identities and new lives (and a little bit of toy money). If the referee knows the class some prior thought should be given to the next stage, which is allocating either British (white badges) or Indian identities to everyone, in married couples. The officials are introduced: an immigration officer/Indian pay clerk, an estate agent, an employer, a British pay clerk, and the referee (who can, on request, be a policemen, an MP, the Race Relations Board,[2] the DHSS, or anyone else). Participants then go to their own country and find their spouse.

The object of the game is simply to get the best job and the best house possible. Britain is experiencing a labour shortage and pays far better than Indian employers, but despite this attraction the Indian couples do not have enough money initially for both of them to emigrate. Everyone working is paid their wages annually, "years" last about five minutes each and are signified by the referee blowing a whistle. In this way an incentive is built into the simulation for people to want to enter Britain. What happens, of course, is that from the moment they arrive in Britain they are behind the whites in the promotion stakes, and discrimination keeps them there. Prospects are enticingly offered to maintain motivation, but for most people they are not realized. By 1962 there is an Immigration Act, which becomes progressively more effective at preventing entry and keeping couples apart. The 1965 Race Relations Act makes no difference at all to the things that matter most in the Indians' lives, and the 1968 act reduces the frequency of discrimination without eliminating it. At the end of the simulation, usually about an hour or at most an hour and a half, some Indians are still in India, frustrated and demoralized, one or two, the polite ones who have shown they know their place, have supervisory jobs (but not managerial ones), but most have spent an hour being insulted and put down either explicitly and legally before 1968, or more subtly afterwards.

Various permutations can be built in with groups who grasp the basic idea fairly quickly. Periodic random checks can be made on Indians to look for illegal immigrants, they can be refused a job or their wages if they do not know their passport number, they can be deported for getting angry (causing a breach of the peace), someone could be encouraged to try and start a union or self-help group. If the referee has the stamina, unemployment could be introduced, and one might even keep going until the 1980s to see if there are any uprisings. At that point some Indians could be recruited into the police force.

Clearly the point is then to reflect on these experiences and for participants to relate them to themselves and to real life. The discussion which preceded the learning logs reproduced here used the following guidelines: how did it feel to be called "Paki"? Did you retaliate? Did it work? Did the patterns of employment and housing reflect the patterns in real life? Where were Indians concentrated? How did it feel to be Indian (or British) during the game? How did you feel about the British generally, even those who did nothing actively against you? Did any of the British help the Indians? Why? Or (more likely) why not? Did anyone steal? Did it seem "right"? Would any form of direct action have been effective in changing the system? Was the 1965 act useful? The 1968 act?

Jane: Hello, I thought that the game on Friday was a good idea because it showed us roughly what race is about. I thought that the idea of Indians trying to get over to England to get jobs, houses etc. was quite good, it showed us what it is like to be an Indian and to be treated like one. I think the prejudice was a little exaggerated over in the housing department. We also discovered what it was like to be called Paki etc., that wasn't too nice to begin with but I got over that, probably because I had the reassurance that after the game I would be English again. Although I thought it was a bit exaggerated at the place where we had to get into England, but it was still a good game to play, but in real life it is not a game.

(This is an interesting point. People don't have that "escape" in reality, but I'm glad it made you aware of what goes on. And you're right about the point of saying "in real life it's not a game". You obviously put a lot of thought into your experience of the game.)

Linda: I thought that we were going to have a discussion with some people from another country. But when we got told what to do I didn't quite understand at first. What we had to do was get from India to England and find a job and a house. I found that it was hard to do this because I was an Indian and everyone from England turned a blind eye to us and wouldn't let us into England. I found this made me angry. Now I know what they go through. Why weren't we allowed into England after 1962?

(In reply to your comments and question on Friday's activity.... Yes it is difficult for people isn't it, and I know that the anger you felt about your position is much like the anger many people experience in the same situation. In answer to your question, men weren't allowed into Britain after 1962 because basically if more men came in then their dependents would be entitled to enter and this (as the government saw it) would mean yet more people. So the law stated that men had to have an employment voucher in order to be able to enter. This restricted the numbers of men initially coming into the country and in the long term restricted the number of dependants (i.e. wives and children). Is this answer OK or is it more confusing?)

Marianne: Friday was a good laugh. When I got into the room I thought "God, this is gonna be boring" but it wasn't, not really. I played an English person and I only got around to being a factory worker. I think it was a bit too crowded to really let it work well, as there wasn't enough room. By the time you had reached the Estate Agent's and you were one from the front, the whistle would go, it would be a different year and you were told to collect your wages!
   Another thing is that there were far too many Indian people coming into the English part of the room, which made getting jobs almost impossible! Apart from all that, Friday afternoon was a good laugh, well that's all there was to

do when you were stood in the queues waiting for your wages etc. wasn't there?

Karen: When we started, everybody who was English rushed to where the money was being given out. Everyone got the same job to start with and as soon as husband and wife got some money it was to the housing dept. to buy a house. I was so involved in doing this I really didn't know what was going on for the Indians. I just saw them all behind the "border" standing around. After a while, it began to get a little confusing as people began to come from India and everyone else was trying to get as much money as they could. In the end, it ended up with me getting in the queue for the paying of the house and my husband to keep on getting the money. I think that a lot of people who were Indians just started to take money and jobs because the people wouldn't let them have any. The Indians got called "Pakis" and I didn't think that they liked it. In the end they were so desperate to get money that they began to ask for some off the English people. With the housing situation, the English could put down deposits and pay £50 a year but with the Indians they had to pay it all off just to be on the safe side. I think this was a very good way of showing racialism and I think that everyone just realized how important it was and is.

(Some interesting, clear thoughts here Karen. I think you may be overestimating its effects on everyone taking part; you see racism as bad, many people do, but some who took part in the game don't.)

Lee: I didn't know what was going to happen, I was an Indian. The British didn't mind me coming over but when I was over they wouldn't give me a house, sometimes they wouldn't give me my wages. This was stupid so I stole some money. I don't think it was as bad as that when the British let them over. They might have refused them a house but not their wages. It didn't bother me when I was called a Paki or golly wog etc. I think a lot of people are racialist because they don't know the reasons blacks are over here or just do because everybody else is. But some blacks take offence even when it is not meant or said as a joke. Why couldn't they send them back for free, because they let a lot in for free.

(You've mentioned some very interesting points Lee, particularly when you say that a lot of people are racist because they don't understand why people are here, and because they follow everyone else. Can you see why some blacks take offence, if all the time they are continually on the receiving end of other people's thoughts and feelings about them? Lee, it isn't a case of sending them back! What would be your reason for wanting to do this? If there is a problem somewhere connected with black people, surely we should identify where the problem lies (and it's usually in white people's misunderstanding as you said earlier) and tackle it, not appear to want to get rid of people! What do you think? You say we let them in free, well that's not strictly speaking true. They had to pay fares to get here; find work to support themselves once here...so I think you're exaggerating a bit, don't you?)

In my own teaching I have always found this game very effective. Admittedly it does have a few organizational drawbacks which should not be underestimated in real schools. It is not useable with pupils under 14, as they seem to be too young to take "playing" seriously! It requires a large team of people to run it, and although a couple of these can be from the class itself some of the official roles have to be both forceful and resourceful. (Once they have been participants themselves it is often possible to find sixth formers who can play these roles.) Finally, one may not have convenient parcels of time longer than an hour in one's school, and even to do the whole thing in a hour is probably to rush it too much.

There are other problems. The "Indians" get more out of it than the "British" and so some sharing of experiences has to be built into the discussion afterwards, to try and maximize the learning for the Britons.

Part of the role of the officials is to legitimate racism in the game, and this is partly done by name calling. The prospect of teachers initiating this kind of thing, apparently encouraging it among young people who, as black people know, hardly need much encouragement, fills some people with apprehension. In my view, and certainly that of the black people with whom I have played the game, this anxiety is misplaced. The experience of being called a demeaning name when in a less powerful position cannot usually be described to teenagers, nor easily to adults. This point always comes across in a far more effective way than it ever would do by explanation, and some of the comments in the logs testify to this. Pupils in white areas often ask after doing some work about race "but what can we do in an area like this?" A simple but worthwhile first step I always suggest is to get rid of words like "Paki" and "Wog" from acceptable white language. After playing "Passport" they are more likely to agree.

Another potential criticism of this kind of technique is that it presents Indians, and by extension obviously any black people in

Britain, as helpless victims. This is partly the point of an article by the Council for British Pakistanis:[3]

Perhaps... (naive and intrusive questions asked of Pakistani children)... are becoming things of the past, as teachers decide to tackle racism head on. We do not disagree with the sentiment, but we have strong reservations about the method. The danger is that ideas are presented to children that they may never before have entertained, either as victims or as persecutors. Often, violent, explicit stimulus material is used. A stereotype of the underprivileged "Paki" is built up. It is possible that this stereotype will be accepted while the message is ignored. Also, it seems to us, from reports filtering back from children, that anti-racist programmes can be patronising, with the message: you must be kind to our poor brothers.[3]

This is not the intention or the effect of either "Passport" or of the programme as a whole, and the discussion in chapter 1 should show that as far as the pupils here are concerned, no new racist thoughts are being put into their heads. As far as is possible, it is up to readers to judge for themselves whether this is the case. It should be said, however, and this will become a familiar point, that because teachers in white areas do not yet have any great expertise or experience in this field, it is important that courses of action, especially mistaken ones, are written down so that they can be corrected.

Another problem with "Passport" arises when there is a single black pupil in the class, or a very small number. This is a crucial issue throughout the course and will be taken up in more detail later, but personally I would never want to be in the situation of making a child black or white for the purposes of the game if I did not know them, had not talked to their teacher beforehand, and preferably talked to the pupil and her parents. Such precautions are difficult, but to do otherwise could make one guilty of well-meaning but lumbering, flat footed, and insensitive racism.

A final comment on this game. Feelings can run high, there can be some physical pushing and shoving, though I have never had anyone actually come to blows. Some people may withdraw and sit it out because it has become too much for them, some may be close to tears with frustration. Obviously, this has to be handled in a context which the pupils know to be caring, but I have few reservations about using such a potentially dramatic technique. "Race" evokes strong feelings, it is highly emotionally charged for many white (and black) people, and I know of no other technique which gives a flavour of what discrimination feels like for black people. The fact that it hurts is one of the most important concepts that the students have to grasp, and although it may be controversial and explosive, we are scarcely really touching the issue unless we grasp the nettles involved. One of these is pupils' feelings.

Terminology

At some stage terminology has to be discussed and agreed upon with a class. In the case of a word like "Paki" it takes some pupils a while to recognize it as an insult; they often seem to need a clearer idea of the geography of the subcontinent to appreciate that it is senseless to apply the term to all "Asians", and they need some empathy to grasp that it is more than a simple abbreviation even when only applied to Pakistanis. Even then they have to care enough to bother not to use insulting terms, including the more obvious ones like "wog" and "nigger". If all else fails, I fall back on teacher authority, because I would find frequent use of such terms in my classroom too offensive to tolerate. It is a matter of regret if pupils are unwilling to accept this, but in the last analysis teachers have to consider the black children, potential or actual, in the school, who have a right to expect that powerfully insulting terms of abuse for them are not common currency.

The use of the term "black" is rather more subtle, however, and while there is a strong argument for its use[1] it cannot be presented in that form to the average 4th year class. As a first step one can get pupils to simply word-associate on "black", perhaps having previously prepared a list from a dictionary of the terms, almost all negative, which include the word. The point is simply to start pupils thinking about their own resistance to the word, and the subtlety of the attitudes involved. It is not a point which all pupils will write eloquently about, but two extracts demonstrate that the point can be made.

Lorraine: I never really thought about how it was the slaves that made us feel superior. Then when we thought about all the words it seems funny how so many mean so much about black people, so they've ended up with a stereotype.

Steven: We wrote and discussed images and information about black people and all these images are negative. Having all negative images of a person or race is not a good thing as it encourages others to be negative as well. If we gadually introduced facts and images about black people that are positive then perhaps people's ideas of these people would change.

The Enemy Within

The next item listed on the course outline is *The Enemy Within* tape/slide programme.[5] This is referred to in chapter 5 for use with adults, and it is undoubtedly the case that it is pitched at a relatively high level and is not ideal material for use with younger pupils. The first twenty frames, however, contain some powerful material, and are worth using to get a black viewpoint very early on in the course. There is no easy answer to how whites in white areas can presume to speak for black people, nor is there an easy answer to which black people's views on a white teacher should present. Whatever one does, someone can legitimately argue that all black perspectives are not being presented, they never could be, but in areas where black people live there at least some checks and balances built in. *The Enemy Within* is a black view, an uncompromising and very clear one, and since few teaching materials with such a pedigree exist this one should be used. The opening parts of the programme concentrate on feelings of exclusion, whites' rejection, blacks' fears, and contain some first-hand experiences of the kind of brutal direct racist attacks which are seldom seen (or believed) in all whites areas. What pupils make of it can be judged from the following:

Jane: Well, I don't think that coloureds should be treated like an outsider. OK, their skin's darker than ours, but does that make them different from us? I don't think so. As for people saying go back home to them, that's rubbish, a lot of them were born here. I think that prejudice is a load of rubbish, because all humans have feelings, and that it hurts them to have to face prejudiced people every day of their life. It must hurt them a lot. Bye.

(Hello. It does hurt them a lot, but most black people have learned to contain their reactions and not to show how they feel.)

But do all of them learn how to cope with it and not show how they feel?

(No, it's not really easy for us to make generalizations about people's feelings;

it's obvious that some (particularly young) people are refusing to stay quiet and accept this.)

Linda: Hello. In today's lesson we saw a film strip on black people and the way they felt about us. Black people feel left out. I don't think there is any reason why black people should be left out. What is different between us except the colour of our skin? In the film a boy said how he went for an interview and while he was there two coloured girls came into the shop and asked if there was a job going. The first thing the manager asked was "Are they black?" Yes they were, so they got turned down. What happens if a white person went into a black man's shop and asked for a job and he got turned down? There would be uproar.

(An interesting thought in your final point, Linda. You're right about the fact that the colour of a person's skin shouldn't determine what happens to them, but as we will see, it does.)

Steven: From the lesson we found that people are prejudiced against the black race although they don't realize. It's mostly because of the way they were brought up. I think if books, the media and your parents gave an equal account of whites and blacks the country wouldn't have the problems of prejudice and discrimination against the blacks, although liberal discrimination is not really noticed a lot by the whites but noticed a lot by the blacks.

(Interesting thoughts again Steven. The way we are socialized does affect the way we see other people, and as you say, if we don't give equal treatment to all races in the media etc. people will grow up prejudiced. Liberal racism is frightening to black people because they can't easily identify it, it exists and is part of our society's way of life.)

Immigration

Teaching about immigration is probably the hardest part of the course. Many people have argued that to discuss immigration and numbers at all is to allow the racists to define the terms of the argument, and that such debates often end up as the "liberal" trying to prove a lower figure than the racist, implicitly conceding therefore that "the fewer the better". This is certainly a risk, and it has to be looked for, but I would argue for its inclusion in a course for five main reasons.

First, although it may be marginally less of an issue now, our pupil's parents have lived through a time when "race" meant "immigration" (and immigration, of course, meant "blacks"). The mass media and politicians have fed this interpretation for twenty years, and it is an assumption that is rarely questioned. It is a myth, however, and we owe it to our pupils to expose it.

Second, if it can be successfully exposed, it can be used to plant a seed of doubt. Assuming a degree of trust between teacher and pupils, it is possible to go through the doubts and hostility which result from questioning their beliefs in the usual immigration myths, and emerge on the other side with pupils trusting the teacher more. That will come in useful, since their beliefs and preconceptions are going to be challenged again, and if doubt can be established in one sphere they may be more inclined to be critical of other myths.

A third reason relates to the film which I use as the core of the section about immigration.[6] It is fairly shocking in parts and with a reasonably receptive audience brings them face to face with some of the realities of immigration control. On a general level it points out the strength of the law and how it really focuses on black immigration, but it also has some personal case studies showing how individuals are affected — by being separated from spouses for seven years in one case, and being precipitated into a miscarriage in another. The film was made before the discovery that "virginity tests" were being performed on young Asian women at Heathrow. Details of this are in Amrit Wilson's book,[7] and the relevant extracts are well worth using in lessons. Newspapers also furnish a constant supply of cases to demonstrate the severity of the law, such as the Begum case, where a woman was deported because the fiancée she had quite legally entered Britain to marry had died before the wedding. These case studies demonstrate the human consequences of sloganeering about "control", and this is something important which 15 year olds can get hold of. It also important to point out that these things are done in their name.

Fourth, I have never found it possible to bring about a clearer understanding of race relations in Britain without first clearing away some of the myths about immigration. In particular, any information about culture or disadvantage is like water off a duck's back to anyone who really believes that all Britain's problems would disappear if only black people could be made to as well.

A final reason for looking at "the figures" is to demonstrate something important about the thought mechanisms of prejudice. As will be seen in a transcript later (p. 77), people twist and turn in a remarkable way to try and fit the world into their preferred view of it. Whenever I have taught this course we have invariably already studied other aspects of society involving statistics, and these are generally taken on trust. Why they have a much greater emotional investment in statistics about black people is something pupils need to examine. It should be counted as an educational gain if pupils are eventually prepared to say "I don't accept your figures because I don't want to", since they are at least recognizing their own blockages. It is also a learning experience for those who are not so committed to believing in "high" figures to observe those who are.

Turning to teaching this topic, a useful first step is to ask pupils to make a mental or written estimate of the number of black (or "coloured") people in Britain, having clarified the size of the total population. This could be done in small groups or pairs, thereby giving some space for discussion and comparison of estimates. The real figure is about 2 million, but invariably pupils (and adults) grossly overestimate — figures of 10 million being common and 35 million by no means uncommon — so there is at once material for discussion, analysis, confrontation or hostility depending on how the teacher handles what follows. (The teacher really does have to be sure of her/his factual grounds here.)[8]

It is difficult, although not entirely impossible, to resolve the disagreements in a whole class discussion. The difficulties lie in the problems of a few spokespeople speaking for the class (or are they?), and/or the situation becoming an oppositional one. For many of the class very strongly held beliefs are being challenged, and if this is not done gently and coaxingly many students will retaliate with hostility, disruptive "humourous" comments, suspicious silence, and withdrawal. In addition, many issues will be raised which simply cannot be resolved all at once, so they will have to be shelved until later in the course without it appearing that they are being sidestepped. Some indication of this problem as well as some kind of solution can be seen in the pupils' logs.

Small groups are probably a better medium for pupils to talk about the disparity between their views and the statistics. Some will want to say they simply do not believe that the true figure is 2 million, so the atmosphere has to be such that this can be said without anyone getting outraged. The kinds of questions I get groups to examine are

Do you believe me? − on the whole they do not, so, Why not? Why did you believe other sets of figures I have given in the past but not these? Where do you think these figures come from? Where do your own figures come from? Are the proportions you suggest true of this area? Which areas are your suggested proportions true of? After these discussions each group could report back, perhaps with one conclusion or question each.

To give some flavour of what can happen I can offer an edited transcript of one of my own lessons.

Eddie: There must be more than that sir.

Teacher: Okay, are there more than about 4 per cent of Swindon's population that are black, that's 4 in every 100.

Peter: Yes, course there is, quarter of the population, I reckon.

Teacher: Well, if I draw a rough map of Swindon, can you tell me where they all live, which quarter of the town is full of black people?

Jeanette: No need sir, they all live in Beatrice Street (laughter).

Debbie: Yeah, that's right.

Teacher: So is all of Beatrice Street occupied by black people?

Eddie: Yes.

Teacher: Would others agree with that?

Several pupils: Yes! Yes! (laughter).

Teacher: Are these people West Indians or Indians and Pakistanis?

Peter: They're all Pakis, Pakis.

Jeanette: We're not allowed to say that.

Peter: Well, I dunno, Parkistarnees then.

Teacher: So would their names be different to English names?

Eddie: Yes, course they would.

(At this point I dropped the discussion and went on to something else, but that evening I went to the public library and photocopied the electoral roll for Beatrice Street. I brought it to the next lesson.)

Teacher: Now, about Beatrice Street.... We were talking about it last lesson. I went to the library last night and took a photocopy of a thing called the electoral roll, or electoral register. ELECToral register, what do you suppose it's for?

Ann: Something to do with voting.

Teacher: That's right, it's a register of everyone who is allowed to vote, and it gives a list, street by street, house by house. They get the list updated every time there is an election so they know who is allowed to vote, people go round every house with forms and get them filled in. No form, no vote.

Julie: Why are you telling us this Sir?

Teacher: Yes, the reason I've photocopied this is that it tells me the names of almost everyone over 18 in Beatrice Street, so by looking at it I can say how many people with Indian or Pakistani names there are.

Peter: Go on then, tell us, I suppose there aren't any at all.

Teacher: Well, there are 187 houses in the street, and there are 13 occupied by people with Indian or Pakistani names.

Jeanette: How do know that?

Teacher: Because I recognize Indian and Pakistani names, I was hoping you'd take my word for that at least.

Eddie: I don't believe it.

Teacher: But this list has to be very accurate, it has to be reliable otherwise elections could never be held at all.

Debbie: Yeah... well... some of them must have given false names.

Teacher: Why would they do that?

Jeanette: They're probably illegal immigrants or something.

Teacher: Do you not think someone would have noticed if most of Beatrice Street were illegal Asian immigrants pretending to be called "Smith"?

Debbie: Yeah, but sir, they have loads of people in their houses, my gran says they even put beds up in the loft.

Teacher: Well, okay, let's suppose there are more people in each of the Indian and Pakistani houses than the English houses. How many in the average English, or "white" house?

Jeanette: Four.

Peter: No, three, they won't all be parents and children.

Teacher: And how many in the average Indian or Pakistani house?

Jeanette: Ten, no, eight.

Teacher: What, two parents, six children?

Jeanette: Yes.

Teacher: No older relatives? Grandparents?

Jeanette: Two of them.

Teacher: So that makes 10 people in each of 13 houses, 130 black people in all. That leaves 174 houses in the street occupied by white people, with three people in each house, 522 in all (writes on board). So even if your figures are right, which I don't accept by the way, that still means that less than a quarter of the street are Indian or Pakistani.

Debbie: Maybe lots of them have English names?

Teacher: I think that's very unlikely. I can think of only five Asian people that I know in Swindon with partly English names, but even then only one of their names is English.

Eddie: When was this register thing done?

Teacher: October last year.

Eddie: Oh, well, that was 4 months ago. They've all moved in since then.

Teacher: Aha.

This account is illustrative of several things. One important point is that it was all done in a good humoured way. I tried to avoid sarcasm, "I know better than you", arguing aggressively, or too domineeringly, and simply pursued the argument whichever way it turned. There was clearly some element of a game in it, several of the arguers knew on a rational level that they couldn't support their case, but their emotional conviction was still in there fighting. It was interesting to keep an eye on those not participating, because they began to realize one by one how absurd the argument was, and once freed from the idea of Beatrice Street being full of Asians (most of the class, after all, never having actually *been* to Beatrice Street), they could watch and listen with some detachment to the prejudiced mind in action. For them I felt the session was valuable, though I am not so sure about the arguers.

A second approach, which seemed more appropriate with another class, was to argue about numbers locally on the basis of schools. The position being taken by a couple of girls was that at least a tenth of the town was black, because that is how it seemed to them walking round the shopping centre. I suggested that if that were the case then 10 per cent of all, say, 30 year olds would be black, 10 per cent of all 20 year olds, and 10 per cent of all 15 year olds (their own age). (Demographers will know that this will not necessarily follow, but it is not seriously inaccurate.) Conveniently, at the time Swindon had 10 secondary schools of roughly equal size, and to make their case the girls had to agree that one in every ten 4th year classes in the town, or one entire 4th year in one school, had to be black. From their own knowledge, contacts and experience this was demonstrably not so, and the information I was presenting seemed to be more readily accepted without the contortions of the "Beatrice Street saga".

As indicated in the overall course outline and in what the pupils say in their logs, some written work is involved. There is no reason why the laws, figures, case studies, geography and history relating to post war immigration cannot be studied with as much academic rigour and with the development of as many skills as the study of industrial land use, the Industrial Revolution, or the development of the United Nations. Since this is a course designed, in principle, for everybody at 16+ it needs to be constantly pointed out that it is not in the tradition of discussions and vague projects which some people see as "social studies"; as such the pupils' work and activities do not present too easy a target for those concerned about "standards".

There is still a lack of good published course materials, so for this kind of study, so we used "home grown" booklets etc. which I had produced. In the meantime, materials which are generally available are listed in the appendix about resources. For this part of the course there are good parts in the booklet which accompanied the original *Our People* TV series, extracts from Wilson's book (already mentioned), Mercia Last's *Race Relations in Britain,* and AFFOR's teaching pack. Maps of India, Pakistan, Bangladesh and the Caribbean are not too hard to find, and they are essential to enable most pupils to know where one is talking about. Teachers need to read in more detail about the causal factors of immigration, in, for instance, Hiro's *Black British, White British.*[9]

Among those teaching about immigration, methods naturally vary, not only in how direct a teacher wants to be, but diagrams, simulations, role plays, chalk and talk or printed notes will be favoured by different people. Whatever the methods, I would want to argue that the key things for the pupils to understand, the key knowledge objectives, are as follows:

1   The willingness for and encouragement of immigration on the part of many institutions in Britain in the 1950s.
2   The economic context in which that took place.
3   The sectors of the economy experiencing labour shortages in the 1950s.
4   Figures about post war immigration.
5   An idea of the strength of Immigration Law, and recent changes in (tightening of) the law. The effect of the law on individuals.
6   The colonial background of both push factors and pull factors.

The interplay between these knowledge factors and the affective domain is, as before, best judged from what the pupils wrote.

Jane: Well, I think that this programme has showed me what it is like for them trying to get over here, all the questions they are asked etc., but I don't think it is right that, say, if a white immigrant comes here it is more easy for them to get into the country.

(No, it doesn't seem right, really.)

Linda: We learnt in today's lesson that if you are black you are not allowed into Britain. But if you are white and you want to come into Britain, you can. If blacks are not allowed in, no one else should be allowed in. White people who come in from Ireland etc. should not be allowed in as well because the country is becoming overcrowded.

(Think about your last comment. Is the country becoming overcrowded? Particularly when each year there are more people leaving than entering?)

In today's lesson we read through a book called *Immigrants to Britain,* and we were asked 4 questions. And then we read a newspaper report on a pregnant woman. Why wouldn't they send for a doctor, she was entitled to one?

(They thought she wasn't being serious, so they took no notice.)

Now the baby died she is allowed to stay, but she was going to be sent back. Why?

(Originally they didn't believe that she was married to her husband, they changed their minds because of what had happened.)

If a white woman had gone into labour they would have sent for a doctor.

(Most likely, and she would have been able to speak the language. Zahira couldn't speak English, so no one really bothered to help.)

Why is it hard for blacks to get into this country when others like the Irish can get in with no problems at all? I think it is all wrong.

(The answer to this question isn't easy! It is hard to get in because our country of white people is generally anti-black.)

In today's lesson we finished off the questions, and we talked about illegal immigrants. Why is there such a tight security on blacks coming into England? That's all I want to say, sorry!

(Basically the answer to your question is "because that's the way the laws in a white society work".)

Marianne: I think that this lesson has just been a repeat of last lesson, but just talking more about the immigrants in Britain. It is not fair on black people who want to come into Britain to be refused or sent back, they have as much right as anyone else.

(True.)

In today's lesson we have been talking and learning about the amount of immigrants etc. that were allowed into Britain in 1968, 1977, etc.
  I think that the way they are treated is or was completely for the immigration bureau's pleasure, especially the sexual examinations which had nothing at all to do with them anyway. If Britain would accept the fact that there were people who really wanted or needed to come to Britain to marry or work or stay with relations I think it would be better. There is no need to act like they do.

(This seems like a reasonable idea. Marianne.)

Today, when writing answers to those questions it made me think that "black" or "coloured" people have a really bad time trying to enter Britain. There are limited people allowed in and even those who are allowed in have to wait a good 1–3 years, which is ridiculous.

(Yes, it does seem a long time.)

Karen: In this lesson, it showed me how bad it is for a black person to get into the country. I don't think this is fair because the white immigrants get in all right, but because they are black, people probably think that they are going to cause trouble, and they are going to get picked on. Sometimes they do it for their own good, but I don't see what they have against black people.

(Who do it for whose own good? I don't quite understand this bit? Can you explain this a bit more?)

The white people do it for the blacks' own good, but because of this they might think that everyone is against them.

I have realized that Britain is taking in a lot of immigrants both white and black, but because of the black people's colour they are recognized much more than white immigrants. The census in 1971 showed that there are just under 3,000,000 people who have entered our country, which is a surprising amount. Though there are about half of that leaving the country to live somewhere else.

(Yes, when you look at it in these terms it seems strange that people complain doesn't it.)

In this lesson I have found out that people from Asia etc. who are "black" have a very rough time. People don't complain though because: a) when they arrive at the airport they think it is natural for them to be searched, b) if they complain then they could be sent back to their own country.

(Yes, I think these two points are very true. And put yourself in the position of being a stranger in a country. You want to arrive with as little fuss as possible, and settle in as soon as possible, so you are quiet and accept certain things that officials do as routine.)

Lee: Nearly all the Empire's countries wanted independence, now they want to come over here. This is a white country as well.

(So, Lee, what are you saying exactly? That because these countries have asked for independence they shouldn't expect to come here? If this is what you are saying, think carefully about whose countries these places were at first, before the British Empire went in on them!)

Miss, the Government should be more strict with the southern Irish coming over because of the troubles. If a lot of them don't want to belong to Britain why should they get over easier than blacks?

(I think you're mixing up Southern Ireland with Northern Ireland. This is quite different. Southern Ireland (Eire) is a different country with a different government from Britain. Northern Ireland is part of Britain and has the same laws and government. There are many N.Irish people who aren't that keen on being part of Britain, and I think that is what you're saying. As far as I know, the S.Irish come here and don't complain in the way you're suggesting.)

I think it would be easier to tell an immigrant if he/she is black, e.g. if he has a turban that is not a British religion.

(Hallo Lee. This comment seems rather muddled, I'm not sure quite what you mean. If you're saying black people are more noticeable and therefore to be suspected more of being illegal immigrants this is really a very unfair statement. If you were black and born here you'd be British, with as much right as any other British citizen to live a free life in this country. Many blacks don't feel they have this safety because of the kinds of doubts and suspicions some people have about whether or not they are legally here. To look at black people and wonder if they have a right to be here is a racist idea because it assumes that everyone black is an immigrant; you and I know that only one in three immigrants to Britain are black. And, just because someone wears a turban it doesn't mean we should assume they aren't British... Roman Catholicism isn't a British religion, but that doesn't mean the people who follow it should be suspected of being illegal immigrants.)

If they didn't make out that Britain was so brilliant in their letters, then perhaps they wouldn't give false impressions and a lot of them would have stayed there. If I was one of the Asians and used to living in villages and used to all their customs, then came over to the UK I would have wanted more of my traditions brought with me.

Steven: From this lesson I found out that Britain's migration laws are easier for whites than blacks. Statistical evidence of this is that out of the immigrants coming to Britain only a third are black. The biggest problem for the black race is that the home office asks long difficult questions and you have to prove you are who you say you are. Why don't they ask the same questions to white people, because they might not be who they say they are, and if there are more whites it's more likely to happen than in the black cases.

(An interesting point you've made here Steven.)

West Indian and Asian culture

The section on culture is the least satisfactory in the course. It arose in the form it did because of the level of knowledge evident in the 2nd year writings quoted in chapter 1. It was not within my own power to do anything to change that at earlier points in pupils' school careers, so that level of knowledge had to be taken as the norm and responded to in some way. It is probably not necessary to expand on the information contained in the extracts already cited, and it is not the pupils' fault — they have had little if any education about ethnic minorities in Britain, so on one level it is hardly surprising that they are confused or ignorant.

Yet there is more to it than that. The fact that "culture" comes after immigration is deliberate, and reflects what happens if one naively tries to teach about black British cultures as if there is no emotional content in the subject. Teaching about culture, I have already argued, does not necessarily do anything to racist attitudes, since many pupils simply do not want to know or are applying (perhaps unconscious) filtering mechanisms. They do not listen to the distinctions between Sikhs and Muslims, Gujeratis and Bengalis, West Indians and Indians, because they are not interested; they do not want to know because the most important thing to them is that these people are not white, and the students believe that they are responsible for all the unemployment, bad housing etc. If these things were true, we would not expect anyone to be particularly interested in the differences within the peoples responsible for all our ills. Because many people believe they *are* responsible, this has to be tackled first.

Having explained in the Immigration section that these people are not responsible for society's ills, the next problem is how to teach about culture in a very few lessons without being oversimplistic, patronizing, and racist. It is probably impossible, and black people living in areas where they can expect at least some white people to be respectfully conscious of their cultures will be appalled at the digest offered to many white children in their name. As a short-term measure I am not sure there is any alternative. In my own course I had to raise pupils' awareness of the distinctions within the black populations of Britain, because it is more important they know such things than many of the other things they learn in school, but I cannot give anything but a "Cook's tour". "Bringing in an ethnic minority person" does not solve the problem either, since there are simply not enough black people to go round to come into everyone's classroom as walking cultural curios, even if they want to, are available during the day, and feel able to condense "Bengali culture" into 40 minutes. (Studying a religious faith is easier than studying a "culture", and it might be a significant educational advance if we stopped defining the task in terms of teaching about culture at all.)

The major educational problems with "teaching about cultures" can be put this way. There is no such thing as "West Indian" or "Asian" culture. The harder one looks for them the clearer three things become. First, one becomes more aware of the differences within the broader headings. Thus, in certain company it is offensive to speak of "Asians" because Gujeratis, or Punjabi Sikhs, or Sylhetis would be far better descriptions, just as "European" is seldom a usefully precise label for anyone. Similarly, Trinidadians tire of the assumption that all "West Indians" are Jamaican. (So do Jamaicans.) Second, how does one choose a particular cultural feature as an important one, and who chooses? This leads to a third realization: it is difficult to make many generalizations without being racist.

Even with an apparently homogeneous group, cultural generalizations are suspect. The generalizations people make about the British are generally recognized as simplistic stereotypes, unless we believe them ourselves. In such cases they are usually favourable: thus we are inventive, defenders of freedom, appropriately reserved, patriotic, and animal loving. We are not debilitatingly nostalgic, over-hierarchical, or jingoistic, though others think we are. What, then, can we legitimately say about Pakistanis? They are likely to be Muslims to be sure, but as a group of British Pakistanis have said:

Muslim piety is not exactly a myth, but it has certainly developed new dimensions under the flood of material about Islam as a religion, and the dearth of material about Muslims as human beings. We don't exactly take our religion for granted, but we can feel sufficiently comfortable in it to spend much of our time trying to earn our living, raise our status, and even enjoy ourselves. It is our duty to defend our religion as need arises, but we believe that many multicultural enthusiasts have been misled by the fanatical fringe that has fostered the religious theme to the exclusion of all else.[10]

If we have to exercise caution when generalizing about religion, when at least some basic precepts are written down and people formally agree to them, then all generalizations about a group's attitudes, abilities and tastes must be suspect. If one can say, however well meaningly, that Gujeratis have a good business sense, or that the

Hong Kong Chinese "make good restaurateurs", or that West Indians are "easy going", one can by the same token say that the Irish really are thick, Jamaicans are lazy, Pakistanis are money grabbing, and of course the Jews are mean.[11]

All such generalizations are not so tenuous, of course. Two which could easily support themselves with sound statistical evidence are that a relatively high proportion of Jamaican mothers are unmarried, and that a high proportion of British Asian marriages are arranged. How does the presenter of other cultures deal with these? As a political decision I would make no mention of the first, since the only point in mentioning it is to understand it, and to understand it requires a greater knowledge of the legacy of family structures left by slavery than is possible in the short teaching time available.

The issue of arranged marriages cannot be avoided since most white pupils find it intriguing at least, and it is indeed a favourite "problem" for many white people interested in "Asians". The way I teach about arranged marriages, and indeed the related pet topic of the position of Asian women, depends on a specific perspective, which needs to be explained.

It seems a curious priority for white men to concern themselves about black men's sexism. It often happens in training sessions with adults, for example, that men want to test out my "view on Asian women", hoping presumably for some kind of authoritative non-racist condemnation of their inferior status. I do not think it is possible for anyone in my position to give such a view without it being seen as coming from a position of power. It may be a measure of the mess we are in, but the fact is that white people cannot make public judgements about black people and expect to have them taken at face value. As one British Pakistani woman put it, "Leave our men's sexism to us, you deal with racism, that's your problem." Optimists might say that the time will come when enough trust exists for such things to be encountered together, but for myself such trust only exists at the moment at a personal level. In the meantime we have to be very wary of the evident enthusiasm to "help" Asian women, since it can be an unconscious white strategy to avoid looking at ourselves.

With that perspective, all one should be prepared to do as a teacher is to let some Asian people speak. The interviews with Punjabi girls (why is it always girls?) in the *Tomorrow's People* programme about marriage[12] do this in a way that makes possible the beginnings of an understanding for white pupils who are obviously light years away from the value system in which arranged marriages can take place.

Other materials are listed in the appendix.

It is also possible to do something which is important to many black youths, and frequently of great interest to whites. Using some filmed interview material, books written by Rastas or with their consent, the words of Bob Marley songs,[13] and the historical context of the oppression black people feel, white pupils can gain some understanding of the Rasta movement. Since it is so identified with youth it may even be a more effective way of communicating what it is to have a religious view of the world than some conventional RE approaches. One cannot pretend, however, that this is central to every British Afro-Caribbean's life, nor that they all have the same views about Rastafari, since a new stereotype will simply be created.

Of the two formal assessment tasks set for this work, one is aimed at hightening awareness of the differences between some British Asians (based on research by a Pakistani), and the other is constructed so that pupils have to try to write an explanation of something they can seldom agree with, arranged marriages, as an argument against someone who simply condemns them. Here are some pupil responses to this part of the course.

Jane: This piece of work made me wonder if all the people who believe in these religions stick to them, or maybe they go astray a bit. But I think they would stick to the same religion.

(This is an interesting point you've raised. Just like with any religion, some people stick more strictly to the rules than others, for different reasons. Certainly with Asians in Britain there are people who try to follow their religion as they were brought up to in their country of origin, but their children, who are British, may find it very difficult, because they would like to be "British", because the pressures Britain puts on them imply that the only way to be "British" is to be like everyone else! Not an individual. So some people have given up what they believe in in order to be accepted. The awful thing is, they haven't been accepted!)

Linda: In today's lesson we answered questions on the types of Asian people and where they come from and we found about what they wear. Why don't Muslims wear white or bright colours? Why are they not allowed to wear gold but can wear silver? Why must animals be killed in a special way not like we do it?

(You always ask extremely interesting questions which I find ever so difficult to answer. 1) I don't know. It's obviously bound up with religious belief, is it possible for you to find the answer? 2) Once again, I don't know. 3) Religious reasons again, sorry I can't be more specific.)

Lorraine: Ullo. I think that so far this has been the most interesting piece of work we have done. I like to do work on the Asian people and find out how they live, what they wear and eat etc. I think that it is a bit stupid that the Asian men and boys can't cut their hair or beards because when a young Asian boy is growing up he might want to be like English boys, and he might not want to wear a turban on his head and not have a shave when he needs one. I wouldn't like to be an Asian because I like short hair and I like to be able to wear the clothes that I do.

(Yes, I agree that some Asian boys would maybe prefer not to wear a turban, but think about this idea... if we accepted Asian people for who they are instead of telling them who they ought to be once in this country, Sikh boys wouldn't worry about whether they wore a turban. But because there are pressures on them from us, to be like us, some have been forced to give up their religion or some aspects of it, and still haven't been accepted. PS. I'm glad you found this piece of work interesting.)

It's me again. The film which we saw was interesting and I think taught us quite a lot about the Sikhs, their way of life, religion, and why they came. I don't think I would like to be a Sikh girl and have my husband and marriage planned out for me. But saying that, if I was a Sikh girl I might feel different. The English might as well accept the fact that the Sikhs are here. That this is their home as well, because if they don't the racist problem is never going to end. I think if the Sikh people are going to live here they should learn to speak English, because when they talk in their languages out in the street the English people don't like it very much and this doesn't help the racist problem. Bye for now.

Marianne: I think that the programme about Sikhs was interesting. The Sikh people who came over here to Britain both thought that Britain was a wonderful country, but when it came to actually moving here they found it very different. For example the nephew thought he would be able to keep his long hair and beard when in fact he could not. You could see the upset look on his face when his uncle cut his hair, he looked like he was in pain. The woman too, as soon as she arrived didn't expect to see so many white people. She looked totally disgusted with the white woman on the train who had the "mini skirt" on. I wonder what she expected a British person to be like?

Karen: In this lesson we have found out how different the religions really are. It surprised me to find out that they are so different. It is a shame that when they come to this country then most of them drop their religious beliefs, but I suppose that's the way it is. Because of this, if Pakistan etc. did crumble or something and all the people went elsewhere and had to give up their religion, then the whole religion would probably die out. It's funny that they are really strict in their own country, but as soon as they get here they probably think that no-one will know, and so carry on in our culture. It's bad luck when a Sikh or someone is born in our country because of the difference between the two cultures, and they don't know which is right.

(You've mentioned some interesting points here Karen. Some young Asians are torn between two cultures.)

From this lesson and TV programme, I have seen what the reactions really are for a Sikh coming to this country. It must be really hard for them to accept our country as it is, though we are now accepting them and their cultures. It's a shame that it has taken so long for things to be this way. Down the road to me, there are a full family of Sikhs and they live in two houses next door to each other and they also drive cars. The women still wear their long dresses etc. but the men wear suits and do not wear turbans. Really they have accepted our cultures by doing this, but also it isn't fair that they should give up these things when we do not accept any of their cultures. Sikhs or people from the these countries (the New Commonwealth, Pakistan) also find that they have very poor living conditions and not much furniture but they live with this because that is all they need, if they have to send money back to their families in their own country.

Steven: Not all people from Asia are the same, they have different languages, diets, religions, family life, which all goes to make up their culture, so why then do we treat all Asians the same and persecute them for what they wear and do? As it is their religion why should they give part of it up, it's like asking a Christian to give up Easter or Christmas, and so if we learnt and understood their cultures and didn't interfere perhaps people would get on together better in Britain instead of fighting and racialism.

(Some interesting and sensitive thoughts here, Steven; you have obviously understood the need to be aware of the importance of people's cultures, and just because we are all in the same country we shouldn't be expected to be all exactly the same.)

Stages of intolerance, or the extent of racism

This is the part of the course where pupils can begin to build up a fuller understanding of racism, rather than simply have their own ideas challenged, and thus it ought to be the most productive.

The JMB syllabus could be seen as a constraint in this section as it more or less prescribes the framework of Gordon Allport in examining "Persecution and prejudice". This suggests that racial hostility is progressive, beginning with spoken dislike, moving into physical avoidance, then to acts of discrimination, to physical attack and ending with systematic extermination. This is a descriptive framework not an explanatory one, it makes no essential reference to the origins or the maintaining factors of racism, but as a framework for pupils to locate their developing awareness it seems to be quite effective. At this stage of the course the question is still How bad is racism? rather than What causes it? This may be the wrong question, and whether it is or not will be taken up later.

Allport calls his first stage "antilocution", a word so obscure I feel 14 year olds can live without it. We put together "antilocution" and avoidance and referred to them by their more common name, prejudice; that is attitudes and behaviour which stop short of discriminatory acts.

It may be thought that it is labouring the point to get pupils to investigate this themselves, but many at this stage would not accept that there is much racial prejudice in Britain, despite what they have seen of state racism in the material about immigration. Pedagogically there is obviously something to be said for pupils finding out rather than being told, so they listen to, watch and read a good deal of material from black sources about their perceptions of white attitudes, [14] then do a simple survey of their friends and relations. The surveys seldom confirm the black people's views, which is hardly surprising and teaches something about the problems with surveys. The pupils get quite ingenious with their questions, though on the whole they are not, finally, surprised that many people will not state their unwillingness to sit beside black people on a bus. As indicated on the course outline, the method, problems and results of this survey work, together with their findings from the other sources, are written up as a formally assessed piece of work.

There are sometimes strong reactions to the survey. One girl who got her mother to distribute some questionnaires in her office brought back several irate replies about how disgraceful it was for pupils to be looking into this sort of thing. One woman assured me "on the basis of working for many years alongside coloured people in the RAF and in the civil service" that giving attention to "the problem" only makes it worse.[15]

Discrimination is easier to deal with factually since there are many good source materials available. My own favourite TV materials are the *Our People* edition called *The Facts* and the newer *Black*.[16] Both are uncompromising, and give black people a voice, and can lead to productive follow-up work at different levels. There is a danger, of course, of presenting all black people as helpless and disadvantaged victims, and it is not one easily avoided. Both the programmes already mentioned seem to steer clear of giving this message, although there is a general problem with social science teaching that pupils tend to find generalizations which are new to them, and individual exceptions they already know, very hard to integrate. One has to keep stressing that a tendency does not mean a universal pattern, while at the same time insisting that exceptions do not invalidate the generalizations.

Equally, there is a risk exemplified by one of the logs, namely that of simply inducing guilt. This is unproductive on its own, could hardly be defended as a worthwhile educational goal, and can easily produce a backlash of resentment in a class. This could come out in various ways, hostility is one, boredom another.

There are no materials published with school use in mind which really deal well with discrimination, at least none which stand out as clearly as the TV programmes already mentioned. Once again, therefore, this part of the course depended on our own booklets, though an annotated list of materials for teaching about discrimination is given in the appendix.

If there is a paucity of school material about discrimination, there is none at all about physical attack. Most of the material we used is not generally available so they have not been listed in the appendix. There was a useful BBC Radio 4 documentary in 1980 about racial attacks in East London, which has some chilling comments from youths intent on making life too unpleasant for local Bengalis to be able to stay, and a transcript of this with discussion and questions is seldom forgotten. Swindon can reasonably be called a largely white area, but its black population is certainly not free from the harassment from youths found elsewhere. (The family of the "well integrated" girl quoted in chapter 1 went through a period of having their windows smashed in the small hours of the morning about every two weeks.) Any local CRE or CRC would be able to furnish a school with details of local incidents, as long as they were happy with the use to which it would be put. A free booklet about racial harassment on London housing estates is well worth using, and is available from the CRE in London. As with anti-deportation campaigns, it is not hard to find new examples in the newspapers every month.

There are legitimate questions to be asked about whether introducing this topic might encourage some pupils to carry out the kind of racial attacks they are reading about. Sometimes this kind of objection is a smokescreen for a teacher's personal unwillingness to have anything so unpleasant and contemporary as part of "school knowledge", but in some areas, in some schools, in some classes, it has to be seen as a risk. If I saw it as a risk with my own classes I would not do it, and I would want to be sure that local black people did not see it as a risk, either. (Although anti-racist white teachers, even in provincial Swindon, have not been immune from such assaults in the past.)

The most powerful resource in this unit of work is generally available, namely the TV programme *The Politics of Racial Hatred* in the *Politics, What's it all About?* series.[17] It is about the Ku Klux Klan in the USA, and contains some unbelievable news film of Klansmen arriving in cars at a black demonstration and simply shooting unarmed demonstrators. They were all acquitted of murder or assault, despite the film being used in court. Interviews with Klansmen spell out very clearly their philosophy of intimidation by physical attack, and the film also has brief scenes from Nazi concentration camps to put the Klan's views in their proper context. (Like the British NF the Klan is in principle more anti-semitic than anti-black.)

The film is about the USA, but it points out to pupils the slippery slope of racial hostility, of which the next stage is the wish to exterminate the victims. The relevance of all this to Britain is partly in the similarity of the views of the Klan and the young fascists interviewed in the Radio 4 programme, and partly in the logic of extermination. The Nazis began by gathering together Jews with the intention of deporting them; the National Front and other right-wing groups want to institute forced repatriation. Calling the National Front Nazis is often seen as left-wing sloganeering, but even if the similarity is accepted it is often said that they are electorally irrelevant and therefore can be disregarded.

There are two reasons why this is a mistaken view. The first is the penetration of "keep Britain white" as orthodoxy into both the main political parties, but especially the Conservative Party. This is not the place to go into the evidence of the Young Conservatives about NF infiltration into even the parliamentary party,[18] but it is worth stating that the Nationality Act would not have been countenanced twenty years ago by the Tories. For the present, under Thatcher, we not only have government funding for voluntary repatriation, we have a law which defines the right of citizenship and abode in terms of colour. It has ways of avoiding saying so, but no-one can seriously doubt that that is what it is about.

The second reason why the NF cannot be safely ignored is that the first and unchallenged reactions of about a quarter of all of my classes was that repatriation is a good idea. The practicalities of such a view are both absurd and viciously inhumane; do we not owe it to pupils, black and white, to lay this bare?

Realistically, of course, we all know that discussing party politics in school is not straightforward, that there are all sorts of questions about bias and indoctrination and balance, and these are compounded in the case of the NF since thousands of people have demonstrated and one, a teacher, has even lost his life trying to prevent them having a public platform. My own solution to these problems was simply to tape record an interview with the local NF leader. I think the result meets the objections above, as well as clearly justifying the label "Nazi" for the NF. Unfortunately, space prohibits including the transcript here, but it was possible in the interview to get the speaker to express her admiration for Hitler, to outline the NF theory that immigration is all a Jewish plot, and to deny the Holocaust, as well as to spell out in detail how exactly the NF proposed to remove 2 million people from Britain on the basis of skin pigmentation (the first step would be put them all into camps...).

The written work which results from this whole Allport section is the most thorough and difficult of all the assessed work. The task is to write an essay suggesting which of Allport's stages Britain is at, giving detailed evidence and examples. Pupils put many hours of committed work into these, and the most common answer was that we are somewhere between the stages of discrimination and physical attack.

Stereotyping

This section aims, on the whole unsuccessfully, to generalize ideas about race into ideas about stereotyping. The *Scene*[19] programme on prejudice is very useful for this, but it seems to be difficult for pupils to transfer what they know about race into an understanding that their stereotypes of Italians or the Scots are unreal. This partly accounts for my reluctance, gone into in greater length in Chapter 9, to deal with "prejudice" as a general phenomenon. It may well be more effective to finish the course after the work on "extermination".

Doubts, fears, problems about teaching "race"

At the end of the previous chapter there were some common questions posed by teachers. Some have already been discussed during the course of this chapter, but there are several which still deserve some comment.

Will my classroom just explode?

No, unless an attempt is being made to cover "prejudice" in an hour. The issue of "race" is like an octopus, hack off one tentacle and the others grab hold of you, worry the thing too much and it squirts ink everywhere. If an hour is all that is available go for one tentacle, gently, and the one which usually goes to the defence of the others is immigration.

Do I have the necessary skill?

Like a lot of things in teaching, teaching about "race" is a matter of technique. A lot of teachers think they have not got the skills to deal with it because they have met the octopus and had a lesson like the one described in chapter 3. Lots of things teachers do are harder.

Do I have the necessary knowledge?

Probably not, or else such a course would not be necessary in the first place. It is too glib to simply say "learn", but the appendix at least says where to look. The quickest way of sorting out a lot of basic questions is to attend a racism awareness course, which is dealt with in the next chapter.

Is it academic enough?

This is answered both by the quality of the pupils' formally assessed writings (not those reproduced here) and by the level of resource material used. We used television a good deal, which will arouse suspicion in those who think the only respectable resource is a hard-backed textbook, but the level of tasks was as high as those in the comparable subjects taken by the same pupils. In comparison with the mode 1 GCE previously used there is no doubt that the pupils worked harder, and the assessment methods meant that they had to work more consistently for two years than they needed to for a mode 1, and a wider range of skills was judged. In addition, of course, the JMB is not generally regarded as a "soft" board. The point has been made once or twice already, but there cannot be any reason, in principle, why "race" is not as accessible to study as the usual occupants of the humanities curriculum.

Is it inevitably doctrinaire and biased?

Readers will have formed their own opinions about this from the course details already given, and little said at this point will alter that. It is probably clear that I have a view of "the truth". I have little time for the standpoint of pretending not to have a standpoint, nor for the "objectivity" which leads so many white people to disbelieve what black people tell them. On the other hand, this debate should not be closed off, and needs a lot of airing among teachers and pupils; space prohibits a full treatment of it here.

Will pupils be negative and hostile because it is "school knowledge"?

Again this can be judged from the learning logs which have been included here. There is clearly a risk that if the material is presented as the way nice people like teachers think, then many pupils will make their own decisions about what to do with it.

Are there any books and resources?

Many of these have been mentioned in passing, full details are given in the appendix.

How will the black pupils feel?

They will vary, of course. It seems to me essential that the course is discussed with black pupils in each class before it begins, and since in our case this work comprised the second term's work it was usually possible to discuss it at a parents' evening too. There are times when it is uncomfortable for a black pupil to be in the class, and it is worth anticipating these occasions and giving him or her the option of working elsewhere. There have been occasions when black children have been upset enough to be in tears at the end of a lesson when the others have left, and at such times it is difficult to be unequivocally sure of what one is doing. On the other hand, none of the small number of black pupils who have gone through this course have wished that it did not take place. There ought to be support systems available so that black adults or older black teenagers can give support to the black pupils, but this is easier said than done in the maelstrom of a comprehensive school.

Does the course duck the real issues?

Yes, if by that is meant presenting a class analysis of racism as part of the capitalist economy, as explored in chapter 2. There is an uneasy fudging of the issue in, on the one hand, wanting to point out to pupils that black people are not their enemies, and, on the other, not providing much of an analysis of who is. This course on "race" has to be looked at in its context, which was partly a five-term course looking at other inequalities and their manifestations in social institutions, and partly a school where the pupils and the "authorities" considered it very radical to even suggest that racism is worth looking at. When you are on thin ice you have to keep dancing.

References

1   The game was invented some years ago by Coventry Community Relations Council, but is surprisingly little known. It is no longer available from them.
2   During some of the period in which the simulation is set this existed, though it does not any longer under that name.
3   *Multicultural Teaching*, **II,** no. 2, Spring 1984.
4   See for instance my own article, 'What do we call people?' *Multicultural Teaching*, **3** no. 3, Autumn 1984, reprinted here as an appendix.

5 *The Enemy Within,* Catholic Commission for Racial Justice, 1981. Avaliable from the British Council of Churches.

6 *Immigrant* in the *Our People* series, see note 25, chapter 5.

7 Amrit Wilson, *Finding A Voice,* Virago, 1979.

8 For a brief, detailed and up-to-date account I would recommend Dickinson's article in John Tierney's book, *Race Migration and Schooling,* Holt Education, 1982, and *Different Worlds,* from the Runnymede Trust.

9 Full details of all of these are in the resources appendix under teaching about "race".

10 *Multicultural Teaching,* **II,** no. 2, Spring 1984.

11 A book which seems to illustrate this pitfall is Nance Lui Fyson's *Multi-Ethnic Britain,* Batsford, 1984. A serious factual error aside (the book states that Sikhs eat Halal food), it makes too many generalizations. Though the book and its author cannot be blamed for the uses to which it may be put, I have a nightmarish picture of classes all over the country, or individuals doing projects, copying out these generalizations as if they are facts.

12 Produced for schools by Yorkshire Television.

13 The ones I use are on an album called *Africa Unite.*

14 These are given in the appendix about resources.

15 I have never understood in what way this experience qualified her.

16 Shown on BBC in August 1983. See Appendix 1 for details.

17 This was an ITV schools series, still repeated.

18 A report about this was produced by the Young Conservatives in 1984, but the details did not receive wide circulation.

19 A BBC schools series. I do not know if this one is still repeated.

5 Racism awareness training

The preceding two chapters discussed teaching about "race" with pupils. To bring about the kind of changes many of us would like it is also necessary for adults to know more than they often do, or perhaps more accurately to consider what they already "know" in a new way. Where this kind of learning has a professional focus it is often known as racism awareness training (RAT). This chapter has four aims. First, to draw a thumbnail sketch of the kind of orientation towards "racial problems" which has been common; second, to explain and illustrate the working principles of racism awareness training (RAT); third, to examine its psychological assumptions; and lastly to look at the various criticisms of RAT which have emerged.

Racism and victimology

A curious feature of racism is the way it manages to focus attention on its victims rather than its beneficiaries. Thus in social science, although a good deal of work has been done on black people's psychology, black identity, black family and urban social structure, and how they are affected by racism, relatively fewer writers have looked at the psychology and identity of whites, as whites, nor at the actual mechanisms by which racism is perpetuated. As far as psychology is concerned there have been some inquiries: Adorno's study of the limited population of "authoritarian personalities",[1] Pettigrew's study of conformity,[2] Freudian derived theories of frustration-aggression and scapegoating.[3] (None of them gave very much support to the idea that racism was fundamentally rooted in mental structures rather than social ones, though this continues to be received folk wisdom.)

Social science's focus on the oppressed can be justified, of course, on the grounds that it was necessary to have the evidence, both of material inequality and to expose the distance which oppression travels into people's minds and the pain it causes, but whatever the motives, this attention has not always been welcomed by black people.[4] In the late 1960s and early 1970s there was controversy in the USA about the "Elkins Thesis"[5] and Daniel Moynihan's analysis[6] of black family life. In different ways they both argued that slavery and oppression had emasculated and damaged the black psyche, to the extent that the image of slaves as servile buffoons may have been accurate (Elkins). This did not go down well.

The educational manifestation of this tendency is the identification of black children (or parents, or culture) as "the problem" and the consequent removal of any imperative to look at the decision-makers. Attention on black psychology has taken the form in Britain of educational programmes, roundly condemned by Maureen Stone,[7] to improve the self-image of black children, already demonstrated as poor by Milner, Coard, and others.[8] Though it was never its intention this has almost become a racist affair in that it keeps attention on black "failings". It pays passing homage to the idea that a negative self-image on the part of black children is generated by the practices of whites, but what actually happens is that committed teachers in black areas are the most professionally concerned with this particular consequence of racism, so they spend the time (and sometimes actually get the money) to do specialist work with black children: multiracial education.

Similarly, an analysis of the funding and the time spent by such people as Community Relations Officers reveals that the biggest single pressure is "black" casework, it is reactive rather than proactive, dealing with symptoms not causes, and again, often funded in such a way that a more fundamental approach would be difficult, if not illegal. Yet it seems to be accepted in at least some fairly powerful white circles that racial discrimination exists in a fairly systematic way in Britain. Various parliamentary committees have confirmed it: Rampton/Swann confirmed it in education, Scarman confirmed it it Brixton, Smith confirmed it in the police, the PEP/PSI's reports have confirmed it in detail.[9] We have a Race Relations Act, and as Dorothy Kuya says[10] "...in British society ...to be racist and to discriminate against people because of their racial origin is the norm. If it wasn't the norm, we wouldn't need laws against it". Nevertheless, a lot of us say "not me, not here"; racism may be widespread but always somewhere else — paradoxically, most often in the black areas, as if whites in other areas had had no part in putting black people there. The response "not me, not here" comes about because white people cannot or will not recognize racism, either in ourselves, in "our" institutions or in the structure of "our" society. As Mohamed Naguib puts it:

Because the concept is one with which white people feel distinctly uncomfortable, and the concept is often an unpalatable one, the use of the term "racism", particularly by black people, often results in psychological barriers being erected on the part of white people leading to a defensive reaction which prevents an honest and frank discussion of the wider issues of and the effects of racism, particularly as black people experience them. Because racism is therefore often perceived only in terms of intentional and conscious attitudes and behaviour, with people holding explicit and negative beliefs about black people, there is often a failure to come to terms with the wider concept of racism, its manifestations and its effects on both black and white people. It is therefore necessary for white people to dismantle those psychological barriers which prevent an appreciation of the totality of the concept so that they may recognise that racism is about much more than intentional and conscious negative attitudes and behaviour before they can begin to combat it.[11]

The focus on white people

It is against this background that we have to see the growth[12] of a body of techniques called Racism Awareness Training. In the main it is focused on white people, which at least represents something of a shift of emphasis, and it aims to produce an active awareness of racism in its personal and institutional forms. With varying emphases, RAT focuses on how a whole battery of white assumptions and practices when combined with numerical and economic power produce racism, on the structure of white attitudes, sometimes the internal harm done, the distortion produced by racism, ways of unlocking particular thought patterns, getting the person to listen and recognize his/her defensiveness about racism, and to plan some action (personal or institutional) towards change. RAT tends to take the form of structured sessions, usually experientially based (role play, simulation, audio-visual of an arresting or emotionally engaging kind, analytic group work, self-reflexive group work, brainstorming, etc.) with the aim of providing insight into personal and institutional racism. Most techniques are for small groups; though some simulations can work with thirty or forty, there is a general preference for intensive sessions of at least two days' duration, rather than, say, weekly sessions of a couple of hours or so. Some techniques throw unconscious white attitudes into sharp relief, others enable whites to empathize effectively with black people, others use these to highlight racism in society. There is always a facilitator or trainer, sometimes two, and these might be black or white.

The difficulties in raising awareness are formidable. People who have tried "straight" education in this field in the past 20 years have repeatedly despaired of progress. Clichés like "education will help" and "give people the correct information", "counter the myths" are known through a lot of bitter experience to be empty hopes, at least for the most part. Of course, education and correct information do help, but there is such a strength in racism that these alone are often ineffective. People do not learn, or change attitudes, or change actions, when they feel attacked, defensive, hostile, angry or guilty. Even the most professionally and convincingly produced TV material about a controversial topic is subjected to a massive amount of selective perception by those opposed to its message. Such programmes, in fact, are more likely to reinforce existing attitudes, whatever the attitude and whatever the message. Talks, lectures films, cajoling, or haranguing by the "converted" can often leave attitudes untouched, and while RAT is mostly used in work with adults, the problems of resistance to "unwanted" messages are in some ways compounded with school children because they do not value the messenger; in other words their experience of class, ability grouping, prospects, and "school knowledge" lead them to reject or just ignore whatever they are being "given". Out of these difficulties a "technology" of teaching has emerged.

Preliminary criticisms

The whole enterprise is criticized from most directions. Some see it as too apolitical and psychologistic, or having too much in common with "human growth" techniques which they see as self-indulgence:

...although RAT can act as a catharsis — for guilt-stricken whites — or as a catalyst, leading even to a change in their treatment of individual blacks, its pretensions to do more is at once a delusion of grandeur and a betrayal of political black struggle against racism and, therefore, the state.[13]

Others (especially in contexts where it is compulsory) see it as redolent of the thought police, authoritarian, and destructive of thought. Both kinds of critic also misrepresent RAT, inevitably, because of the great range of activities going under the name. The list of techniques given above varies a great deal with different trainers, and the personal style of the trainers makes categorization hazardous, but it is fair to say that there is a rough divide beween those who focus on personal racism and those who put greater emphasis on its institutional and political life, reflecting what Ahmed Gurnah[14] suggests are RAT's two apparent theoretical underpinnings: Rogerian psychology, and Marxist sociology. Black and radical white commentators have more often concentrated their criticisms on RAT's psychological "style" and emphasis.[15] More reactionary attacks have been with a scatter gun; lacking a coherent analysis of racism (at least one they care to spell out) they have tried mockery, oversimplification, and "academic freedom".[16]

My own suspicion is that even this division in types of RAT between the political and the personal is partly one of misunderstanding; RAT cannot help being "psychologistic" in one sense because it consists of structured activities about something threatening and emotionally loaded in intensive small groups, the techniques therefore can be mistaken for the analysis. Nevertheless, there is a species of RAT (bred, perhaps in sterile conditions away from the outside world) which seems to concentrate on the personal. In so far as this chapter suggests RAT as a strategy, it is not this kind. It has too much in common with some "human growth" techniques if it just puts people through a mild trauma, a cathartic experience, and leaves them feeling better. Anti-racism requires action, not groups of people self-indulgently wallowing in their feelings and guilt about "race", accepting wherever each other is "at", and then going home feeling purged. Such training is founded upon and spreads an entirely individual and psychological conception of racism.

A further criticism of RAT comes when it is presented as some kind of panacea. It is not one and should only be seen as sometimes complementary to and sometimes just different from action of a political or institutional kind. It is not always necessary to change people's minds to change their behaviour. Rules and procedures may be drawn up in such a way that discriminatory practices are exposed and reduced, monitoring of job applications and appointments (with supporting sanctions) can expose and prevent racism, a threat of non-validation for degree programmes concentrates the mind wonderfully on curriculum reform, the collective black vote can force change at local council level, burning police cars can force changes in policing procedures. Many changes were brought about in the USA in the 1960s by the successful struggle of black people on the streets, not by coaxing white people out of their racism in specialized (and expensive) training. This is part of two of the most cogently argued radical critiques of RAT, those of Sivanandan and of Gurnah,[17] to which I shall return later (see pp.115-17).

I felt it necessary to give this detailed background information before cautiously saying that I think RAT is a worthwhile strategy to try, in some places, alongside other steps. It can have a particular role to play in institutions not subject to democratic control, and many educational establishments are like this, especially schools. With a head unwilling or unable to implement certain changes from above, the only way to move may be to try to change some people's minds. It does not rule out democratic pressure group action, it may initiate it. In my limited experience, in so far as one needs allies and one needs a common understanding and analysis of what is happening, the "right" sort of RAT moves people along faster than anything else which works at the level of individual and small group consciousness, except action. But the kind of action which radicalizes people in London is not available in Sussex and Suffolk. A school which campaigns with pupils who are threatened with deportation is engaged in a process which inevitably radicalizes its perspectives, but if the anti-racist struggle can be carried on at all in all white areas it will not be by that means. RAT may have a particular usefulness in such areas.

Course rationale and content

To give a little more weight to this assertion it might be valuable to give a more detailed picture of the kinds of things that often form the basis of racism awareness. The standard work on the subject is Judy Katz's *White Awareness*[18] which is both a rationale and a training manual for trainers, based on her extensive work in the USA. She seems to adhere to a psychological model which holds that to varying extents racism structures white thought and is hence unsettling or threatening to give up. Her evident encounter group/T group training also gives her a particular sensitivity to the starting points and needs of group members. She offers a kind of political analysis in so far as she sees white society as fundamentally racist with some possible connotations of that word in terms of domination, discrimination, privilege and power, and she says RAT is only part of a process not an end-point or a solution. She is usually interpreted more psychologically than politically, but to some extent this is due to the reason mentioned earlier, technique is confused with analysis.

Katz has a thoroughly worked out hierarchy of approaches: she takes groups through graded steps, each one building upon the preceding ones. Although some of the items listed below look like simple information-giving, the point is that techniques are grouped in sequential categories, the later ones being deemed more effective when preceded by some of the earlier items. What may appear as simply a TV programme becomes more than that when it is part of a coherent overall plan. Her notion of a graded sequential hierarchy of techniques seems to be followed by most RAT workers in Britain. The logic is clear, groups should not be expected to run before they can walk, and to miss out stages or get them in the wrong order can be counter-productive.

The stages of development of anti-racist consciousness that she suggests are as follows:

1   Naming and defining key concepts.
2   Describing and examining racism in institutional and individual forms.
3   Identifying and articulating personal feelings and fears on racism, taking up the feelings and fears brought to the surface by stages 1 and 2.
4   Exploring cultural racism.
5   Exploring whiteness, how people's own attitudes and behaviours are representative of racism.
6   Developing and acting upon specific strategies against racism.

If Katz's stages of development are translated into British terms and British materials a list like the one which follows is produced. If she has got the progressive stages right then it is vital to place new materials or activities in the right stage, and not get them "out of order" or use them in isolation. Which techniques are used and how long is spent on each stage depends on the nature of the group, as does the choice of exercises from each group, though in general only one would be used. The list may seem to mean rather less to those who have not attended RAT. Many people will, however, know of particular resources and I hope the list shows where they could be located in a larger "package", perhaps as a starting point for discussion in designing RAT for particular circumstances. It will be understood better after participating in RAT, though it can profitably be read in conjunction with Katz and the BBC video and book mentioned in note 18.

1   Naming and defining key concepts, other introductory strategies

	Numbers	Time
a Why I am here and what I expect of the course.	18	varies
b Defining terms "prejudice" and "racism".	4	45m
c Draw a cartwheel on a large card, "racism" written in the middle, free associate on spokes, discuss in larger group.	4	15m
d Examine names whites use to refer to black people (when not intending to be offensive), perhaps using photos.	4	15m
e Show opening sequence of *Anglo Saxon Attitudes*[15] to identify issues.	18	30m
f Two concentric circles of people, outer one rotates and shares either definition of or experience of racism with succeeding opposites. An alternative, as a general introduction and ice-breaker, is to do the same but exchange anything important that's happened this week.	18	2m
g What I have done in the field of race relations that I am pleased about.	2	4m

2   Describing and examining racism in institutional and individual forms

	Numbers	Time
a Passport game.[20]	30+	2h

(Most of the following involve watching something, usually with one or more specific questions raised first, followed by reactions in pairs or small groups before larger group discussion.)

	Numbers	Time
b *Enemy Within* tape/slide.[21]	18	1h
c *Recognising Racism* tape/slide.[22]	18	1h+
d *Institutional Racism* tape/slide.[23]	18	45m
e *16UP* video.[24]	18	45m
f *Our People* video (immigration).[25]	18	1h
g *Our People* video (discrimination) (see note 25).	18	1h
h Salman Rushdie *Opinions* video.[26]	18	1h

i *The Testimony of Chief Seattle* tape/ slide.[27]	18	45m
j Designing a racist school.[28]	6	1h
k Role plays about decision-making.[29]	6	30m
l Mini-lecture about forms and levels of racism.	18	15m

3   Dealing with feelings

Stages 1 and 2 help raise participants' consciousness of what racism is and how it functions. Many people enter stage 3 sitting on host of feelings, overwhelmed with new data, confused about what is really the "truth", and feeling helpless about what to do about it all. Other people may be feeling guilty about being a racist or about being white. Some may feel a responsibility for racism because they are white or angry about the way the system has treated third world people. In stage 2 many of these feelings must be brought out and dealt with; otherwise they will begin to immobilise the participants and stifle growth in any positive direction. The exercises in stage three help participants get in touch with their "here and now" feelings, deal with them, and move into a process of change and growth (Judy Katz).[30]

a "Here and now" wheel — each participant quarters a circle and writes in one feeling so far in each. Discuss supportively.	4	varies
b List fears about dealing with own racism, or about accepting that facts given about racism in society are true.	6	45m
c "Whose fantasy?"[31] A story with unfinished sentences to tease out people's real feelings.	2/18	varies

4   Exploring and unlearning cultural racism

a Free associate on black/white/red/yellow (could use dictionary). Try also black/black foreign.	6	30m
b BaFa BaFa simulation.[32]	30+	2h
c *Crosstalk* video.[33]	18	1h
d Posters analysing words and images in textbooks.[34]	18	45m

e	Posters on black/colonial history.[35]	18	1h
f	*The Whites of Their Eyes* video.[36]	18	1h
g	*It Ain't Half Racist Mum* video.[37]	18	1h
h	*Black* video.[38]	18	1h+
i	*The Testimony of Chief Seattle* tape/slide (see note 27).	18	1h

5 Exploring whiteness, the meaning of individual racism

a	Pick from list of adjectives 5 to describe self, then 5 to describe "whites". Discussion.	6	30m
b	"Being white in UK today is like...." Complete sentence 3 or 4 times. Repeat for "black" and note differences.	6	45m
c	Respond to statement "white is beautiful". Discuss problems, anxieties, hesitations.	6	45m
d	Read "After you Alphonse" and discuss.[39]	6	30m
e	"30 statements". Examine to see which are/ are not racist. Discuss.[40]	6	30m
f	"Vision of Equality" responses to statement by "tolerant white liberal".[41]	18	30m

(The purpose of this stage is to get people to own their whiteness, recognize any guilt or ambivalence they feel about it, identify attitudes and preconceptions they need to work on, and finally to realize the importance of taking active steps to go beyond this and to combat racism in themselves, in others and in society.)

6 Strategies for action

Whatever other stages are missed or skimped because of lack of time or the level of awareness of the group, this stage has to be included in some form. The stage can take various forms, dividing into interest groups for example. The energy and awareness created by the course has to be harnessed; Stokely Carmichael's phrase "If you're not part of the solution you're part of the problem" is worth displaying.

a Continuing to learn can be action. Set up a continuing group with a schedule. Trainer must make resources available.

b Be positive. Show rest of *Anglo Saxon Attitudes* video.	18	1h
c Keep a journal about events/actions/ personal steps to do with racism.		
d Work through checklist of "personal commitment against racism".[42]	18	1h
e Work through "costs/benefits to oneself" exercise.	2	30m
f Make a flow chart involving specific goals, risks, obstacles, time scale, support needed. Discuss.	1	30m

Some practicalities

Since the essence of RAT is experiential I do not propose to try to capture it or equip anyone to lead it by pages of written guidelines, but since very little has been written about it in this country there are several observations I think are worth making.[43]

Numbers matter. One trainer can reasonably cope with a group of up to ten, with more than that the possibility of giving adequate attention to everyone in the group begins to recede. With more than eighteen (easily divided into two or three sub-groups) the group dynamics are likely to become unworkable, even with two trainers.

"Race" matters. Trainers in this field can never expect anything other than constant and repeated questioning on who is doing the training. Katz (herself white) takes the view that it is exploitative to expect black people to run RAT, since racism is our problem to sort out. Others argue that since RAT inevitably involves giving a "black perspective" this cannot or should not be attempted by whites. That aside, some black people argue that in any case they want "real jobs", not "race jobs". On the other hand, many would see it as a strange enterprise to have a group of white people with a white trainer closeted away doing some work on racism, especially given the historical tendency for white men, in particular, to subtly colonize even people's oppression and to make careers out of it.

Group make-up matters. Most RAT in Britain has been done with volunteers. Bradford Council is the best known exception to this. There everyone who makes appointments is systematically being put through training. There is as yet no data about its effectiveness, nor even how we might judge it, but clearly a group of conscript heads or senior officers, well used to manoeuvring and holding their own in groups and not being used to compulsory attendance, will behave differently to a group of volunteers from a union branch. There are such things as black RAT groups, but they serve a different purpose. To some extent they sensitize black people to racism they were not conscious of or chose to ignore, but the dynamics of such groups and the kinds of action which result from them is entirely different from white groups. It is not common to have mixed groups, especially where the black people would be in a small minority.

Time matters. Some organizations set up to run RAT, like London's RAPU,[44] will not do less than three days, and most trainers accept that the surface is barely scratched in a day's course. This is partly a function of group dynamics and the defensiveness we usually have about race means that things simply take time to warm up. The times noted above for the examples of activities are often too short; many trainers would double most of my estimates. With some groups stages will be cut short or omitted altogether, particularly stages 4 and 5, although anyone focusing on institutional and structural racism can hardly omit stage 6.

Specificity is favoured by many trainers, that is, working with a homogeneous group and tailoring the training and the action plans to fit the group. One organization spends time in the workplace with the group for a while prior to the training, so that they understand the mechanisms and practices which are relevant to that particular group. (This inevitably increases the cost.)

Group dynamics and group work skills matter. Recognizing one's own personal racism or the racism of one's workplace, the education system, or society as a whole is very threatening, and the recognition of this is part of the "technology" of RAT. Many people, both black and white, are suspicious of the "softly softly" approach which might be implied by RAT; is it not too cautious about white sensibilities? Certainly for anyone who has been on the receiving end of racism, or even involved in much work fighting it, the frustration at its pervasiveness and its resistance to change makes a gentle kind of approach *feel* wrong. It smacks of compromise, of letting oppressors off the hook, when it seems imperative to hammer them mercilessly. There are two answers to this. First, working off one's own anger and changing other people's attitudes are analytically different things and should not be confused. The rather unsatisfying psychological truth seems to be that verbally crucifying people may be good for the anti-racist but it rarely produces increased awareness in the subjects. A second answer, and a more psychologically satisfying one, is that several awareness techniques do actually give people a hard time. The approach of the trainer may be supportive and, to some extent, accepting, but the experience for the subject can be threatening and acutely uncomfortable. If the atmosphere is nevertheless a "safe" one then the discomfort can be productive.[45]

There is fear here of the power of group dynamics and the partial origin of RAT in encounter groups. There is an argument that the power of the group is such that it can be authoritarian, cause the suspension of judgement when a person is very vulnerable, and impose interpretations to an extent which almost amounts to "brainwashing". There is a certain authoritarianism in anti-racism, in that racism is no longer seen as a legitimate "point of view", when this is put together with intensive small group work and the emotional charge in the issue carried by most people, the dynamics are seldom low-key. While I hesitate to give them weapons it is noticeable that the Right have not yet employed this criticism.

RAT's psychological assumptions

To turn now to the third purpose of this chapter, it is worth saying something about the model of psychological processes employed in RAT. Clearly the "technology" of RAT has to pay some heed to psychology, but it is worth noting at this point how "psychological" the discussion becomes; is this form or substance?

At one level it is possible to see "prejudice" as an extremely basic, "natural", human phenomenon, easily generated and directed at any convenient group. One can thus be prejudiced against new neighbours, brown-eyed people, an opposing sports team or a different dormitory on a summer camp.[46] At its most basic this is hard to dispute, although the awareness RAT ought to be trying to promote is more than simply an awareness of self, and even if prejudice as a basic structure of human thought is not going to be eradicated, that is not to say that its most virulent and pernicious forms cannot be reduced or even dismantled. Prejudice can be habitual, if we do have some kind of predisposition towards it then we can easily slot into the ideological structures presented to us about "race", gender, and other categorizations, but is also based on scanty, non-existent or contradictory evidence so it can be undermined and exposed.

A model of racial prejudice as (partly) misdirected learning shades into a second one which holds that the learning of erroneous facts is so extensive as to structure the person's other "knowledge". (One can take this view with or without the neo-Marxist wider perspective that this structuring of thought is no accident, that the construction of racist "knowledge" serves a purpose.) It is therefore hard work to "unlearn" racism because doing so at least sends unsettling winds through one's mental furniture and at most can blow the house down. How far one takes these "knowledge" structures to "be" the person depends on whether one sees any great mental trauma in shedding or restructuring them, but clearly other features of a person's identity enter in here, so that, for instance, a teenage boy uncertain of his identity is going to be at least resistant to having his mental furniture rearranged.

Taking this a stage further, a third model would see prejudice as to a greater or lesser extent the refuge of a crippled personality, a crutch leaned upon by other inadequacies. In its extreme form one only has to talk to a Nazi in one of our ultra-right parties to see the accuracy of this portrait when applied to some people, and RAT will certainly have no effect upon them. For a larger group of people, it follows that because prejudice is a difficult thing to shed it must be serving some purpose beyond just structuring thought, it seems to be a walking stick, if not a crutch, and RAT is going to be of limited effectiveness on them, too.

These ways of viewing the psychology of prejudice to some extent shade into one another and share common assumptions. A rather different approach has its roots in Re-Evaluation Counselling, a counselling technique with quite a long history in the USA, although it really mushroomed in the 1960s and 1970s alongside encounter groups and "personal growth".[47] This approach holds that racism is hurtful, damaging, and personally limiting on the racist, and that it is actually a liberating and rewarding experience to dismantle one's own prejudices. Whereas the other approaches would point to resistance to anti-racist overtures as evidence of how defended people are about their basic mental structures, the re-evaluation counsellors would say the overtures are simply being made in the wrong way. Deep down racism causes "hurt" to the racist because people are basically disposed to be loving and accepting of other people, and this has been suppressed in us by the lies and half truths of our society. A lot of energy is used in blocking off the systematic experiences of misinformation and the denying of basic humanity, often by the significant others important to us as children. This is a very brief outline of an approach which takes about a day's work at experiential techniques to really come to grips with, and while trying to avoid a really detailed exposition I do not want to do the approach an injustice. My objections to it as a "world view" (which it almost sets out to be) are, first, the assumption of a basic loving co-operativeness in people, and, second, the view of prejudice as a painful experience rather than one which is positively welcomed by some people. If, however, the totality of the view would not suit everyone[48] it has a wealth of humanity and sensitive techniques in it, and states in a powerful way that white society makes white people victims of its limiting ideologies, and that the parading of blame and guilt is a luxury that will make little progress. Its style of working has certainly penetrated the RAT field, although Gurnah (see note 14) would argue that in Britain at least many trainers use its background assumptions as mere slogans.

On a less psychological level, RAT works with some people because it highlights a tension between many professed beliefs, personal and institutional, and actual practice. There is such a thing as unintentional racism, and when it is highlighted for the first time some people are prepared to act upon it. Twenty years ago in Britain such people used to preface the most outrageously bigoted statements about black people with "of course, I'm not prejudiced", and then try to maintain this fiction by suggesting that black workers were slower, could not work beside white workers of the opposite sex, or use evidence of their supposed incompetence to justify black people's exclusion from certain jobs.[49] Even then it would seem that some British notion of fair-mindedness, or of being the Mother Country of the Commonwealth, made declarations of overt prejudice unacceptable. (Or it may have been that they did not actually dislike black people, they just thought they were like children.) Although it still happens, explicit racism is less formally unacceptable than it was in the upper echelons of the education world, and by now so are some of the comments mentioned above which could have been made so freely twenty years ago. This is partly because the law makes it impolitic for anyone in a position to discriminate to show any disposition to do so, and partly because British middle-class values are still such that overtly prejudiced attitudes are inconsistent with other beliefs.[50] The unacceptability of actually saying you're a racist is important in British culture, and has importance for the kind of training outlined in this chapter. I do not want to make too much of this, nor argue that it really detracts from an analysis of Britain as a profoundly racist society, but the highlighting of contradictions is an effective spur to *some* people. There is a contradiction in Britain between the rhetoric exemplified in the Race Relations Acts and the real intentions of the Nationality Act, Britain is not yet, in Rushdie's words "cleansed of the filth of imperialism"[51] but these contradictions are not easy for white people to deal with. RAT can provide a learning structure where people can listen to Rushdie rather than just hear him (or more likely, turn him off). Gurnah argues, however, that having listened to Rushdie white officials then simply learn the acceptable language of anti-racism to disarm black criticism. This brings us to the fourth intention of this chapter.

Reactionary and radical criticism

I now wish to deal with the two main kinds of criticisms identified earlier (pp. 103—4), and perhaps best characterized as reactionary and radical. As far as reactionaries are concerned, I have already referred to the *Daily Mail* (see note 14), but on the strength of his most recent book, I would also have to include Robert Jeffcoate.[52] Beginning with an argument that racism may be less pervasive than many claim, Jeffcoate's chapter on "Combatting racism" then moves to a section called "Anti-racism as illiberalism". In this he warns of the threat to the autonomy of teachers, the "gross infringement of teachers' rights" involved in making RAT courses compulsory, and the "simple-minded" foregone conclusions like "racism and racial inequality are endemic in Britain". From reading the account in the BBC's referred to earlier (see note 43) he concludes "The participants appear to have been subjected to a brand of the Marxist version of racism... purveyed through the unlikely methodology of encounter group behaviourism."[53] The core of his argument is what he calls "liberalism", but he fails to distinguish between the evidence and manifestations of racism and people's subsequent response to it. In his wish to defend the right to be racist he seems to want to allow teachers to ignore the evidence, if they so choose. Whatever his motives, Jeffcoate's argument seems to add up to saying "racism is not so pervasive after all" (something often said by white people), "and anyway I can be racist if I want to be". If RAT is "illiberal" because it works from different premises to Jeffcoate, then so be it. I shall return to the issue of teachers' freedom in chapter 8, on teacher training.

Turning to radical objections to RAT, Sivanandan would accept the claim made earlier that it can make people more willing and able to listen to, for example, Salman Rushdie's talk, but only in so far as it applies to individuals and their response to individual black people. He denies any claim that RAT may have a wider effect, and it is important to see why. The nub of his argument is that all RAT, whatever its claims to look at political stuctures, is nevertheless a part of them. Thus, it is the wrong kind of action in the wrong place run by the wrong people. This analysis, like Mullard's in chapter 2, is a Marxist one. Perhaps from this point of view using RAT may be a bit like running classes to improve the human sensitivity of pre-revolutionary Russian aristocrats, or German officials during the early years of Hitler's regime. With hindsight, we might look at such endeavours as pitiful attempts at the reform of something unreformable by people trying to have their moral cake and eat their material one. With his insight (or foresight) Sivanandan looks at RAT in just this way.

There is thus a close correspondence between the radical critiques of Education for Racial Equality (or "weak" anti-racism) and of Racism Awareness Training: to Mullard and Sivanandan RAT is, in fact, "weak" anti-racism. In both "...oppression is severed from exploitation, racism from class, and institutional racism from state racism".[54]

To support his case Sivanandan draws on the most psychological passages in Katz, saying that she reduces the "white problem" from one which actually inheres in the capitalist power structure to one which is purely personal, "a problem of individuals". It reduces "social problems to individual solutions, passes off personal satisfaction for political liberation". That is a legitimate reading, or application, of Katz's techniques, but I have said enough earlier to indicate that in my view that kind of reductionism is not inevitable. If racism equals racial prejudice plus power then RAT has to look at both. It must, at least, examine the outcomes of unexamined white power, and some RATs will extend this by linking racism with the structures of capitalism. If they do, they are carrying on Sivanandan's argument by a different means; if they do not, they either have a different understanding of racism ("weak" anti-racism, for instance) or they have a (psychological? tactical?) eye on what is possible within their training time.

If one way of interpreting the significance of RAT is to examine its methods and ideology, another is look for its effects. Sivanandan and Gurnah both argue that the mushrooming of RAT after Scarman has made no difference to the position of black people. Unemployment is up, racial harassment is still increasing, the quality of housing has not improved: "...the Police, multi-culturalism and RAT are used by the central and local state to manage blacks".[55]

All that has happened is that the centre of gravity of the Race Relations Industry has moved from the central government and the Commission for Racial Equality to the local state — and with it, the black struggle, not for community and class any more, but for handouts and position. And Racism Awareness, not black power, is the new ideology.[56]

This is good rhetoric, but in Britain RAT is not the new ideology any more than black power was the old one. A different sense of black power, simply the involvement of black people in decision-making, is a central plank of "weak" anti-racism, but to the extent it has happened Sivanandan castigates this too. "The white left now believes that any self-seeking middle class group that calls itself black... is automatically political or progressive." And "Scarman has changed the terms of the debate from the material effects of racism on poor blacks to the cultural effects on and the job prospects of middle class ethnics."[57] This does not represent progress since it is within the rules of the state, it does not challenge them, and certainly it would be hard to point to recent material improvements in the lives of poor black people. It is worth quoting Sivanandan at length to get an idea of what he envisages instead, since for him the only use for analysis is to guide action.

The fight against racism is, therefore, a fight against the State which sanctions and authorises it — even if by default — in the institutions and structures of society and in the behaviour of it public officials. My business is not to train the police officer out of his "racism", but to have him punished for it.... Nor does changing the attitude of an immigration officer stop him from carrying out virginity tests — but changing immigration law (or merely the instructions from the Home Office) would. Nor can (middle class) housing officers who have undergone RAT change housing conditions for the black working class, as long as the housing stock is limited. Nor, finally, does disabusing the minds of the editors and owners of the yellow press of their "racism" prevent them from propagating their poisonous ideology of racism (when it sells papers); only a concerted continuing, public and political campaign can do that.[58]

It should be reiterated that where RAT is "the new ideology" those holding to it are mistaken, as are those who see it as a panacea. However, it is interesting that Sivanandan includes the phrase "albeit by default", indicating that at least some things happen because they are examined and unchallenged. Immigration officers cannot change the law, but RAT can make other people see what the law allows in their name. Housing officials cannot increase the housing stock but how does it help class formation for them to continue to distribute even poor housing inequitably?

A role for RAT

I am arguing that RAT has a role to play, at least in education. If one is running courses anyway this kind of course deserves more than a dogmatic rejection. It ought to be part of what Mullard calls "The

Three Os" of anti-racist education: orientation, observation and opposition.[39] Although he says that "orientation" does not mean "some psychological re-examination of self, a re-vamped gestalt or encounter group type racism awareness course", he does acknowledge that even with the necessary willingness, ability and moral strength "this kind of reorientation will be as disorientating as it will be painful". It means, he says, "...the changing and repositioning of existing self within and against the context of an informative and interpretive history of past self". It also means looking at the world in a new way:

...looking entails the looking at all situations, relations, processes, structures, people, groups, curricula, agencies, textbooks, associations, school materials, traditions, customs, governing bodies, policies, practices, special events, and all else that goes on overtly or covertly in education. It is a kind of sensitive and sensitised looking through eyes trained in the detection of injustice, inequality, and all the large and small oppressions, discriminations and exploitations which are part of normal daily life in a racist institution and/or society. It is the looking at the common place, the normally unnoticed or taken for granted; all those things which go to make up the texture as well as the substance of schooling, pedagogy, and education.... To achieve this kind of sensitive and sensitised looking it is necessary to look with the ears as well as the eyes. The listening to all educational talk...[and] more important than verbal talk is all that goes on and which is often described as non-verbal talk. From sneers to gestures, dress to haircut, shoving in the dinner queue to bullying in the playground, distancing to closeness, staff silence to staff rowdiness, and the ordering of library materials to the selection of the football, rugby, cricket, netball, lacrosse and croquet teams all non-verbal talk, once identified, is in fact extremely noisy.... The listening to this sort of talk together with that commonly recognised as talk calls for the development of a special skill; one which permits the ears to come together with the eyes in order to listen to the driving hail and deceptive snowflakes of racism as they form in the sky before they fall to cover the ground completely white.[60]

Mullard is talking about consciousness here, albeit a consciousness transformed by practice. Though scathing about many of its assumptions and practices, even Gurnah says "This is not meant to imply that all anti-racist education and anti-racist consciousness raising is ineffectual and harmful. Quite the contrary: both are extremely important but need to be done in the context of concrete action."[61]

RAT can be a part of the process of arousing and refining this consciousness. It can also be, as Sivanandan argues, a gratefully accepted way of avoiding a challenge to the structural roots of British racism, and a way for hapless white liberals to convince themselves they are playing a part in the struggle.

References

1 J Adorno et al. *The Authoritarian Personality*, New York, 1950.
2 'Personality and socio-cultural factors in inter-group attitudes', T.F. Pettigrew, *Journal of Conflict Resolution*, 1958.
3 L. Berkowitz, *Aggression, a Psychological Analysis*, 1962.
4 See, for example, J. Ladner (ed.), *The Death of White Sociology*, Vintage (Random House), 1973; J. Bourne & A. Sivanandan, 'Cheerleaders and Ombudsmen', *Race and Class*, **XX1**; Errol Lawrence, 'White sociology, black struggle', *Multiracial Education*, **1X,** no. 3, Summer 1981.
5 S. Elkins, *Slavery, a Problem in American Institutional and Intellectual Life*, Chicago, 1968.
6 D. Moynihan and N. Glazer, *Beyond the Melting Pot*, Cambridge, Mass., 1965.
7 M. Stone, *The Education of the Black Child in Britain*, London, 1981;
8 D. Milner, *Children and Race*, London, 1975 and Ward Lock, 1984. B. Coard, *How the West Indian Child is Made Educationally Sub-Normal in the British School System*, New Beacon Books, 1971.
9 *West Indian Children in Our Schools*, Cmnd. 8273, HMSO, 1981, *Education For All*, Cmnd 9453, HMSO, 1985. Lord Scarman, *The Brixton Disorders*, Cmnd 8427, HMSO, 1981; David Smith, *Police and People in London*, PSI, 1984; *Black and White Britain*, London, 1984.
10 In *The Enemy Within*, Catholic Commission for Racial Justice, 1981.
11 Mohamed Naguib, 'Racism and anti-racism in education', a paper for the 1985 NAME Conference.
12 This may explain its growth in Britain, but not its origins. It began in the US forces; all ranks found an unsegregated military hard to take.
13 A. Sivanandan, 'The sentence of racism', *New Statesman*, 14.6.85.

14   Ahmed Gurnah, 'The Politics of Racism Awareness Training', *Critical Social Quarterly*, **11**.

15   For example, A.Sivanandan, 'The sentence of racism'; and 'In the castle of their skin', *New Statesman*, 7.6.85 and 14.6.85. See also C. Mullard, *The three Os, Anti-Racist Education*, NAME, 1985.

16   A couple of examples are to be found in the *Daily Mail*, of 24.10.83 and 15.3.84. It is a feature of these and of some other "discussions" of RAT I have heard that this kind of opposition has trouble calling it racism awareness, the word seems to stick in their throat and "racial" or just "race" is used instead. An article by Ronald Butt in the *TES* 24.5.85 suffers from the same disability.

17   A. Sivanandan, op cit. and in *Race and Class*, spring 1985.

18   J. Katz, *White Awareness*, University of Oklahoma Press, 1978.

19   *Anglo Saxon Attitudes*, BBC, produced by John Twitchin. A series carries this name, as does a 50 minute compilation which is the one referred to here. It is held by most teachers' centres and by the NUT head office. The rest of the series, but not this compilation, is available from Concord Films, 201 Felixstowe Rd, Ipswich, Suffolk.

20   The game is no longer available from Coventry Council for Racial Equality, who invented it.

21   Produced by the Catholic Commission for Racial Justice, and available from the British Council of Churches, 2 Eaton Gate, London SW1.

22   Available from the Multicultural Support Service, Bordesley Centre, Camphill, Stratford Road, Birmingham.

23   Available from Lewisham Council.

24   Produced by the BBC.

25   The original series was shown in 1979, and most of it was re-broadcast at least three times in the schools *English Programme* series. For availability contact Thames Schools Television, Publications Office, 149 Tottenham Court Road, WIP 9LL.

26   Broadcast by Channel 4 in December 1982. *New Society* published the text on 9.12.82.

27   Published, perhaps surprisingly, by the United Society for the Propagation of the Gospel.

28   Katz, pp. 46-7. One example of this exercise is filmed in one of the BBC Multicultural Education series: *Teacher, Examine Thyself*, and the 1985 edition of the accompanying book outlines how to set it up (J. Twitchin and C. Demuth, *Multicultural*

Education, London 1985). In my experience it is the single most effective exercise for producing new insights, and it is one which participants do for themselves.

29 These are quite easy to make up, with role cards for different "characters", and tend to highlight assumptions and attitudes.

30 op. cit. p. 94.

31 Katz, p. 104.

32 Originated by OXFAM, and reprinted as D. Hicks, *Minorities*, London 1981, pp. 82-5.

33 Made by the BBC, now available from Concord, address as in note 18 above.

34 Not available for hire, but best made by a group of teachers.

35 From Poster Film Collective, BCM PFC, London, WC1N 3XX.

36 Made by Thames, as part of their *Viewpoint* series. Address as in note 24 above.

37 Made in the BBC Open Door series by the Campaign Against Racism in the Media.

38 Shown on BBC in August 1983. See Appendix 1 for details.

39 Katz, p. 148.

40 Katz p. 157. Another useful list with a British context is in J. Twitchin and C. Demuth, *Multicultural Education*, London, 1981 and 1985, pp. 167−9.

41 Katz, pp. 161−3.

42 See, for example, the chapter on RAT in the 1985 edition of Twitchin and Demuth.

43 It is worth reading a complementary account of the mechanics of RAT in the 1985 edition of Twitchin and Demuth (see note 40).

44 Racism Awareness Programme Unit, 5−5a Westminster Bridge Rd, London SE1 7XW.

45 In a way, although they are designed to combat racism, the techniques themselves may be an example of cultural classism in that they create an ambience which owes at least something to "human growth" techniques which were always middle-class dominated, and something to management training too. They are extremely verbal and in a loose sense "intellectual" techniques. People like teachers can be good at evading and rationalizing and ducking the issues trainers raise, even if the trainer successfully gets past the blocks, because the whole enterprise takes place more or less within a set of rules recognized by those with lots of formal education. I have no idea how they work with people whose stock in trade is not talking, and since

most RAT is aimed for obvious reasons at middle-class decision-makers perhaps not many other people know either.

46   A well known and dramatic simulation of this is the film *The Eye of the Storm,* an extract of which is shown at the beginning of *Black* (see note 38) and available from Concord (address as in note 18 above).

47   Re-Evaluation Counselling was developed by Harvey Jackins and explained by him in *The Human Side of Human Beings*, Rational Island Publishing, 1978. This work on counselling about racism seems comparatively recent, although a lot of work has been done by members of oppressed groups counselling on their oppression – notably and mostly in the USA by women, black people, Jews, and children. Gurnah would include Jackins in his label "Rogerian" although Jackins would probably deny a specific connection.

48   In the kind of authoritarian way referred to later anyone's rejection of this approach is seen as confirmatory – it demonstrates the strength of repressive patterning if one cannot see the basic loving co-operativeness of people. The fact that you cannot see it proves even more strongly that it is there but repressed.

49   Some dramatic examples are given in *Black* (see note 38) from 1950s documentary footage.

50   The recent slip by a senior policeman and adviser to the Home Office on race relations, when he used the term "nig nogs" to a conference, clearly demonstrates the depth of racism where we ought reasonably expect not to find it. It also demonstrates that this is supposed to be a secret, since he had to resign.

51   Rushdie, p. 418.

52   R. Jeffcoate, *Ethnic Minorities and Education*, Harper & Row, 1984.

53   Jeffcoate, p. 151.

54   A. Sivanandan, op. cit.

55   Gurnah, p. 16.

56   A. Sivanandan, op cit.

57   ibid.

58   ibid.

59   Mullard, p. 44.

60   ibid., p. 44.

61   Gurnah, p. 17.

Part Three
Policy...Making Long-Term
Changes

6   Getting a school policy

This chapter is about anti-racist policies in white secondary schools, their usefulness, the reasons in principle for having them, the arguments that might persuade people to adopt them, and the possible strategy differences in this between "black" and "white" schools.

The focus and value of a policy

It should be made clear at once what I am suggesting such a policy ought to be about. My starting point in chapter 1 was that the majority of white pupils have considerable levels of confusion, misunderstanding and hostility about "race", and that it is the duty of schools to tackle this in all the ways open to them. (If they do not then we will continue to fail both black and white pupils, and any attempts to locate the problem solely in inner-city areas will not succeed.) Thus any policy ought to set out to deal both with the manifestations of racism against black pupils (and this can be an issue even when there is only one black pupil in the school), and with the contribution the curriculum and ethos of the school can make towards eroding pupils' racism and replacing it with something else. As the DES says in respect of the preparation for life which secondary schools should offer, pupils "will need to resist tendentious influences".[1]

The Swann report commented:

We... see education as having a major role to play in countering the racism which still persists in Britain today and which we believe constitutes one of the chief obstacles to the realisation of a truly pluralist society... we believe that the education system and teachers in particular are uniquely placed to influence the attitudes of all young people in a positive manner.[2]

To those who see this as a negative and therefore unhelpful way of posing the issue, let me restate one of the points of chapter 2, namely that the failure to recognize the extent of white racism has bedevilled educational responses in multiracial areas (where there have been any responses at all), and that if the white areas are to avoid such a painfully slow evolution of their own responses they have to stop thinking that racial education is about immigrants.[3] One training strategy to facilitate that is examined in chapter 5, since to look at a white pupil's attitude is often to look at a white adult's, too. LEA power politics are examined in the next chapter, where educational racism is placed in the realm of institutional processes and policies and beyond the sphere of simply attitudes.

This discussion of school policies has to be set in the context of the other chapters, and a distinction made between how points may be phrased here and how they may be phrased in the early stages of discussion in a particular school. My basic argument in a school would, in principle, be the same as that above. In other words there is no real option other than to define the issue as racism and to define the school's task as responding to it. This is a negative and threatening educational task to present to people, and could be opposed on the grounds that it is strategically better to present challenges as positive rather than negative (it always feels better to be creating a new world rather than reacting to the problems of the old). Thus a broader and richer curriculum could be the carrot, and a more effective incentive than the stick of racism. This may, on occasion, be a good strategy, but it should not be confused with our basic understanding of the problem. In fact, I am not convinced it is even a good strategy, since my own experience has been that teachers do not really get to grips with a new, "multicultural" curriculum until they have recognized the racism of the old one, and the most effective way of showing the penetration of racism into their daily work is to show them what their pupils think. Hence chapter 1, but we shall return to that.

However else one may be tackling the issue in one's own classroom or curriculum area, a school policy about "race" is a useful thing. To state this is not to claim that all policies are effective, or that their establishment is any kind of end in itself, but it is to claim that given the structure of most schools' decision-making and the struggle for legitimacy that anti-racist work has to go through, getting an institutional policy is both a useful process and a worthwhile target.

Paraphrasing some comments of Robin Richardson's about LEA policies, we might say the following about a school policy:

1   it is a resource for advocates, in that it provides legitimacy for their

concerns, that is, it gives them protection from certain criticisms and scepticisms, and it gives them a fuller and more rational hearing in debates and deliberations;
2 it is an internal communication between different levels of power in the school, and may contribute to procedural, structural and cultural change within the school.[4]

In addition it is worth adding that many people have found that the process of debating and deciding upon some sort of policy has been valuable in itself, it seems to clarify issues and make people think out where they stand.

Such advantages may appeal to "advocates", but there are also arguments which can be put to those who are initially uninterested. One might be that in a contentious and newly recognized area of concern staff both need guidance and the process of debate to clarify their aims and practices. Another is that a school's principles need formalizing and setting down — they often are nowadays in prospectuses in any case — so that pupils, parents, and new staff know what the school stands for.

As arguments of principle these are uncontentious enough, but efforts to get a policy statement on something the staff as a whole think is irrelevant will fall on stony ground. Although as Richardson suggests a policy confers some legitimacy on the debate, some degree of legitimacy has to be established in the first place for there to even be a policy. "Race" may be a newly recognized area of concern nationally, but for many teachers it is not locally. Thus the problem is how to get "race" on the agenda in a white school, how to get past the inertia produced by the statement "but there's no problem here".

Perhaps there are some lessons to be learnt from multiracial schools. It may be thought that there is a difference between successful strategies for getting a policy in schools where there are black pupils and those where there are few or none, yet surprisingly this does not appear to be so. The expectation that it might be arises from the assumption that those working in black schools would see some issues more clearly, and, in particular, would recognize the curriculum opportunities of a multicultural society more easily. As I have already argued in chapter 2, however, there is a sense in which although the presence of black children has made "race" an issue, the issue has been mostly conceived as being to do with *them* and not with *us*. Many substantially black schools now recognize the implicit racism of this formulation of "the problem", but as long as white schools see the issue that way they will understandably see no implications for themselves.

By no means a majority of largely or substantially black schools have policies about "race", but of those which have there are some patterns to be seen in how the policies are phrased and argued. These give some indications of what the formulators and the staffs which accepted them saw as the primary issues which they ought to be dealing with. Space forbids reprinting school policies in their entirety here[5] but it is worth noting the sort of things they contain. Their authors and supporters in my examples, all from London schools, would make no claim to having produced the last words on the subject; these policies are simply the best known, two having been reprinted for national reference by the National Union of Teachers (NUT)[6] and all but the last circulated in many ILEA schools as useful starting points. They were also among the first to be produced. The last one is included because it is newer, and because it achieved the unwelcome attention of a hysterical national newspaper.

A simple content analysis of these policies reveals some interesting emphases. They all begin by stressing the existence and undesirability of racist attitudes and behaviour either in the pupils, or in the immediate locality.

Holloway's policy begins "Due to the increased electoral success of the National Front, Holloway staff... [should]... make a special effort to combat the evils of racism." It then details an NF leaflet which was found in the school, arguing that its discovery makes it necessary to have a school policy. "Racialism outside schools is becoming gradually more respectable and this development will inevitably have repercussions inside schools." The rest of the document scarcely mentions the curriculum, it is couched in terms of reacting to the threat by using harsh discipline and guidance. This threat involves both black pupils in the school and the assumed values of the school by the rejection of them by many white pupils.

Quinton Kynaston's begins with an account of an Asian pupil having his throat cut by skinheads. The remainder of the document is, like Holloway's, almost entirely about the containment and reaction to expressions of racism by pupils.

Hurlingham begins a letter to parents about its policy by saying "Recently, in the community at large, there has been increasing pressure, particularly on young people, to adopt a racialist viewpoint and to express it wherever they happen to live or work."

North Westminster details the forms of racism encountered by its pupils. It briefly mentions the fact that it acknowledges and values all pupils' cultures, and its first point is about getting people's names right. The discussion then turns to physical attacks, intimidation, verbal abuse, racist literature, and racially exclusive behaviour. What is suggested for incorporation into the school's code of practice is a set of guidelines for dealing with racist incidents.

Abbey Wood's says a good deal more about the curriculum and its role in combating racism, but it sets the agenda initially as being a response to the "racist incidents and expressions of racism that have occurred in and around the school", such as verbal abuse, physical attacks, distribution of racist publications, wearing NF and BM insignia, and graffiti.

Mayfield argues the same way. Its policy statement begins with the question "Why the need for a policy statement?" and answers it by pointing to the frequency of racist incidents like name calling, graffiti, racist jokes, and the threatening and carrying out of violence.

Those schools which did not, at first, mention the curriculum, soon come to do so. A later version of Quinton Kynaston's policy, for example, has much more about the implications of an anti-racist approach in the curriculum. Despite the lack of any substantial discussion of the curriculum in the early policy statements, the point is that these schools, and by that I mean the activists in the schools who actually drafted the policy statements, either conceived the main imperative as dealing with the expressions of overt racism in the pupils, or decided that defining the imperative that way would be more persuasive and compelling to others.

The imperative does not seem to have been conceived in terms of golden new enriching curriculum opportunities, the possibilities of broadening the cultural base of the classroom to make education more fulfilling for everyone. This kind of rationale is often advanced, but in many schools well known for their work on "race", it does not seem to have been a strong enough force to get anything changed.

I should like to make it clear that this is not intended as any kind of criticism of those who worked to bring about these policy statements in the schools mentioned above. When faced daily with the victims of overt racism there should be no doubt where the first imperative for action is. Having raised the issue this way, the schools have all gone on to reappraise their priorities in the curriculum. This shows something of the differences between the older "celebrating diversity" and integrationist approaches and an anti-racist one. The extent of racism among whites ought to be an incentive for us to do something about it, to do otherwise is really not to grasp the educational nettle.

That being the case, we have to try to clarify the most effective strategy for those in white areas concerned to raise the issue of "race". We must be clear what the issue is. Is it that a richer, broader curriculum awaits us if we only had less ethnocentrist eyes to see it? This is positive, optimistic reasoning, presenting a multicultural approach as an opportunity, not a threat. There are times when it must be sold this way, and if presented like this it may reduce the anxiety and resultant hostility in many teachers. We should not be under any illusions, however, that the world is really such a happy place. If multiracial schools have failed to respond in this way for the past twenty years or more, if they find that even with black children in their classrooms they can only now begin to get policies when these pupils are the victims of racist violence, it may be naive to think that a more positive approach will work elsewhere. If it took people having their throats cut by young fascists to enable anti-racist teachers to get multi-racial schools' policies through, one has to be an optimist to expect a more far-sighted approach in white schools.

In addition, the key "political" factors which have brought about school policies seem to be one or more of: pressure from black pupils or communities; right-wing political activity in or around the school; a core of committed anti-racist staff; a committed anti-racist senior member of staff; and amalgamation or reorganization leading to a significant change in the ethnic composition of the school.

Only three of these factors are likely to ever apply in white schools. Schools with a large proportion of black pupils but without one of these factors (or probably two) at work are entirely capable of, in the late 1980s, having a "colour blind" approach. Swann disapprovingly quotes a teacher who gave evidence to the committee:

We have no distinction in this school between pupil and pupil, that's our first objective.... I should have put it – if all the Asians... evaporated tomorrow, it would not make a scrap of difference to the curriculum.[7]

Policy formation in a white school

Having thus argued for posing the issues in a certain way, it may be instructive to look at the process of trying to get an anti-racist policy in a largely white school. Some reflection on a case study coupled with the experiences of the schools mentioned above may produce some general guidelines for action.

The school concerned was a large comprehensive in a town with a population of about 120,000, with a small proportion of black people and a smaller proportion still in the school. A very small number of staff out of a total of about seventy were concerned about racism to the extent of seeing it as an educational issue which affected them. Its most common expression would be found in the kind of attitudes expressed in the pupils' writings included in chapter 1, but this was also acted out in the kinds of ways described by the Indian pupil in the same chapter (see p.11). The kind of racist political activity noted by several of the London schools mentioned earlier, and researched at the same time by the Centre for Contemporary Studies,[8] was also in evidence in the area outside the school. A small core of boys were members of the National Front or had some allegiance to the now defunct British Movement, and they were not only evangelizing among the other pupils they were doing so in an informational vacuum left by the school. The evangelizing was not on a large scale and was fairly secretive, but this capitalized on the slight glamour these organizations already had as tough and violent, it gave affiliates a feeling of being one of the elect.

Although several staff would have described themselves as anti-racists, and were indeed involved in anti-racist work outside, it took this growing racist activity to focus the issue for them inside the school. They would have welcomed an earlier catalyst, and today might not need one, but at the time they saw this as a personal and institutional spur to action. This particular spur to action would have been hard to present as a positive opportunity for enriching the curriculum; it was unpleasant and pernicious, and the only way to get any kind of staff support for action seemed to be to show them the kind of racism that was coming to the surface in the school.

There were regular staff meetings where almost anything could be discussed (after the most vital issues of corridor supervision and the best system of queueing for lunch), but action was more likely to follow if the matter had first been discussed by, and perhaps been the subject of recommendations from, the meetings of two of the centres of power in the school: the Year Heads and the Heads of Department. Accordingly, a file of National Front and British Movement literature was put together, not all of it taken from pupils in the school but all of it certainly available to them, and a special meeting was asked for with the Year Heads.

The extent to which such initiatives seem to depend on individuals is disturbing, but it was clear that just anyone could not go to the Year Heads' meeting and expect to be listened to with much patience. Teaching is often tough and wearing, and committed, concerned and hard working as these Year Heads were, it was understandable that they should want to minimize any new problem if at all possible. Thus, whoever presented this "new" problem to them had to be credible in terms of hard work, competence, experience, and realism. Fortunately there was a head of department (also thought of as a future year head) who was able to able to attend the meeting and speak about the issue. Although the convenor of the year heads' group, the pastoral deputy head, was politely accommodating while actually being cynical, there were two clear allies amongst the group of eight who were pressed in advance to attend and to be supportive in the meeting, which in the end lasted no more than 25 minutes. It was nevertheless valuable to have the examples of racist leaflets, since none of the year heads had actually seen any of the material before. (It is remarkable how many people of liberal persuasion give lip service to opposing the NF, but support their "freedom of speech" in the belief that they engage in the same kind of political discourse as the other political parties. They are usually shocked to read the kind of thing printed in the fringe right-wing press, which does not mince words.)

This was the first step, and, clearly, all that was being done at this stage was to sensitize people to the crudest, most blatant forms of racism and to try to get them to take action against them. Perhaps the more subtle manifestations need a tuned ear. The Year Heads felt that the racism of the kind in the literature was the most visible and pointed tip of an iceberg, but that there was a limit to what they could do about it. They could confiscate racist material, they could suspend distributors (or those with the little stickers which had begun to appear around the school), but they preferred to rely if possible on the existing school ban against any political activity rather than to act explicitly against racism. The head was reported to be willing to back temporary suspension for offenders.

The Year Heads were right to say there was a limit to what they could do about it, and there is also a limit to how much the policies cited earlier can do about racist pupils. In so far as the school has a role in creating and reinforcing racist beliefs reflected elsewhere in pupils' families, the media, and in peer groups, all those with pastoral responsibilities can do is mop up after the mess left by the holes in the curriculum. The Year Heads in this school accepted that they had a role to play, but they were quick to say that the manifestations of racism which they, as links in the disciplinary chain had to deal with, had their origins and proper solutions elsewhere.

The issue of racist attitudes was then raised at a staff meeting, after a half-hearted attempt by the head to "forget" about it by pretending it was the subject of a local heads' meeting. It was not, but what was going on was the well-known management ploy of sitting on or ignoring controversy if at all possible. Heads cannot do much right in the eyes of the "public", and if a school is at all worried about its reputation (and this one was) it does not do to be making a stand about anything "controversial".

Plans had been too well laid, however. Half a dozen staff had been asked to state their concern about racism among the pupils if the opportunity arose in the staff meeting. They were all people who recognized that there was a problem, but were not necessarily those who always came to or spoke at staff meetings. They were asked to couch their comments in terms of asking for guidance from the head, rather than attacking him with demands that he should do something. They were also asked not to sit together so they would not appear as an identifiable group.

It is interesting to note the way in which many school staff meetings work. Most have no formal system of voting, and reflect the essentially autocratic nature of school management. Balances of opinion are hard to quantify, and their quantification by voting is frequently resisted by heads because they can then listen to whom they want to and still claim to be "sensing the feeling of the meeting". (This is not meant to sound as if all heads are by nature dictators, it is often a role which is forced upon them.) At any rate, such a way of conducting a meeting is open to manipulation by several staff agreeing to all speak in the same way and a small number of people can thereby create "the feeling of the meeting". There is no doubt that such a technique is undemocratic, even machiavellian, but so is the usual alternative.

At the meeting some staff felt this was really nothing more than a general issue of politeness, and that pupils who did not open doors for staff were the same ones who called others names. Others saw the racial abuse as no worse than fat children being called names. All the same, the stage had been set, and more people than had been expected to joined in, so it would have been hard for the head to have made no response. The response was to ask the head of departments' meeting to discuss the matter — the matter being fairly loosely defined as overt racism among the pupils.

It was fortunate that there was someone among the HoDs who had considerable credibility with the others and who took the problem of racism very seriously. The overall perspective being employed was that it is of little practical use to try and furnish an overall societal analysis of racism; teachers have too many investments in the status quo for such a thing to be accepted easily. A more persuasive argument is one which highlights the fact of pupils' racism on the small number of black pupils, and on the white pupils themselves. The fact that they strongly believe something so antithetical to liberal values can be a useful lever on otherwise conventional staff. Their liberalism can be mobilized, since if they can be convinced of the strength and the nature of pupil attitudes they cannot but seek to respond in some way. By this time, unfortunately, the folder of racist literature was no longer available, since the head said he had lost it.

Each department head was asked to take back to their department meetings four case studies, and to come back with a departmental response to each one. This was intended to provide a focus so that people were talking about the same thing, and to tease out more of what people really thought. The case studies were:

1   A black pupil comes into your classroom with a message, and someone makes an audible offensive remark like "get back to your tree" or "bloody Pakis", or mutters "National Front, National Front".

2   A swastika and the words "BM, fight for a white Britain" are written on a desk. It's fairly easily cleaned off and you can identify the culprit. Do you leave it at that?

3   In a class discussion about jobs (or discos, or school buses, or anything), perhaps in tutor time, a girl uses "Paki" in the common way, as a descriptive term. Another boy uses "nigger" in apparently the same way.

4   There is almost a fight between a black boy and a white boy. On investigating it you find the white boy called the black boy a "jungle bunny" because the black boy had first called him "honky". Fair enough? Leave it at that?

Although two departments reported that they had never come across such incidents and that there was therefore not much of a problem (all the case studies had actually happened in the previous few months) no one recommended inaction. There were anxieties about blowing things up out of proportion, and about heavy-handed responses to such incidents, but no one was prepared to just let them pass. Not surprisingly, the same kind of comments were received from some black people who were also given the case studies.

The following paper was then circulated by one head of department to the others before the next meeting, with a suggestion that a small group of three or four look more closely at the wording and produce a final version for formal endorsement.

A school policy about race

Some time ago I asked all HoDs to discuss with departments four possible situations involving racial hostility between students, they are set out again below:

1   A black student comes into your classroom with a message, and someone makes an audible offensive remark like "Get back to your tree" or "bloody Pakis", or mutters "National Front, National Front".
2   A swastika and the words "BM, fight for a white Britain" are written on a desk. It's fairly easily cleaned off and you can easily identify the culprit. Do you leave it at that?
3   In a class discussion about jobs (or discos, or school buses or anything), perhaps in tutor time, a girl uses "Paki" in the common way, as a descriptive term. Another boy uses "nigger" in apparently the same way.
4   There's almost a fight between a black boy and a white boy. On investigating it you find the white boy called the black boy a "jungle bunny" because the black boy had first called him "honky". Fair enough? Leave it at that?

Almost all the departments gave a written or verbal reply, for which I am grateful, since if nothing else it shows staff regard it as an issue worth noting.

The replies also show quite a striking degree of agreement. (Two departments have never come across incidents like those above, possibly because of the content matter of the subject, possibly in one case because of a very strict policy about graffiti of any kind on folders etc. I did however gain the impression that those departments would not dissent from the reactions of the others.)

Although many felt that standards of mutual respect between students were generally poor, everyone thought that the suggested incidents were serious and had to be dealt with, not ignored. As one would expect, there was also an awareness of the difficulty of the issue from the "craft of the classroom" point of view, so that people felt at times such incidents should be dealt with head-on but that they ideally require a careful talk, without an audience or a confrontation. Several people mentioned the risk of over-reacting, and giving the issue the kind of public attention that could rebound on black students. Almost everyone thought all such incidents should be reported to senior staff and that strong support should be forthcoming from them.

Bearing in mind the degree of unity, at any rate among HoDs, I would like us as a school to formalise our views into a brief race relations policy statement. The Education Authority is currently discussing a county policy, and is likely to approve the wording set out below. I am not suggesting any departure from this (since I was involved in writing it) but it is necessarily pitched at quite a general level, and we need to be more specific:

Educational commitment within a multi-cultural society

...County Council recognises the cultural, ethnic and religious diversity of contemporary British society. Therefore, it affirms its commitment to an education which acknowledges the particular needs arising from such a society and will endeavour to make provision to the best of its resources. The committee therefore accepts the following objectives within its general policy:

1   To educate pupils and teachers towards an understanding of, and respect for, one another's cultural, ethnic and religious differences.
2   Within its many different educational activities, to draw upon, encourage and support the cultural heritage of the communities within our society.
3   To take positive steps to promote equality of opportunity and harmony and to combat discriminatory practices.
4   To endeavour to meet the particular needs of all children within its schools, having regard to their diverse cultural backgrounds.

Suggested school policy statement

1   Since we regard all students as being of equal value, racism must be opposed because it is diametrically opposed to this belief.
2   Racism may be expressed in actual physical assault or threat; racial name calling, teasing or abuse; expressions of prejudice or misinformation about minority groups; or graffiti around the school premises.
3   Teachers have a responsibility to combat such racism in some way whenever it occurs.
4   Staff must be vigilant and report to the Head or Deputies any racist behaviour.
5   Racism = Prejudice + Power. Given the balance of numbers in this school it is not possible for whites to be the victims of racism. This does not give a free hand to black students to be offensive, but staff should be aware of the inequality.

6   The curriculum should reflect the fact that Britain is a multi-cultural society and will remain so. Where appropriate it should promote a respect for other cultures and educate against racism.

7   It is important that students involved in racist incidents nevertheless believe that they have an equal opportunity with other students to follow their studies.

8   Racist literature should be confiscated on the same basis as pornographic literature, both are offensive and degrading to sections of our school community.

9   We need to be clear that our opposition to racist practices in school is qualitatively different to our official impartiality on politics in general. It is inconsistent with our aims as a comprehensive school to be neutral about racism, and there times when we have to say so, though it may bring ill-informed criticism.

The school was really not a radical or especially left-wing one, but the strategy worked. There was discussion, naturally, about the proposed policy statement, especially point 5, but by this time discussions were becoming fruitful. These processes are by no means only valuable for their end products. The exchanges, alliances and insights which arise during the consultation and discussion stages are of lasting value. Typically in a busy school the discussion was guillotined by the caretaker since it had been the last item on a long agenda, but a small group was asked to spend some more time on the wording.

Ironically, having gone so far along the road of being one of the first white schools to have such a policy, it could go no further. The proposed LEA policy statement quoted in the paper came up at the Education Committee soon afterwards, and in circumstances described in the next chapter (see p.150) was unexpectedly rejected. The head had been nervous all along about the school producing anything in writing, in case the papers or the governors made something "controversial" out of it, so the LEA's decision was taken by him as a prohibition on schools to have policies.

This was an unfortunate ending to a well orchestrated and effective campaign to raise the importance of racism in the school, and points to the factors which can frustrate developments. On the other hand, the account provides suggestions for how other schools might proceed. The key elements in the success of the strategy employed seem to be:

1   The involvment of someone relatively senior and respected among the staff, so that it cannot be written off as the naive concern of a few scale one "youngsters".
2   The presence of racist activity in the school.
3   The involvement of the key power and opinion blocs — the heads of department, the pastoral heads, and the staff meeting.
4   The opportunity for all staff to discuss the matter in department meetings, thus increasing the chances of any final decision feeling "owned".
5   The provision of two focuses for discussion, the racist literature, new to most of the staff, and the case studies.
6   In areas where there are black people in any numbers, obviously pupils and black organizations would be involved. This was not the case here.

Equally, we can see the key obstacles to progress, the first being the head's nervousness. One can be critical, but heads have a tightrope to walk between their own convictions, those of their staff, the gleeful sensationalizing and myth-making of the local press, and the governors and LEA, their employers. At the time there was a paranoia about the relative success of pupils from this particular school in finding jobs, and it was feared that an unfavourable portrayal of the school as an anti-racist one would have given pupils' job chances with many local employers the kiss of death. The head actually said, though not in public, that however good the "cause" he would not let the school have a public policy because it would be misunderstood and the school's reputation would therefore suffer.
 Another obstacle could, then, be summed up as the range of pressures bearing on heads, or at least their interpretation of them. This is the sharp end of any debate about schools being answerable to society, however ostrich-like or bigoted the often self-appointed spokespeople of "society" may be, schools do not have the power to ignore them.
 The final obstacle in this case was the LEA, although this was more a matter of choice than the head admitted. Since LEAs have great difficulty in pressing schools to have policies at all, it is hard to believe that they possess any more formal power to prohibit them.

Complementary approaches

In a sense this school was "helped" by the growth of racist activity in and around the school, as it seems were several of the London schools whose policies have been examined. It would be absurd to "hope" for overt activity by racist groups in the school before pressing any initiatives. One other effective way to raise the issue is to do the exercise in chapter 1, that of getting pupils, without any prompting, to write something about "race". With few exceptions, classes will produce the same kinds of things. If these are printed out, preferably in full so that it is a recognizable class and no-one can be accused of selectivity, and then circulated among the staff before a meeting, they may still argue that the best thing is to let sleeping dogs lie, but they can no longer deny that there is a dog.

Once again, it is probably important which member of staff does this. Another convincing kind of evidence is a tape recording of a black pupil describing their experiences, rather like Balvinder's in chapter 1. It requires a lot of trust on the part of the black pupil (or ex-pupil?) to do this, but it is hard for staff to argue with it.

The spur used to initiate action here was unambiguously pupils' racism, and while that is the most pressing reason for change it would be wrong to ignore opportunities to present the issue more positively at any stage. Since there are numerous statements of principle encouraging all schools to recognize that Britain is a multicultural society[9] these can be quoted and used to try and spell out the curriculum opportunities. This is more likely to be a successful strategy in a school where there are more than just a few black pupils, since, as has already been argued, the mere presence of black people somewhere else does not on its own strike teachers in white areas as much of a reason to change.

Individual subjects can have their horizons widened if there is the happy chance of a TV series or exhibition like *Africa* in 1984. It can be no coincidence that the subjects commonly given low priority on the timetable, like the creative arts, are often more amenable to a less ethnocentric approach than the real subject repositories of our culture, but their contribution is not to be ignored. Some more specific suggestions about various subjects are made in the appendix on resources.

To raise the implications for the curriculum, some schools have tried a questionnaire, designed and worded in a way that is not threatening or accusing, to ask people to consider the role of their own subject in multicultural education. There are enormous problems of definition in this, because unless many hours have been spent agreeing about terms (in which case a questionnaire would not be necessary) people will understand the issue in very different ways. Some will see it as educating against prejudice in general, others as a matter of strangeness, so that pupils must mix with other cultures as much as possible, others will want to encourage pupils to feel sorry for "the third world", and still others will want pupils to study "primitive cultures and their contact with civilisation". I have quoted these understandings because they are real ones from a real school, although clearly some of these good intentions will have racist effects. If nothing else, such an exercise shows the level of interest, however misguided, in a school.

A good way of defining the debate in unambiguous terms from the start is to include a brief preamble to any questionnaire. This might be extracts from the better LEA policy documents such as ILEA's or Berkshire's, or it might be the curriculum guidelines suggested in the appendix on resources. Colleagues will not automatically agree with these, and there is a danger that if their printing and circulation defines the debate too much people's doubts and questions may not emerge. One cannot wait for every member of staff to have an unambiguous understanding of racism, but one has to avoid steam-rollering and allow at least some colleagues to get hold of some new ideas and make them their own.

There is no short cut to a more coherent anti-racist stance, but if a core of staff can be persuaded to go on a racism awareness course the resulting acceleration of progress is likely to be considerable. This may be a large claim, but the written evaluations of teacher after teacher following one of these courses suggests that there is no better way of getting agreement about key terms, concepts and perspectives in a relatively short time. (The NUT has taken a lead in organizing national racism awareness courses for teachers, and is now prepared to mount them locally where there is demand.)

Where there is an active union branch in a school they are clearly a group to work with. As the unions are sometimes the only cross-curricular groups who are allowed to meet without the hierarchy setting the agenda, and often have clear national guidelines to back them up, union members are a potential force for change. Schools vary enormously in the relationship between unions and formal organization and decisions, indeed there are many schools where building up the strength of the unions would be a longer task than establishing a coherent response to racism!

A working party is the almost inevitable outcome of a school taking the issue seriously, although one has to be conscious of the frustration many people feel with working parties. The working party in the school featured in *Anglo Saxon Attitudes*[10] had undoubtedly made some progress in its three year life, but the core of members' reasoning about why it would be unwise to move any faster was an anxiety about upsetting the rest of the staff, i.e. upsetting white people. This makes sense, of course, but it is also an example of how racist outcomes are embedded in the decisions we see as entirely reasonable. There is no answer to this except that white resistance is a real matter to be reckoned with; for those of us who sit in staffrooms and try to negotiate and press for change, the working party may be our best vehicle.

Such a group can look for spaces. It may press lots of departments at once with some kind of questionnaire based on the curriculum suggestions in the appendix on resources, it may see an opportunity in active tutorial work and build on that to get at staff's teaching identity via their tutorial one. It may circulate or gather examples of good practice, it may manage to define the role of the head as central and crucial and even get her/him to go on a course. It may be able to give support and advice on the teacher's eternal cry "Where do I get the resources?" Between its members it may be able to employ a variety of approaches, some subtle and unthreatening, some direct and uncompromising. It may be able to ultimately define the issue as beginning with a problem but presenting an opportunity. Finally, it can give support and solidarity to those engaged in the isolating business of anti-racism.

To conclude, I would simply like to list the factors which seem to impede anti-racist progress in schools, and those which, in different schools at different times, have moved things in the right direction.[11]

Obstacles

Frustration and uncertainty.
Other pressing problems in school (reorganization, GCSE, pay dispute....)
Some teachers are as racist as the pupils.
Belief that "coloured pupils are well integrated".
No slot for anti-racist work in the curriculum.
Career/promotion prospects of activists.
Activists associated with other challenging issues.
LEA or governor opposition.
Staff's unwillingness to recognize issue.

Staff anxiety about controversy of any kind.
Head's/key staff's apathetic or wilful obstruction.

Obstacle removers/circumventers

Commitment of at least one key/senior member of staff.
Involvement of key power/opinion blocs.
Racist activity in or around the school.
Planning, with time scale, avoiding damp squibs.
Powerful support from outside (some parents, a governor) even if only nominal.
Working party, wide ownership of key ideas and strategy.
Helpful outsiders.
Formal legitimation (LEA policy, union policy, Swann Report, HMI reports, phrases in school prospectus).
Pressure from black organizations.

References

1   *The Curriculum 11-16,* DES, 1981.
2   *Education for All,* HMSO 1985, Cmnd 9453, p. 319.
3   "...the fact that attempts to develop educational policies designed to prepare all pupils for life in a multi-racial society often appear to be restricted to schools or authorities with ethnic minority pupils — as though the actual presence of such pupils was the major catalyst for such initiatives rather than any broader educational justification — has we believe not only tended to distort discussion of this aspect of educational development, but has also contributed to the generally disappointing degree of progress in this field, especially in 'all-white' areas." *Education for All,* p. 326.
4   From a paper given to the day conference "Match and Mismatch", June 1983, at London University's Institute of Education.
5   Some copies of school policies may be available from ILEA, but they scarcely have the resources to respond to many requests.
6   Two examples can be found in the NUT booklet *Combatting Racism in Schools,* NUT, 1984, available to members from Hamilton House Mabledon Place, London WC1H 9BD.

7   *Education for All*, p. 107.
8   *Nazis in the Playground*, Centre for Contemporary Studies, Ingersoll House, 202 New North Rd, London N1 7BL.
9   About half of all the LEAs now have policy statements of some kind, and of necessity many of these take a "positive line". The Schools Council series *Examining in a Multicultural Society* can always be quoted as authoritative (see the appendix), as can AMMA's booklet and, of course, Swann.
10 In *School Report* in the BBC series *Multicultural Education*, and in the compilation called *Anglo-Saxon Attitudes*. Full details note 19, chapter 5.
11 In this connection see an excellent article by Robin Richardson, 'Each and every school, responding, reviewing, planning and doing', *Multicultural Teaching*, 3 no.2, Spring 1985.

7 Local education authority policies — some strategies

There must be a massive amount of energy up and down the country being used up by people trying to get multicultural education policies or anti-racist policies into their schools. I say "used up" but I might just as well say "misused" since a good many of the people involved have spent months, or years, grinding away and feeling they are getting nowhere. Individuals will identify different causes for this: opposition from the LEA, the head, key senior staff, advisers, inspectors, governors, parents; too many other bread and butter issues around for the staff even to be able to lift their noses from the grindstone for a moment (the "doctrine of the unripe time" as Frances Morrell calls it); lack of credibility or seniority of the people promoting the cause; a widespread feeling that "it's not an issue"; inertia among the staff; a right-wing racist staff; no tradition of new developments except from certain quarters, typically the "top"; constraints of the traditional/examination curriculum. I hope many people will recognize the causes of their own despair in this list.

Lessons from existing policies

Several panaceas have been held up in the recent past, the main one of which is the local authority policy. "If only", people say, "we had a policy like Berkshire's or Bradford's or Brent's or ILEA's then we could use that as a stick to beat unwilling colleagues with". There is some truth in this, indeed this chapter will argue that such policies can be indispensable to teachers working for racial equality in education. However, there are several characteristics of the best policies which have to be borne in mind when considering their export elsewhere, especially their export to white areas.

The first is the pressure which produced them. In each case there was a loud enough black voice, sometimes a voting voice, to bring substantial pressure to bear on the LEA to do something coherent — piecemeal and often wrongheaded things having been done for years.

(The exception to this may appear to be Berkshire, though in fact 10 per cent of its pupils are from ethnic minority backgrounds, and their parents are concentrated enough in Reading and Slough to be able to make a political noise.)

Sometimes this "pressure" was more dramatic, notably in Avon. Despite an active NUT group pursuing racial injustice in education from within the service it took the St Paul's uprising to set the stage for their booklet *After the Fire* and to make some LEA response inescapable. Despite that, the resulting policy is not among the more far-reaching. Most policies with any kind of implications for practice date from the early 1980s, and although a particular DES circular[1] and the Rampton Report are often quoted by LEAs themselves as spurs to or legitimators of action, it is difficult to discount the effect of the national attention on "race" produced by the uprisings. In some LEAs it is doubtless the case that they provided the final "push", the final proof for those who had been pressing for action for years. It would be ahistorical to see support for policies emerging full grown without any antecedents in each area, but these antecedents only seem to have developed enough in areas with substantial black populations to have tipped the balance in decision-making. Mullard, Bonnick and King at the London Institute of Education, in their analysis of policies,[2] state unequivocally that in the case of the first policies produced it was the presence of black people which provided the initial rationale for their formulation. This can equally be the case with Conservative authorities like Bradford and Birmingham, where "race" policies can be seen as an exercise in social management, or "keeping the lid on".[3]

A second factor is the political balance in the LEA. Berkshire was a "hung" council at the time it passed its policy, so was Brent; Bradford was only just Conservative. Thus, in each case a few people held the balance of power. When its policy was passed in the early 1980s the ILEA was not just a Labour council but a strongly-committed-to-educational-change Labour council. That, combined with the fact that the catalysts and resources for recognizing "race" in education are walking around the city in substantial numbers means that some LEAs will inevitably be in the vanguard.

It is these factors which make it unlikely that better policies will be passed in other LEAs in quite the same way, although there are metropolitan districts like Sheffield, Manchester and Liverpool which have both a black presence and a Labour educational tradition and these are taking them along the same sort of road as ILEA.

Mullard, Bonnick and King also note that the metropolitan districts in general are more responsive to national trends and redirections in education than other authorities.

Money is another factor. Bradford has for a long time had to spend money on "immigrant" education. It does not need "immigrant" education (ESL teaching actually) as it used to do, so it is relatively easy to gradually move the expenditure into multicultural education and anti-racist initiatives. ILEA has a long history of being the highest spending LEA per pupil — it may be argued that it needed to be because of the scale of disadvantage and deprivation of the capital's population. But despite the fact that 31 per cent of the schools' roll is on free meals (only substantially beaten by Liverpool's Knowsley at 41.9 per cent), it also has a resource production and teacher support wing that are head and shoulders above any other LEAs, and better pupil/teacher ratios than almost anywhere else.

A fourth key factor can sound like a kind of "great person" theory of history. It is said of several LEAs that if a key individual or two were taken away the "race" policy would collapse, and I have no doubt that certain chief education officers (CEOs), in particular, but also individual advisers and elected members, have had a vital and unique part to play in getting policies through. With due modesty they would probably deny this, and rightly if really presented as a "great person theory". They would point to the blend of historical and political factors, the money, the awareness, the community pressure which makes a certain time ripe. But for practical purposes it is as well to remember that key individuals can be crucial, because, without detracting from the other forces which make a particular time "ripe", if these people (who are usually powerful) are not taken account of the policy proposal will fail. It goes against many people's democratic instincts, but the fact is that CEOs, in particular, can get their way — less senior officials can be directed by them or have obstacles to their work removed, elected members may defer to their judgement. This is seen more clearly when they are obstructive, and some of the strategies suggested later may be useful in clearing the blockage, but there will be many LEAs where for years activists will chafe at the power exercised by one bureaucrat to frustrate their efforts. This may be because s/he knows the time is not ripe to get committee approval, it may be her/his motives are less sympathetic or concerned.

Fifth, the formal and informal structures of an LEA are also crucial factors. It is pointless to be too definite here since LEAs differ considerably from each other, but even a formal description of an

LEA structure does not necessarily tell you how power and influence is distributed. It could be that a particular adviser or officer is very influential on the CEO, or that some useful informal links exist between some elected members and some officials, or that the opposite is true and they are all at daggers drawn. In this connection Mullard et al. looked at the authorship of policy documents, finding that the CEO (sometimes called Director of Education) had formulated eighteen of the thirty-six existing statements, as against three from multicultural education advisers, thirteen from working parties, and two from elected member sub-committees. They add, however, "It should be noted that Director of Education is a formal title reflective of authority rather than the actual formulator", presumably suggesting that in many cases other officers/advisers/ inspectors had actually written the thing but that the director was prepared to put his weight behind it. The effect, I suppose, is the same.

It is rather surprising to learn, again from the Institute report, that most policies have not, in fact, got elected member approval. At the time of that report (October 1983) there were only seven policies in this strict sense of the word.

Interestingly, there are at least half a dozen LEAs which have "position statements" not formally ratified by the committee which are as comprehensive as many formal policies. All the LEAs involved have a history of substantial black populations so perhaps the local traditions are such that officers are free to make explicit position statements (involving expenditure) without fear of opposition from elected members, i.e. they can redirect "immigrant education" monies. Perhaps they can successfully keep members in the dark. Whatever the reason for this state of affairs in places like Birmingham it is unlikely to be workable in whiter areas. A position statement which addresses even a few substantive issues is not going to slip by unnoticed or with tacit approval in Dorset, or Devon, or Sussex.

An abortive attempt

Trying to get a policy in white areas is more likely to be a problem with the elected members of the education committee than with anyone else. In terms of effectively shifting day-to-day educational practice, the heads, advisers/inspectors and education administrators are the key people, but to give them space to work a policy is needed, and getting a policy generally needs the support of the elected members. Worse, if the opposition rather than the support of the elected members is aroused, they can close off any space to work and set back anti-racist action for years.

One case study of this is provided by an authority which did not have a policy (in 1982) but which had an advisory group on multicultural education, consisting of the heads of the three or four schools with more than a handful of black pupils, a couple of local CRE people, and a sprinkling of interested advisers and officers. In practice, in most authorities officers and advisers usually have a reasonable degree of autonomy, especially if the CEO is supportive or uninterested, and one or other of these was the case here. A few courses had been run, Section II posts had been successfully applied for, some covert help had been given to mother tongue classes. It was felt, for the sorts of reasons already mentioned, that the group could "come out" a little more if there was a formal policy legitimating its concerns. Accordingly, various other LEAs' policies were examined, and a first discussion draft was produced as follows:

Draft:

The County of Blankeshire Education Committee acknowledges (affirms?/ recognises?) the multi-cultural, multi-racial and multi-ethnic nature of British society which contains a variety of languages, religions and cultures. The authority will make every endeavour to meet the needs of such a society and adopts the following general policy:

1.   To prepare all pupils to live and work harmoniously with an equality of opportunity.

2.   To recognise the richness and diversity of the complex contemporary society and to portray this diversity in the most positive manner by adopting a multi-cultural approach to education.

3.   To define very clearly racism, its effects, and to take positive steps to counter racism wherever it arises.

4.   To promote equality of opportunity.

5.   To make every endeavour to meet the specialist needs of all pupils/ students as far as resources will allow.

6.   To identify resources available to further this work; including Section II (of the Local Government Act 1966), urban aid, EEC funds etc., and to maximise the use of these resources to meet the above needs.

7.   To encourage and support the work of those individual teachers already striving to meet the above objectives.

At the time when this document was written (1982) it was thought impolitic by the advisory group to leave in the word "racism" because it was too "hard", too "left-wing", and a milder, more general policy statement was suggested, rather similar to Avon's:

Educational commitment within a multi-cultural society.

Blankeshire County Council recognises the cultural, ethnic and religious diversity of contemporary British society. Therefore, it affirms its commitment to an education which acknowledges the particular needs arising from such a society and will endeavour to make provision to the best of its resources. The committee therefore accepts the following objectives within its general policy:

1)   To educate pupils and teachers towards an understanding of, and respect for, one another's cultural, ethnic and religious differences.
2)   Within its many different educational activities, to draw upon, encourage and support the cultural heritage of the communities within our society.
3)   To take positive steps to promote equality of opportunity and harmony and to combat discriminatory practices.
4)   To endeavour to meet the particular needs of all children within its schools, having regard to their diverse cultural backgrounds.

More interestingly, perhaps, the policy proposal was preceded by a brief summary of "multi-cultural education" in the county in the previous fifteen years, to enable the poor old committee to know a little of the context. This read as follows:

EDUCATION COMMITTEE

Schools Sub-Committee
15th November 1982

MULTI-CULTURAL EDUCATION

1. Introduction
1.1   Multi-cultural education has its origins in the response made by schools to the influx of families from the New Commonwealth in the 1960s. The most immediate needs of these children were in learning to read, write

and speak English and also in adapting to life in a country and culture which vastly differed from their previous experience. The emphasis therefore was placed on language work and on assimilation into the dominant culture. As time passed the perspective began to change. Schools in areas with large concentrations of pupils from ethnic minority groups began to examine what was taught and to consider its appropriateness bearing in mind the background of their pupils.

1.2   During the 1970s there was a gradual movement away from the notion that multi-cultural education concerned only those schools with significant numbers of pupils of ethnic minority origin. The Department of Education and Science document "A Framework for the School Curriculum" (January 1980) recommended that the curriculum should foster:"Respect for the religious and moral values and a tolerance of other races, religions and ways of life, to help pupils understand the way in which they live, and the interdependence of individuals, groups and nations".

1.3   It can be seen, then, that multi-cultural education has two broad objectives:

> (a) to ensure that children of varying ethnic origins are able to reach their full educational potential and,
> (b) to ensure that all pupils, of whatever ethnic origin, have an understanding of, and a respect for the varied cultures and life styles which make up our modern society.

1.4   This approach to education is a preparation for all young people for life in today's multi-cultural and world society, promoting respect for, and understanding of people whose life styles, religions and backgrounds may be different from one's own. The approach applies both to primary and secondary schools and crosses traditional subject and age boundaries being important for the social and personal education of all children. It should therefore permeate the whole curriculum although in some secondary schools examination based courses in Multi-cultural or World Studies have been developed.

2. The multi-cultural education team

2.1   In 1968 two "Teachers of Immigrant Pupils" were appointed to cater for basic language needs of children who were arriving in Blankeshire in significant numbers at that time, and to offer help and advice to schools on the specific problems that these pupils might face in adjusting to their new environment. In 1979, the Authority began to experience an influx of Vietnamese and Cambodian families who were being accommodated primarily in the north eastern area. In order to meet the educational needs of these children, a temporary team of four was created and subsequently disbanded in 1981.

2.2   In January 1982, a Multi-Cultural Education Team was appointed using a central government grant under Section II of the Local Government Act 1966. The purpose of the Team is "to meet the specific needs of children from ethnic minority groups and to make a positive response to the implications of a multi-cultural society for all pupils in the County". The Team consists of three full-time teachers: an Advisory Teacher and two full-time peripatetic teachers. The Team operates in a variety of ways.

2.3   The Team has established a small unit for relatively recently arrived children who are in immediate need of a concentrated programme of basic English. At present there are 10 children attending the unit on a part-time basis.

2.4   The Members of the Team teach about 30 children within their own schools on a peripatetic basis. These children may be taught individually, or in small groups, depending on the level of teaching necessary. A further function of the team is to advise Heads and other teachers on appropriate strategies for teaching English as a second language. Equally important is the building up of good relations with parents of children who are receiving help.

2.5   The Team fulfils various other functions in addition to meeting the demand for teaching English as a second language in schools in the....... area. It is, for example, in the process of building up a collection of learning materials for use by teachers in........ One of the team helps teachers with translations of material into certain languages. Advice is also given on the use of English as a second language in the classroom and on the cultural backgrounds of certain ethnic minority groups within the area. In addition, the Team is engaged in discussion with a number of outside groups, such as those associated with local churches and with various community organisations. Finally, the Advisory Teacher has also been involved in the preparation of in-service courses and conferences.

3.   Support for mother tongue teaching for ethnic minorities

Three small grants were awarded to the following groups in the area which undertake voluntary mother tongue classes out of school hours:

(a)   Hindu Samaj Mandal
This group provides Gujerati teaching for about 30 pupils using the.... School premises.

(b)   Sikh Temple

About 60 pupils at present have Punjabi lessons in the Sikh Temple.
(c)　Pakistani Muslims Association
The Association conducts Urdu classes for about 30 pupils.

4.　Policy statement on multi-cultural education
4.1　A number of Local Education Authorities, including Berkshire and
Avon have now adopted a Policy Statement on Multi-Cultural Education.
The purpose of the Statement would be to recognise the field of Multi-
Cultural Education and to incorporate the objective within the general
policy.

In the models of racial education outlined in chapter 2 this summary
and the argument for a policy which it is supporting are clearly in the
tradition of multicultural education, with the occasional reference to a
"needs of immigrants" perspective. It quotes the DES, it mentions
mother tongue teaching, it stresses cultural diversity,
interdependence, mutual respect and to be fair, discriminatory
practices. The argument is overwhelmingly a low key, positive one;
who can oppose mutual respect and celebrating diversity?

The committee did. This was apparently because there was
something unresolved from a previous item, or a maverick move by
one councillor, or a misunderstanding. There were comments like "If
they come over here they should assimilate and learn our ways, I
don't see why the education policy has to be changed to accommodate
them." The statement did not even go to a vote; it was not worth it
since there was no chance of it being passed. The officers (and it is the
CEO and his team who are primarily responsible for when and how
matters are put to committee) were surprised, and the short-term
effect was serious in that it had sensitized the committee to anything
about "race". Any new expenditure, courses, meetings, even a
newsheet for some teachers, technically did not have committee
backing so could not happen. After a while such things were possible
again, but often with some anxiety lest some committee member
raised an objection. It should be said that although this particular
education committee, like most others in shire counties, was
dominated by Conservative ladies and gentlemen with more than a
sprinkling of ex-military and other titles and precious little experience
of state education, the Labour members were not necessarily more
helpful. Old guard Labour stalwarts, heading a party mafia in their
own areas and more concerned with their own power than with much
else, can provide much less innocent opposition than the gentry.

Liberal party policy is less racist than either Labour or Conservative, so Liberal councillors ought to be potential allies.

A plan for a white area

So how does one get an LEA policy? I have a few suggestions and guidelines culled from the experiences of several LEAs. The suggestions are more or less sequential but not strictly so, and they are all based on things which have actually been tried.

1   Have a core of key strategists, who meet privately and independently of any formal meetings and procedures. By its nature this group is not formally constituted and may not even be known about by the people it seeks to influence. Essentially it is a group of friends and allies who want to have a policy, so there is going to be as a minimum some teachers and some black people, some of whom may be both. If there is a tame adviser/inspector, officer or head so much the better, since their working lives give them training in institutional procedures, how decisions are made etc., and at times such a person can influence or persuade someone else with some useful power.

2   This unofficial core of strategists has to work out a beginning-to-end strategy, with meetings planned, with whom, dates, alternatives, and so on, being careful not to try and work too quickly (as with most educational change in Britain it will only be brought about through the free time of the committed), or to try and account for every eventuality.

3   In principle black organizations have to be involved at an early stage, earlier than anyone else. This might be considered to have been done as soon as the strategy group has some black people in it (it might, of course, have no white people in it, but since I am writing about entirely or largely white areas it is likely the group will start off white). It is one thing for black people to be involved in all the central strategy planning and another to actively consult whatever organizations there may be. Groups will disagree, have contradictory demands, unclear demands, and will vary in the extent to which their "leaders" represent general opinion (just like white groups). Some groups will not want to talk to you. A way has to be found through this minefield or the whole process has an internal contradiction, it is the pursuit of racial equality from a white perspective. That having been said, it is worth adding that anti-racist education in white areas is primarily going to affect white people, it is in a way for their benefit, it

is to remove the inadequacies and debilitating aspects of their education, so there is a legitimate and important place here for a white perspective as well as a black one. Getting back to black organizations, however, the issues likely to be raised by them or with them are likely to be rates of achievement, teachers' attitudes, contacts with schools, racism, rocking the boat (or not), pre-school provision, RE, single sex schooling and responding to bilingualism.
4   The next stage is to get a key and large group of other people interested, in order to get the issue on some kind of public agenda. This might be done by a day conference with local Council for Racial Equality/Community Relations Council/black organizations involvement, maybe with some LEA involvement, depending on the point on the ignorance—opposition continuum occupied by the LEA officials. The publication of the Swann Report in 1985 has started this process in many LEAs where it has not been possible before, but its usefulness for this purpose could only be short-lived. Parent—teacher associations (PTAs), governors and teacher unions are other obvious groups to consider including.

At this stage people have to be clear about how much they value "democracy" as sometimes defined. I do not suggest the opening conference/meeting above as being necessarily to involve or consult "appropriate" groups. The only groups which have to be involved and consulted are black organizations, since the goal of a county policy is presumably about defending and promoting their interests. The rest is pragmatism. Who might be powerful opposition? Can she/he/they be won over? If not, can they be ignored or controlled by a more powerful group? If the PTAs are likely to cut up rough and keep to the safe ground of fund-raising and "maintaining standards" then let them. If some PTAs appear to be supportive (and hence useful parental ammunition) involve them. If individual school governors are likely to be sympathetic make sure they attend by issuing individual invitations; if they are not likely to be supportive then do not invite them. It is necessary to have the support of perhaps two of the education committee, maybe only two (there is likely to be a full committee of thirty or so), because someone on that committee has to be more informed than the others. It may be a Liberal with no national party record to defend, or a councillor who sits for an area where there are some black people, or perhaps a member who is married to someone born abroad. Someone at least is going to be sympathetic, so build on that by involving them, too.

Thus, this initial process is not about democracy, it is about getting a power base. If we aim to convince the majority of constituents before we try to get a decision out of an education committee we will have a very long struggle. An influential group who will be respected (or feared) by the education committee will give some kind of wider authority to the pressure for a policy statement. It is not the job of a pressure group to be democratic, in the usual sense of representing or consulting everyone, but in the true sense of protecting the interests of everyone, including minorities. A pressure group has to put a case for a particular interest, if necessary in conflict with or to the exclusion of other interests — white middle-class PTAs for example. A fairly basic tenet of those concerned with anti-racist work in education is that the distribution of resources (money, teachers' time, textbook interests, legitimacy) is inequitable, that it serves one set of interests rather than another. That being the case it does not seem like sound strategy to painstakingly consult those who are structurally inclined to oppose you.

5   Another useful strategy to get support and understanding for the policy-making process is in-service training. If there is enough support from someone influential in this — the in-service co-ordinator, a teachers' centre warden, an adviser — then a group of teachers can not only be given help in meeting their classroom needs but can also become part of a larger group supporting policy change. Obviously there is a range of inset possibilities from a one-hour 4.30 to 5.30 talk to a three term Further Professional Studies certificate. Again, Swann might be used as a starting point. Some sessions might be set up to be explicitly about racism or multicultural education. In some areas a back door might have to be used such as "project work in primary schools", "issues in Social and Personal Education", "history teaching in the eighties" or "guidelines for buying new geography textbooks". With the right input or speaker and a degree of support afterwards this could give rise to another supportive group.

Setting up an in-service course is not always easy, however, and in cases of outright obstruction or a lack of credibility for the would-be organizers through age or experience (or sex?) or political affiliation (real or imputed), try the union. A relatively small number of people can get a small grant from a union branch meeting to pay for a speaker and to publicize her/him. The NUT has several conference resolutions[4] which should give direct authority to such a move, and AMMA has an excellent little book on multicultural education (free to members)[5] extracts from which could be used to great persuasive effect. Rather than a specific subject meeting a union could finance a racism awareness course for interested members, although this would almost inevitably have to take place over a weekend. The NUT financed three weekend courses in the 1983/1984 academic year at their conference centre; the time ought to be ripe in some white areas to run a local one.[6]

A local RAT course can be an excellent opening move in linking the teachers' struggle to other groups, and if individuals from other organizations can also come the gains in terms of widened support and understanding could be exponential rather than arithmetic. Perhaps the Trades Council could support a RAT course rather than a single teachers' union, and send personnel. What about a joint course with a women's group? Or the members of a school governors' course run by the local Workers Education Association or a political party? Why not, come to that, the Rotary Club? You never know.

This is as close as I can get to the demand expressed in some of the literature for "forging links with other groups" and "building a broad-based struggle" because it is the only way I can think of to give such exhortations practical expression.

6   Officers and advisers may have a crucial role to play in getting a policy through, although this varies in different LEAs. They may have individual contacts with elected members, or they may put concerted pressure on the CEO, or it may be very useful for the CEO and a few supportive elected members to be able to say there is strong adviser/officer interest. I would argue that the quickest and most efficient way of getting this group talking the same language is a racism awareness course. This is easier said than done, of course, and it amounts to getting the issue on the agenda before it is on the agenda. If the group is keen and interested then there is little problem (they will get something from good RAT whatever their existing level of interest), there are usually days set aside when advisers can undertake training, so unless there is obstruction from a senior officer this might operate quite easily. If the officers and advisers are not interested, how do you get them to RAT so they are interested? If a senior officer is keen enough, or a small group is keen enough, a two line whip or a lot of persuading by example would probably get most of them to a RAT session. Perhaps it is over-optimistic, but I do not envisage a huge problem with officers and advisers. With some gruesome exceptions they usually seem to be people of considerable abilities and vision in education, and part of their job is, of course, to be informed and to know where education ought to be going. The field may not be quite as threatening to them as it is to practising teachers, since it does

not necessarily imply changes in what they do the next day. They are also better paid than teachers, so perhaps they can more easily afford to be self-critical. In addition, most of them have spent a large proportion of the past few years administering cuts, therefore they might welcome being for once involved in a growth area, and for a while, at least, "race" and education is one of these. In day-to-day practice they have less directive power than heads, but their influence, though not as deep, is far wider.

7 Advisers and officers may have their minds concentrated on the issues by HMIs. It is not yet possible to tell whether Swann will affect the thinking of HMIs working in white areas, but there have been a few instances of individual HMIs noting a lack of "multicultural" perspectives in their school reports. Therefore, we may soon see the unfortunate advisers and officers squeezed between the HMIs (to whose reports they must now respond within a given period) and their reactionary committees. It might be productive pressure.

8 At some stage a group of people has to formally constitute itself, unless the support from the LEA people is strong enough for them to stage-manage the formal writing stages, the committee, and the voting. An obvious step is for the formal group to become a branch of NAME. It may not be politically possible for elected members to be seen on this group, or LEA officers (though they could be on the strategy group, which could be almost the same people as those in the formal group). It is likely to be the case that political objections from a nervous CEO or an obstructive elected member to officers/advisers being involved in a pressure group for change can be answered in terms of good management practice. The officer is simply keeping her ear to the ground, making a contribution to the community debate about education, ensuring that the education service is keeping abreast of grass-roots developments. This may be all lies; the officer is actually being a political activist pressing for radical educational change.

This may take off and develop very well, so that potential political or senior official opposition sees the meetings as a containment exercise, while what is actually happening is that some good policy principles are gaining wider credibility and acceptance. It is then possible that in the end some elected members get a shock when faced with not only a good policy (which they may not like) but also a policy supported with clear argument and evidence and demonstrably wide support.

9 It is worth remembering that members of education committees do not have much contact with ordinary people concerned with their

children's education. They from time to time make the most fantastic generalizations about what people think and want based on remarks one or two people have made to them. Their mail on educational issues is not very great except during crises. Thus a carefully orchestrated letter campaign raising the issue of multicultural education, or different aspects of it, would both raise their awareness and make them see that here was an issue in the public mind that they must know more about. One has to be careful not to overdo this, the committee gets so few letters that it will smell a rat (or a RAT) at once if there is a sudden rush. Having sensitized them, you may get more to meetings and consultations than would otherwise be the case.

10   Know your education committee. A list will be easily available from the council offices and information has to be gathered from political party contacts, union representatives on LEA committees, and anyone who has seen them vote or heard them speak. Letters could be written "from an interested parent" simply asking for their views on a couple of specific items to do with multicultural education. You will soon learn that some can be spotted from the start as inevitable opposition, but others may be useful allies, and useful for further information on who else can be swayed and how.

11   Consider whether one particular issue may be "safe" enough to get some committee members' interest without panicking them right from the start. It might be mother tongue teaching, though in very white areas this is unlikely to be a live issue. If mother tongue classes run at all, the argument around their provision seems to be a good one to draw attention to a specific need, align it to good educational practice, and challenge a few racist preconceptions too. If it were possible to set up a small meeting about mother tongue teaching, with a respectable, clear and learned case being put by someone respectable, clear and learned — ideally from outside the area — then it might change a few minds.[7] The thing about mother tongue provision is that having heard the educational arguments in its favour it is almost impossible to oppose it without being demonstrably anti-educational, suddenly a county councillor whose knee-jerk reaction was "they should learn English" finds herself agreeing with a black community demand.

On a less positive note, it may be possible to get some real concern from elected members if you can gather evidence of potent racism in white school children. This is covered in more detail in chapters 1 and 6, though I should add that to have any effect on committee members it must not be possible for them to see it is simply an issue or a problem in one school or institution. If they can they will blame the school (poor discipline), or the area's parents (what do you expect from those homes?), or the teachers (it's all stirred up by left-wing agitators). The section of the Swann Report which looks specifically at this might make such responses harder.

12   There are not many other things you can do except hope that on the day the vote is taken the members get out of bed the right side and are not in a hanging mood. Ideally the policy statement should be clear about racism and not hide behind wishy-washy apologies like "cultural diversity", but despite all I have said about this in preceding chapters it has to be recognized that this may not be possible in some areas.

Who are policies for?

I said earlier that LEA policies are sometimes seen as a panacea. Although, even in their mildest form, they can confer legitimacy on work in a school, it is a decision to be made in many LEAs at the moment whether the whole process is worth the trouble. Of course, the discussions and alliances formed must count as progress, but for individuals slaving away in particular schools it may be the right decision to forget the months (years?) of planning and pressure-grouping on a wider scale and concentrate their efforts in their own school. At the time of writing the prognosis is both good and bad; well over half of the LEAs now have policies, but at a time of mounting cuts. On the other hand, many councils which have been solidly Conservative for years are now "hung", with Alliance members or independents holding the balance, and in that sense the time must be ripe.

A final word about the LEAs with good policies. Teachers in such LEAs probably do not know how lucky they are in terms of legitimacy. At least heads do not have official backing to stamp on the mildest developments in celebrating cultural diversity. But there is a book yet to be written on how, if at all, the policies will shift the unwilling and downright hostile powerful elements in the education service — and this usually means heads. The national press tells us gleefully that recalcitrant heads in Bradford are taking early retirement rather than attend RAT courses; there are heads in Berkshire and in ILEA who have sent the briefest of formal replies to their authorities' requirement for a school response to their policy, and who boast of the fact. But that is the state of the art at the moment;

in this field as in others, schools' autonomy is being challenged, and we do not know what the outcome will be.

Troyna and Ball asked in an article in 1983[8] whether policies are worth the paper they are printed on. If they are going to be then (in an ideal world far from the reality of already overworked campaigning teachers) the policy has to be written so that "it is a launching pad for change and not the target". Berkshire is a useful model here. Although not traditionally a high spending authority and not one which in the past has put large sums into "immigrant education", one vital feature of the negotiations, consultations and planning which went into Berkshire's policy was the recognition that a policy had to have clear spending implications, approved with the form of words, if it was to be effective. Berkshire managed this primarily through 24 Section II posts; which were cheap because such posts only cost the LEA 25 per cent of each person's salary, but indicative of the recognition of the staffing needed to even begin to put the policy into effect. (In whiter areas Education Support Grants, section H, can be used.)

This is by way of saying policies are all very well, but they need to be backed with money to give more than just moral support to teachers, and to signify that the elected members mean it when they vote for the policy.

Mullard et al. argue that whatever the genesis of policy documents and their official rationale, they are actually used by LEAs in four different ways. The first of these they call "procedural informative utility", a bureaucratic/legal perception that the LEA should inform educators of their broad legal duty and of any key report, but that they should not spell out specific practices as either desirable or undesirable (especially if to do so would impose on school autonomy).

The second use of policy they call "corroborative–legitimating utility", meaning that LEAs use a statement to pat themselves on the back, affirming that new reports or laws simply support what they themselves have been doing for years. This use of policy tends not to identify LEA practices which need changing.

The third utilization is called "innovative problematizing". The authorities adopting this approach

...appeared to be conscious of the opportunity open to them to set standards only by their own example of attempting to develop an adequate conception and practice in the field of multicultural education.

Lord Scarman's report and thus the uprisings which occasioned it was the spur for the last need/use of an LEA "race" policy: "reactive—corrective". Here concern was focused on the threat to public order presented by "race" in the early 1980s, and education's role in reacting to and correcting this. Several policies' preambles refer to the necessity of avoiding overt conflict seen on the scale of Brixton, Toxteth or St Paul's, and as a possible example of crisis management and containment it is instructive to read the comments of one of Bradford's officials quoted by David Selbourne in a *New Society* article:[9]

For 25 years the local authority could get away with letting sleeping Asians lie. Racism was a taboo subject. At the time of the riots in Toxteth, there was panic, fear and ignorance in Bradford. No one knew what was going on in the streets, no one knew who in the community to turn to. There were no institutional bridges, no structures to negotiate with. Now we can cope with Moslem demands. We have trained people to shout, provided they shout acceptable slogans. Halal meat, mother tongue teaching. The issues where we can deliver.

Naturally LEA policies do not fall wholly and squarely within these "ideal types", but the typology contains some warnings against the kind of blandishments that might be put up as "policies". We have to aim at conceptually clear anti-racist perspectives which shed light on practice.

That having been said, a policy is valuable. As Robin Richardson wrote when he was Berkshire's multicultural education adviser:

It is a resource for advocates in individual schools and communities, for it provides legitimacy for their concerns: that is, it gives them protection from certain criticisms and scepticisms, and it gives them a fuller and more rational hearing in debates and deliberations.[10]

Prior to the adoption of a policy are the long months of preparation, planning, consultation and argument. It is usually held that this is a very valuable process in itself because it tends to involve a lot of consciousness-raising and promote a lot of discussion, and can bring together many people who have been in isolation working for and wishing for similar ends.

Most importantly, however, these policy statements and the range of practical initiatives that stem from them are intended to promote and effect changes in routine school practices and procedures. What is more, they are designed to implicate all schools in a process of reappraisal and change ....[11]

Berkshire managed this better than most, though few of the team centrally involved in implementing the policy would say they are going anywhere at speed. The policy is reprinted in Swann as an example, not necessarily of the policy which will have the biggest effect (although it might), but to show what can be passed in an area not known for its educational radicalism. It is also brief, grounded in some theory and principles, and has staffing implications which might be copied elsewhere. It may also stand as a warning. Despite the strengths of its policy and the hopes that many put in it, there are recent signs that Berkshire is less than comfortable with its "radical" image. Some senior officials think the policy went too far too fast; some elected members who never liked it are now in a stronger position; disenchantment has set in with at least some sections of the black community; the interview for a race relations adviser was met with a demonstration, that for the multicultural adviser with a boycott.

Mullard et al.'s study shows that most policies are firmly couched in terms of the second model outlined by ILEA — cultural diversity.

Implicit in this formulation is the conception of a pre-given normative consensus that has been ruptured by the settlement in British society of non-British ethnic groups with different cultures and different value systems.[12]

In principle we should have no time for such policies. In principle, and often in practice, they can be written off as misguided and hence perpetuating the racism we seek to dismantle. My own view is that on some occasions we might nevertheless accept them if they are the best we can get. If, despite months of preparation by the strategy group, a cultural diversity rationale is all that can be got through the committee that does not mean it provides no space for explicitly anti-racist work. One task of activists is to push the limits of conventional definitions and formulations by good educational practice which highlights the contradictions and inadequacies in those conventional definitions, and to find and create whatever space there may be to "do things better". There is a difference between agreeing to compromises and being satisfied with them.

References

1   DES Circular, no. 6/81 The School Curriculum.
2   *Local Authority Policy Documents, a Descriptive Analysis of Contents*, Working Paper 2, Race Relations Policy and Practice Research Unit, Department of Sociology of Education, London University Institute of Education, 1983.
3   I would want to argue that there is a case for examining the curricula of a post colonial society whatever the "Black presence", since it could not do otherwise than reflect at least elements of the world view of a former dominant world power. That aside, what David Kirp calls "inexplicitness as a policy preference" has largely prevailed in areas where there are black people.

If only the newspapers and television would stop harping on race, if only they'd keep quiet, it would all get better, wouldn't it? It only needs time. You can't expect people to get used to coloured people just overnight, can you? But British people are very fair: if the newspapers would only stop, we could get on very quietly with living together.

Quoted from Ann Dummett's *Portrait of English Racism,* 1972 by David Kirp, *Doing Good by Doing Little, Race and Schooling in Britain,* University of California Press, Berkeley, 1979.
4   The NUT has policy statements about "race" going back several years. The following extracts from conference resolutions give some idea of the range of decisions taken.

1979   Racialism

Conference instructs the Executive to define clearly the Union's attitudes towards key aspects of multi-cultural education and to indicate positive lines of action in the following areas as soon as possible:

(a)   The dissemination of good practice in all kinds of schools in respect of multi-cultural educational curricula that would provide:
     (i)   contribution to the multi-cultural awareness and tolerance in all pupils;
     (ii)   ways to improve the educational performance of children from minority ethnic groups;

(iii)   a sympathetic appreciation of the diversity of cultures, traditions, languages and dialects.

(b)   The application of positive discrimination that includes:

(i)   a central fund to meet these needs;

(ii)   the provision of specialist resources and training centres;

(iii)   an increase in the number of ethnic minority teachers;

(iv)   relevant initial induction and in-service training;

(v)   improved careers guidance and counselling;

(vi)   enhanced employment prospects for all school leavers;

(vii)   reorientation of examination courses to cater for cultural diversity;

(viii)   intensified language instruction;

(ix)   the development of close links with ethnic minority parents.

1980   4. Racialism

Conference expresses its grave concern at the problems facing schools due to the inability of the Race Relations Act to prevent the propagation of racialist ideas and the use of schools by racist groups. Conference therefore calls upon the Executive to co-operate fully with the TUC Working Party investigating the work of the Act, with particular reference to the problems facing schools. Conference urges Local Associations and Divisions to oppose, strenuously but within the law, the use of school premises by racialist groups and the dissemination of racialist literature in schools.

1982   2. Racialism

Conference recognises that the NUT as part of the trade union movement, has an important role to play in the fight against racism. It commends the stand taken by the Executive in publishing "Combatting Racialism in Schools" and in opposing the parts of the British Nationality Act which effect the education service.

  Conference condemns any statements which imply that the recent disturbances in inner-city areas were the responsibility of minority communities and supports the right of ethnic minority citizens to live in this country without fear of harassment. Conference asserts its total opposition to all forms of racism and accordingly calls for schools to adopt a clear anti-racist stance, which would include staff discussions to develop a school policy for tackling racism, as outlined in the Union policy document "Combatting Racialism in School".

  Conference supports strategies to enable the teaching of ethnic minority languages within the curriculum to examination level, the development of in-service training courses for all teachers for a multi-cultural curriculum, the training of more ethnic minority teachers and opposition to any discrimination against black teachers.

  Conference calls for Union encouragement and support for members taking an anti-racist stance in support of Union policies and within Union rules, and backing for any member victimised as a result of such activity.

  Conference opposes discrimination in employment against black school leavers and calls for an enquiry into the extent of such discrimination.

  Conference welcomes the TUC's proposals for inner-city investment and the TUC Black Workers' Charter.

  Conference expresses concern at the failure of Government to implement the recommendations of the Rampton Report and the Home Affairs Committee Report on Racial Disadvantage and urges the Government to take urgent action to ensure equal opportunities and fair treatment for both black pupils and teachers.

Note also the other NUT statements on the issue, *In Black and White* (guidelines on stereotyping in materials), *Education for a Multicultural Society* (evidence to the Swann Committee), and *Combatting Racism in Schools* (now a 1984 edition). Free to members from NUT, Hamilton House, Mabledon Place, London WC1H 9BD.

5   *Our Multicultural Society, The Educational Response*, available free to members from AMMA, 29 Gordon Square, London WC1 OPX.

6   A fuller background to RAT is given in chapter 5, and the NUT can be contacted direct about courses.

7   Further suggestions and help would be available from the Mother Tongue Project at Robert Montefiore School, Underwood Road, London E1 5AD. The NUT also have a booklet on Mother Tongue.

8   "LEA multicultural policies, are they worth the paper they're printed on?", *Times Educational Supplement*, December 1983.

9   "The culture clash in Bradford", *New Society*, 26 April 1984.

10   From a paper given to the day conference Match and Mismatch, June 1983, at London's Institute of Education.

11   From Berkshire's policy statement itself.

12   *Local Authority Policy Documents, a Descriptive Analysis of Contents*, Working Paper 2, Race Relations Policy and Practice Research Unit, Department of Sociology of Education, London University Institute of Education, 1983, p. 4.

8 Teacher training

To say that there is no need to educate all students about such matters because, as one college has said, "very few of our students go into schools where they are likely to meet mixed classes" is to miss the point.... Teachers should be equipped to prepare all their children for life in a multi-racial society   (Select Committee on Race Relations and Immigration, 1969!)

It is not the intention of this chapter to give a complete overview of teacher training, but rather to make some observations on the general situation and on initiatives in the two colleges of higher education (in white areas) in which I have worked. (It will become clear that exactly the same strategies and processes will not directly apply to university education departments or teacher training which has a small niche in a large polytechnic.)

In general terms my questions for teacher training are easily put: how do we train students to teach in ways which do not perpetuate racism in both all-white and mixed schools? How do white colleges in white areas achieve any significant level of contact with black people? How do colleges organize themselves so that they are not examples of the kind of institutional racism they want students to recognize elsewhere? I propose to discuss these questions, first in terms of the general situation in which teacher training finds itself, and second by means of the kind of draft policy colleges ought to be working towards.

Teacher training: the general situation

When faced with new challenges many teachers not unnaturally say how ill-prepared they are by their training, and with respect to issues of "race" I have heard many black parents ask "but what do they learn in the colleges?" Though understandable, the expectation of teachers and some parents that teacher training could do very much about racism in education is misplaced, for two reasons. The first is that apart from a brief spell in the late 1960s and early 1970s (when birth rates and new comprehensives meant they were desperately needed), new teachers are not generally listened to, and have usually taken years to get to any position of influence, except, perhaps, in maths and physics. "You may think that way now, fresh from college and all their fancy ideas, but you'll think differently once you've been here a while." And so it was.

A second reason is that even if new teachers' perceptions were listened to, falling rolls and worsening pay mean there are now so few of them they can hardly be effective. The Swann Report[1] observed: "The number of new entrants to the profession who have just undergone initial training is now considered too small to have any significant impact on schools." A further corollary of this is that it will a long time before any recently trained teachers get to positions of formal influence, it is much more a case of "dead person's shoes" than it used to be.

This is only a word of caution, not a counsel of despair, because as far as "race" is concerned we clearly have to put the teacher training house in order, but we have to recognize that on its own it would be a very slow way of changing what happens in schools. As for change, there are several factors in the situation currently faced by training institutions and their students which might either produce or limit worthwhile change.

Over half of all new entrants to the profession have only trained as teachers for a year, mostly in universities via the Postgraduate Certificate of Education (PGCE) route, having already taken degrees in their specialist subjects. Rather more than half of the PGCE students are destined for secondary schools, the majority of primary teachers çome from four year B.Ed courses, typically taught in colleges of higher education. It is a common view that people who have studied teaching for four years will be better teachers, especially in primary schools, than those who cram it into thirty-six weeks, but this is not the view of the DES. The White Paper *Teaching Quality* in 1983 said: "Good teachers need to have a mastery of the subject matter they teach...." and this has been taken very literally by the Council for the Accreditation of Teacher Education (CATE).[2] Somebody, and it is widely presumed have been legitimated by Sir Keith Joseph, the then Secretary of State for Education, had the idea that subject expertise was the foundation upon which all good teaching, secondary and primary, was based. The practical effect of this belief has been that any new B.Ed (they are all renewed frequently) has to have at least 50 per cent of the time devoted to subject study at higher education level. This is not the place to argue with this priority, but the implication for my concerns in this book is that all new teachers will have spent at least half (three-quarters in the case of PGCEs) of their "training" studying an academic subject, and it is this, at least as much as anything they study in education courses or learn on teaching practice, which will shape their educational ideas.

Subject studies (to say nothing of the staff) in university and polytechnic degrees are fairly remote from schools. In teacher training establishments the staff who teach the "pure" subjects have frequently never taught in schools, and many would be in universities if they could. We have the problem, therefore, that the general tone and ethos of teacher training may be fixed by "academic" values which are out of touch with or even contradict what is happening in schools. It is all very well for Swann to say: "...we hope that all higher education institutions, not just those involved directly in teacher education, will be prepared to incorporate a pluralist perspective in all their provision" (p. 566) but that hope may take a while to be realized.

One of the central difficulties will prove to be "academic freedom". It is one thing to argue on a professional basis that we cannot qualify racist teachers, but different arguments are needed when a course is solely academic. There is something of a tradition in universities (and by extension in all higher education) that academics are entitled to their views. If a history lecturer is clearly a Nazi there is nothing any university in this country can do about it; the same applies to an English don who pronounces all Indian literature "primitive" or an economist who advises starvation as a means of population control. A different argument is needed because even if one thinks all such staff should be removed[3] the difficulties in doing so would dwarf those, for instance, of an LEA trying to lose a head who has lost the confidence of black parents.

The issue of academic freedom arises particularly in subject degrees with no necessary link with teaching. In those which are linked, i.e. the subject components of B.Eds, there is more hope of change. Although the directive from the DES about 50 per cent of degrees being subject study amounts to compulsion, there are other pressures too, some of them also from the DES, which can be used to good effect. Recently HMIs have been taking more interest in training establishments, and among other things they want to know:

Is there any evidence to show that teaching studies, education studies, curriculum studies and main subject areas work together? Is there any attempt to develop a holistic approach? Does it all make sense to the students?[24]

DES Circular 3/84, about the criteria for approval of courses, said:

Students should be prepared through their subject method work and educational studies to teach the full range of pupils they are likely to encounter in an ordinary school, with their diversity of...ethnic and cultural origins. They will need to learn how to respond flexibly to such diversity and to guard against preconceptions based on race....

Of the forces outside the DES, probably the most powerful is the Council for National Academic Awards (CNAA), which validates the vast majority of B.Eds and PGCEs which are taught in higher education colleges and polytechnics. As the result of a working party on multicultural education set up a few years ago they now have a policy, and in principle, at least, no new degree submission is validated by them unless it addresses issues of "race". Part of it used to state:

Teachers need ...
   ...to be equipped to prepare all young people for life in a multicultural and racially harmonious society....
Teacher education ought to...
   ...permeate all elements of the course with multicultural and anti-racist considerations...
   ...encourage a critical approach to cultural bias...
   adopt an approach to all subjects... which avoids an ethnocentric view of the world....
Students ought to be...
   ...sensitive to the presence of unintentional racism in their own expectations...and in curriculum materials.... (CNAA, 1984)

(This stood for about three years, but in December 1986 the overall council of the CNAA substituted for "anti-racist" the phrase "provided without racial discrimination". Many believed that this was a bowing to political pressure, and the substitution brought protest and a resignation.)

Sometimes equally powerful are the occasional phrases in government documents, for example:

Teachers cannot reasonably be blamed for failing ethnic minority children if they have not had access to the sort of initial and in-service training which would enable them to perform more successfully. (Home Affairs Committee, 1981.)

The fact that a third of all the institutions...[we examined]...train B.Ed students who, like the great majority of PGCE students, need take no account, during their preparation for teaching, of education in a multicultural society must be a matter for concern. (HMI, 1980)

In the complicated theology of approval for teacher training, CNAA are supposed to look at the academic worth of degree proposals, CATE at the meeting of various professional criteria by the whole college (advised by HMI inspections), and the National Advisory Body (NAB)[5] at the number of students particular courses may admit. All of these gods have the power of life and death (some colleges have been closed down), so institutions tend to move with some determination to live according to the gospel. Anyone who has witnessed the rite of a CNAA visit (perhaps twenty staff from other colleges, reading and questioning for two days) will know that some of this is empty ritual, but not all. Colleges fear these visits, and course writing and the appointment (and sacrificing) of staff is affected up to two years in advance of them.[6]

This indicates the potential effect of particular high level policies; there are other policies which have less god-like power but which nevertheless could or do affect colleges. Many colleges are funded by LEAs, and are therefore subject to whatever policy exists there. Even if it wanted to, Bradford and Ilkley College could not be seriously out of step with the LEA's general line. In addition, about a dozen colleges are "voluntary", which means they retain their religious origins and funding, and the voluntary colleges as a group have a multicultural/anti-racist policy. Finally, most teacher trainers outside the universities belong to the National Association of Teachers in Further and Higher Education, and it too has a policy.

It will be noticed that the universities are largely immune from all this since they are under the direct control of no-one. They are self-validating so they never see CNAA; CATE can refuse to accredit their education departments, but it is only very recently that HMIs have had any right even to step inside the doors (it is still by invitation only), and while NAB does cut numbers in some "duplicated" subjects, there is evidence of a basic assumption that the universities do the best job. The LEAs do not fund them so their policies have no jurisdiction. None of them are voluntary colleges, and their staffs do not belong to NATFHE. It remains to be seen whether much of a gap in practices opens up between universities and the other institutions.

While there are many outside pressures which can be used to advantage to get racism on the agenda in training, some work against this. Whatever progress a college may make, it is, particularly in white areas, likely to be considerably ahead of its surrounding LEA. Though its stance may seem tame to anti-racists working in the conurbations, it will make it seem like a hotbed of revolutionaries to racists working in the shires. This matters partly in respect of funding, but also in terms of relationships with schools. Blatant examples of racist schools or teachers are easy to deal with, at least in principle, colleges can boycott them, but if students were only allowed to go to schools with good anti-racist credentials they would never have a teaching practice. On their own colleges cannot change this, it needs both in-service training (chapter 5) and initiatives at school and LEA level (chapters 6 and 7).

Internal factors in the colleges

So much for the outside forces for change. There are also internal factors which need to be understood.

The first of these is time. One year, or two years out of a B.Ed, is a short time in which to learn a lot. One student recently likened her training to doing 'O' levels; a wide range of subjects crammed into too short a time and inevitably covered only superficially. Language, maths, computers, bits of psychology, learning difficulties, and much more all done to a depth considerably less than that of 'A' level. A PGCE year is thirty-six weeks, including about twelve weeks of teaching practice; the direction B.Eds are going suggests that the education component of them will amount to two years' study, i.e. about sixty-four weeks, of which at least twenty weeks will be in school. We are left therefore with a relatively short time to do major remedial work on the students, if we assume, as I do, that a good deal of racist damage from their own education has to be undone. In the case of PGCEs this is all we can do, with B.Eds we can work on the other front of subject studies as well.

Another internal factor is that this all has to be seen in the context of "multiculturalism", as it is often called, being only one of several "new" issues that colleges must get to grips with; information technology, special needs, and "the world of work" are at least as important to the DES. (Gender may be next, but it is striking how much less sexism has been the subject of official policy.) It is perhaps not surprising then, that sometimes all these things are seen as just fads which will eventually fade away, especially if the right noises are made about them for a time.

A factor which, on the whole, limits change is the students. Someone said to me recently "I can't understand why your students don't force the colleges to change more; I've never met a student yet who didn't want to change the world". With all due respect to them, he had not met many B.Ed students. Things may have been different in the radical sixties, but somehow I think it must always have been the case that many of those who want to become teachers are those who have done best in the education system as it is (or was). Grammar and private schools still contribute a higher proportion than their "share" of graduates or 18 year olds with 'A' levels. Not surprisingly, therefore, most students do not arrive having seen lots of faults in their own schooling which they want to put right, they come because their own memories of school are fairly happy ones and they want to share this with another generation or two. This is not the most fertile launch pad for radical criticism. It is also worth pointing out that a great deal of recruitment to colleges of Higher Education is local, so that colleges in Kent, Dorset and Yorkshire recruit most of their students from their own geographical area, with fairly obvious effects on the proportions of black and Asian students and the experiences of the white students.

It is no exaggeration to say that there are students currently in B.Ed and PGCE training who have seldom if ever met and spoken with a black person. One does not have to hold a naive view that "personal contact breaks down all barriers"[7] to recognize that there is a problem here, yet it is not an easy one to solve. A step which appealed to Swann was the teaching practice in a multiracial area,

We would...urge that as many students as possible should have experience of working in schools of cultural and racial diversity during their period of training in order that this experience might both inform and benefit from

College based programmes...we should emphasise that the main focus should always be on the shared experiences of ethnic majority and ethnic minority communities within our society and on the positive opportunities offered by multiracial schools, rather than on the "strangeness" or on the "problems" of such schools... (p. 565).

It is easy to find fault with this. It could be based on the kind of näiveté suggested above; it says nothing about the many bad practices in multiracial schools Swann details elsewhere; it is self-limiting (there are not enough black children to go round); and for a college which is any distance from black people it is prohibitively expensive. The Voluntary Colleges have an urban/rural pairing arrangement to resolve the distance/expense problem, but the other difficulties do not admit straightforward solutions.

In my own experience college staff have been more amenable to anti-racist perspectives than some others, but I may have just been lucky. Part of the job of a teacher trainer is to be professionally informed, so to that extent there seems to be a certain willingness to accept new issues outside people's direct experience. To the majority of teacher trainers, who have not taught in the big conurbations, "race" and racism is one of these. There is also the cynical view that CNAA, CATE and the rest have concentrated lecturers' minds wonderfully, since to get it wrong can mean closure.

Despite the limitations, however, "multiculturalism" has been discussed for some time in teacher training, mostly with regard to the curriculum, where "permeation" has become the catch-word. Whereas in the past (some) colleges' response was to have a specialist option in "multicultural" education — the "bolt on" approach — the issue has achieved such a high profile that it is no longer thought appropriate for students to be able to opt away from it entirely, so we have the "pepperpot" model instead, the ideal of permeating the whole curriculum with "a multicultural perspective". In principle this is clearly better, though as Swann warned

[The]...strategy of "permeation" may be effective where the level of awareness and commitment amongst course tutors is high, but without specific, detailed plans for compulsory input to initial courses, backed up by specialist options for those who wish to pursue the issues in more depth and widen their expertise, it may be just a paper promise (p. 559).

In other words, things can become so well permeated that they disappear altogether. It also needs to be asked what is being permeated? In the chapter on teacher training Swann correctly identified a common confusion:

What is most immediately apparent...apart from the general paucity of provision, is the continuing confusion of two distinct forms of provision — on the one hand, course provision designed specifically to give student teachers the particular knowledge and skills needed to teach in a multi-racial school, and, on the other hand, the preparation of all students in initial training for teaching pupils in a multi-racial society, irrespective of whether the students concerned will be teaching in an "all-white" or multi-racial school (p. 551).

Until that confusion is well and truly resolved it is quite likely that colleges will unwittingly still be working with an "immigrant education" perspective.

Towards college policies

Thus a formal policy seems like a good strategic target in a teacher training establishment. They are affected crucially by outside policies, they have to formalize what they do into documents for outside scrutiny, and they are partly managed by a network of committees. Paper rules. How to get an internal policy is in a sense already set out in a college's constitution, although a less formal strategy group of staff and students is invaluable.[8] In the current external climate the temporary import of a teaching fellow/seconded teacher with some expertise in this field can be funded fairly easily (or so it would seem, judging from the number of colleges which have done so), and such a person will have the time to concentrate her energies.

  While curriculum concerns are the primary interest for colleges, it does not take long to realize that however good the curriculum, there could be other aspects of college life which are somewhat out of step with it. The most notable of these is student recruitment, but we need not stop there. In principle there is no reason why all the provisions of an equal opportunities employer should not apply to teacher training, so that racism is monitored (and dealt with) in staff applications and promotions, provision of services, dealings with landlords/ladies, and the provision of resources. In a way these things are easier to bring about in a college than an LEA or a school because they are smaller than the one and more self-governing than the other, and they tend to have a longer tradition of apparently democratic boards and committees that have some say in the running of the institution.

So, finally, I suggest a draft policy. The content offered here is a mixture of several documents I have produced for two different colleges,[9] the form is a distinctive one of successive preambles followed by suggestions. I have found this effective because it prevents some straightforward misunderstandings as well as malicious ones. It is also thorough and reasonably clear and precise, and perhaps not quite typical of committee papers. This seems to outmanoeuvre the opposition unless it has a very clear and precise analysis which it cares to spell out, and usually it does not. In neither college did all of the proposals get through, but many did, and in one, at least, the rest will be raised again.

A policy ought to begin with some briefly argued general principles and an interpretation of the usual terms like racism, multicultural, and black. This is to stimulate the initial process of debate, to educate a little, and (if accepted) to be part of the "activists" formal legitimation later on. Following that, policies must be as detailed and specific as possible (the draft presented to my present college's Academic Board ran to twenty-four typed pages). As well as a preliminary target the means of getting there must be spelled out, so that while the statement of general principles might say:

The College will ensure that its curriculum examines the richness of cultural diversity, the importance of good intercultural relations, and the ways in which discrimination is located within the social, economic and political processses of our society.

The policy must aim to set up a mechanism to make sure it happens, for example a monitoring committee to look at all course outlines, reading lists and assessment tasks, with the means to make suggestions for additions and the right to table disagreements in a management committee. Such a proposal might look like this:

The B.Ed management group should require all courses to supply the monitoring group with required and recommended reading lists now in use, so that it may suggest additions.

All courses should also be required to supply the monitoring group with assessment tasks set, since this gives some indication of the importance given to an anti-racist perspective.

This exercise is likely to produce some suggestions of modifications/

additions/deletions from the monitoring committee. Such suggestions must at least be discussed by the groups responsible for course design.

Note   (We are under no illusions about this being straightforward or necessarily welcomed; undoubtedly some will see this as an intrusion into their own academic domain and resist any attempt by "outsiders" to modify what they teach. There is no point, however, in this not becoming a matter of open debate within the college; if there is a policy about the curriculum then sooner or later there will be disagreement about its precise applications. It would scarcely be worth having a policy if this were not the case.)

Conflicts and disagreements about course content between the monitoring committee and those responsible for the course should be formally recorded and presented to the Programmes Board. It is then for the Board to discuss and minute its recommendation or decision.

Every course should be required to report annually and in detail in its evaluation on its progress in bringing about education for racial equality.

Racism awareness training of at least a day's duration should be introduced for all students during their first year.

Staff development is an integral part of the process of curriculum development. The College will therefore continue to support staff wishing to attend conferences and courses which relate anti-racist concerns to their work in the College.

The College should begin a programme of racism awareness training for academic staff at all levels. Two groups of 8 staff per term should participate in this, and training should be of at least one day's duration.

Similarly, while a college might say "In its administration, services, recruitment and staff development the College will strive to become a good example of an equal opportunities organisation..." it has to grasp the nettle of what this means in terms of recruitment and ethnic monitoring. This has often been a contentious proposal in the past, with black people objecting to being counted separately and white people arguing that monitoring highlights the differences they want to diminish. It has also been argued that ethnic record keeping simply focuses the attention of the powerful on how to discriminate better, so a college cannot consider monitoring unless it explains on application forms why it asks for ethnic origin, and unless it has clear procedures for action if intentional or unintentional discrimination is found to be taking place. In practical terms this might mean:

Once in every academic year the Registry shall be required to produce an analysis of:

– the ratio of black and Asian applicants to black and Asian students offered places.
– the reason for refusal of places to black and Asian applicants. Depending on whether any pattern emerges this may need to be continued into reasons for refusal of white applicants.
– where numbers permit, this analysis should be continued into a breakdown by subject/age range.

Once in every two academic years the College Secretary should provide an ethnic breakdown of staff applicants/staff appointments.
All recruiting staff should be made aware of the law relating to unlawful discrimination, and of the college's attempts to prevent it, and that such discrimination would constitute misconduct.
All findings from this process, except the names of individuals, shall be publicly available within the College.

Monitoring procedures may provide a check on what happens to applications from black people once they have been received, but they also need to be encouraged. A positive attempt to recuit more black and Asian staff would bring both a different experience and perspective to course development, as well as demonstrate a college's willingness to engage itself positively with structured inequalities. This might mean that selectors would look more at all a person's qualifications rather than just her/his academic ones but this is not "lowering standards", it is a careful consideration of the most creative and productive balance in a staff training people for teaching in the 1980s and 1990s, and an argument against defining "standards" in too narrow a way.

There are also other recruitment issues. Are prospective staff and students asked about "race", not in a crude and simplistic way but as one index of where they stand educationally? In this regard Swann was a good deal tougher than many colleges are yet prepared to be:

...if a teacher has negative attitudes towards ethnic minorities and the development of a culturally plural society then he or she will in our view remain an inadequate teacher of any child in any school in this country (p. 568).

Another question for a college is whether it wants to take any positive steps to recruit black students. Swann noted

Our own discussions with youngsters from a wide range of ethnic minority backgrounds have...revealed that comparatively few of them actually aspire to a career in teaching. The explanations most frequently put forward for this reluctance...were that:

— they had experienced racism and negative stereotyping of ethnic minority groups while at school and had no desire therefore to rejoin such an institution;
— they were disenchanted by the somewhat limited role which they felt many ethnic minority teachers were asked to play in the system — as E2L or "mother tongue" teachers or simply as supervisors of ethnic minority pupils — and the restricted career opportunities this presented; and
— they did not regard teaching as offering good career prospects in the current economic situation, especially since they felt their own chances in the jobs market would be hindered by the influence of racism (p. 610).

If a college wants to do anything about this it has to do some very deliberate recruiting, as well as to make sure it is attractive in all sorts of ways to black students, such as having access courses, clearly accepting exam passes in Urdu, Bengali, etc., and making policy provisions which protect them.

These things do not exhaust the concerns of a thorough-going policy: there are also resources, research guidelines, careers help, meals provision, in-service work, and many issues to do with teaching practice. It is a long process, and any working group in a college should regard its first proposals as just that. Policies and procedures which get to grips with the real issues will only come about after a long struggle, but it is a struggle which has to take place in institutions which bear such responsibility for the future.

References

1 *Education for All*, HMSO, 1985, Cmnd 9453.
2 Set up by Sir Keith Joseph in 1984 to reform teacher training. As is indicated later, it has considerable power.
3 My own view is that formal institutional steps would take us on to a slippery slope. Pressure from students and colleagues is both more politicizing and perhaps more effective in dealing with such people.
4 This is from an analysis of HMI reports by three colleagues, Kate Jacques, Arthur Horton, and Jeff Williams.

5 The National Advisory Body was set up, again by Sir Keith Joseph, to make recommendations about student numbers and course provision in public sector higher education.

6 I certainly owe my own two teacher training appointments to these pressures.

7 I have nevertheless seen dramatic results from students' residential weekends "touring" a variety of places of worship. They really do return with many funny ideas blown away.

8 In writing the policy, or its preliminary discussion papers, I cannot stress enough the value of a word processor; although it gives a certain amount of power to the controller of the keyboard it means that no suggestion or modification is too small to put into the final document. Long, hand-typed documents make democracy harder if they have to be constantly re-typed.

9 Some points from it are included here. They were collaborative efforts, and thanks are due to Tony Barnes, Clive Behagg, Mark Burton, Owen Cole, Bev Hibbert, Ros Hurst, Ann Miller, Harbans Singh Mudher, John Naysmith, Zainab Nigoumi and Grishna Sutaria for all their comments.

9 Other struggles, theories and practicalities

I'm a black working class woman, so I know what it's like to be at the bottom of the class heap. I'm the victim of sexism every day of my life. But racism is the worst, nothing else eats at my soul like racism (conversation, 1984).

I cannot overturn people's assumptions about inequality all at once, to make any headway I have to concentrate on something. Since I have to choose I'll go for sexism, there are more potential allies in my, white, school...more victims too (white, male teacher).

Trainee teachers are mostly professional liberals, and to our generation racism is not really acceptable, however much we may still need to understand it in ourselves. But to most people feminism is either a pain or a joke (white, female student teacher).

I am opposed to institutionalised prejudice of any kind, on the grounds of race, sex, disability, class or age. We can't have a policy on one without a policy on the others (white, male, able-bodied, middle-class, middle-aged, educational administrator).

I can see race is important to you, more important than other inequalities, but you're a young white man. The older I get I find sexism hits me more and more, perhaps as I get further away from what society says the ideal woman is like. To me, nothing is more pervasive than sexism, and I cannot but oppose it in school (white, middle-aged, woman teacher).

Racism gets at liberal consciences all right, but it does nothing to shake the way working class culture is ignored or demeaned. For some of us, that has been an issue for far longer (white, working-class origins, male deputy head).

I hate sexism. It makes me rage. But the more I read about racism the more I see it's about power. Since I'm white I have to use what power I have to fight racism first (white, female student teacher).

It will be clear from this book that I have one or two working assumptions. One of these is that racism is not just "human nature", another is that like certain other "isms" it is part of our social structure, and a third is that it makes sense to give some priority over the others to the anti-racist struggle. I now want to develop these assumptions a little further.

First, I want to take issue with those who may insist on a generalized notion of "prejudice" which they want to tackle in education. Prejudice covers so many things it is hard to find a sphere of life which is outside its scope. In racism awareness training I tend to look for several key elements in a definition of prejudice: it is emotional rather than reasonable, it is frequently based on little knowledge, it is always resistant to change, it is based upon a judgement of or a stereotype of a group which therefore allows an individual to be pre-judged, and it is usually used in the negative sense. The kinds of groups prejudices apply to are legion: women, black people, other nationalities, upper class, working class, gay people, regional groups, residents of different estates, newcomers, old people, young people, the disabled, punks, non-punks, townspeople, villagers, politicians, second-hand car salesman, school teachers, etc. I use the discussion and the definition arising from it to distinguish prejudice from racism, but on its own where does the definition get us? It seems to lead inexorably towards a psychological view: if prejudice is so pervasive and directed against so many groups by so many groups, it must be a basic feature of human beings, it must be Human Nature. Whether it is or not, it is plain that it is going to be with us for a little while yet, and precisely because it is so broad and all embracing I would argue, from practice in classrooms, that it is impossible to work against it as a generalized phenomenon. Thus I regard it is misconceived to argue for the study of any kind of prejudice (against food perhaps) in the hope of a general spin-off, for the study of newcomers in a village, or churchgoers and non-attenders swapping images of each other, to lead to an understanding of the mechanisms of prejudice and thus greater "tolerance". It can sound convincing to say, "Well, tourists are the group people around here are most prejudiced against, so we teach about prejudice by looking at that. It's much more relevant to the children and I'm sure it makes them more aware of things when they do meet a coloured person. Of course we don't get a lot of that here", but it would be more persuasive if the school concerned looked at gender, yet they almost never do, although presumably there is a lot of that about.

Whereas out-group hostility is certainly a common human tendency which can be directed against all kinds of groups, to see it as simply that is to take a psychological route to an educational (and social) cul de sac, because prejudice is not the same as oppression. To return to a much earlier point, anyone can be racially prejudiced but in Britain only whites can be truly racist, because to be racist requires power. The same kind of thing is true about sexism; women may have "gender prejudices" about men, but it takes an almost wilful blindness to the actual distribution of power to argue that women often have the opportunity to be sexist.

Racism, sexism and "class prejudice" are more than just prejudices because they are forms of oppression which lead to structured inequality. This is not to say that "ageism" or prejudice against the disabled do not produce inequality, obviously they do, but "race", sex and class have much more explicitly political pedigrees, they have been used and are used in the mainstream of political life as key elements in the beliefs of our social order. In varying degrees and in different ways they are beliefs which legitimate inequality and hence a whole string of political consequences. To take racism as an example, its origins are in the need to legitimate colonial expansion. If one society is entering into a relationship of inequality with others, involving economic exploitation and expropriation as well as subjugation of the indigenous population, it has to justify itself. Britain's justifications varied from the belief in spreading civilization and good government to "benighted savages", to furthering a new and progressive economic order, to spreading the word of the one true God. Each of these required a belief of superiority and implied a right on the part of the British to spread their influence.

A good deal of scientific effort in the last century (and this) has gone into the investigation of black people's mental capabilties, genetic origins, and even their mental stability. These questions were not asked in some kind of vacuum, the society which ascribed a social position to black people virtually worldwide also set the agenda for investigation "into" them. On the whole scientists came up with the goods, with the pre-evolutionist Great Chain of Being and the social Darwinism of the late nineteenth century, and the IQ debate of the twentieth. Anthropologists also tended to produce confirmatory findings, pointing to the primitive savagery of child-like colonial subjects. This kind of racism survives to legitimate our relationship with the third world, but newer forms have been developed to cope with changed circumstances. At heart many people still hold beliefs about racial superiority, but nearer the surface we have the common ideology of "the immigration problem" and the responsibility of black peoples for our current economic position. This is a great deal more than the "prejudice" of a group of people's dislike of a new commuter estate in a country village, or a shop assistant's scorn at the advanced RP accents of some of her customers.

Racism can be contrasted with the inequality stemming from disability. Like "race" and sex, there is a law about disability (which actually pre-dates the Equal Opportunities Act), and several agencies have employment policies explicitly protecting their rights. There are several similarities in legal provision: firms can be made to show why they have no registered disabled people working for them (though they seldom are so required), special access courses exist for the disabled, there are attempts at integration in schools all over the country as a result of the Warnock report (accompanied no doubt by liberal glows like my own when I noticed how naturally my 6 year old responded to a handicapped girl in his own class, "What prejudice? They all play very naturally together").

On the other hand there do seem to be some important distinctions between the position of the disabled and those of other groups which have been identified, or which have identified themselves, as disadvantaged. Unless one conceives of the able-bodied as an oppressor group, it is difficult to see the notion of able-bodied as having been developed to maintain and justify a set of power relations, where one group benefits from the oppression of the other. Our system of government and society is not founded upon the "justified" role allocation of able-bodied and disabled people, but it is founded upon such allocations for men and women, blacks and whites, the working class and the rest. (Some may think that this portrayal of divisions is overstated and that structures of opportunity have changed, but such a view would probably still have to concede that there was a past where such divisions did exist and were fundamental to the ordering of society. This was never the case with disability.)

"Disability" is also a deceptively blanket term. Even if we leave out mental disability (and it would be naive to try and give an uncontentious definition of that), the concept still includes both the totally blind and deaf and those who have a slight limp from childhood polio. Although many disabled people can function as well as the able-bodied where their disabilities are not relevant, there are cases where disabilities are relevant. (Which is not to say assumptions of "relevance" are not to be questioned when interviewing someone with a spastic condition for, say, teacher training.) We do not expect to see the police in wheelchairs or blind electricians, and to that extent we are dealing with something real.

This is less often the case with women or black people. Although a command of English is a real criterion for some jobs, the actual refusal of a job on these grounds (rather than on the covert ones of "race") has to be far more rare than a similar refusal to someone disabled. The case may be even clearer as far as gender is concerned. In so far as the justification for "men's" jobs and "women's" jobs is on the grounds of physical strength, it can almost never be a tenable justification — there are always some men weaker than many women. The restrictions are much more visibly social ones, those against women fighter pilots for instance, or until recently against male midwives, are demonstrably a reflection of a set of social attitudes not a physiological imperative. This is even the official view of the state (although it allows itself a few exceptions), and of course there are still those who will argue that a woman's biology predisposes her to different patterns of behaviour, to different strengths and, more often, weaknesses. For both women and the disabled differential treatment is justified by a kind of appeal to physical facts, the consequences of which are starkly obvious to those using the appeal and challenged by those who find their own lives restricted by it. But disability is considered relevant for disqualification far more often, and legally so; parliamentary attempts to extend the same kind of non-discrimination protection to the disabled have not been successful.

I have to concede that whether or not beliefs about disability (or age) arose as part of a legitimating ideology, such distinctions may seem rather abstract to those experiencing unfair unequal treatment. Whatever the cause, the results may feel very much the same. However, we are a long way off any kind of political analysis for the disabled, and it may be counterproductive to lump disability together with sex, "race" and class. It has a distracting appeal for those too anxious about the murky depths of oppression to want to delve too far. It seems like safe ground, it is not political or controversial, it is manifestly possible to do some good in terms of broadening children's perceptions, one can even raise money for the disabled (or for old people) in a way that is hardly possible for black people or women (unless they are in Africa). One can take certain institutional steps to remove barriers to the disabled, literal ones in the case of putting in ramps and doorways, and institutional ones in the form of encouraging recruitment and building out certain assumptions.

None of the above, I would argue, is "periscopic" or illuminating of key processes in our society, in the sense that the educational examination of racism or sexism can be, hence my contention that it is oppressions and not prejudices that we ought to be dealing with. Yet which oppression? Is class the one which really underpins the other two? Is racism simply the worst, as stated in my opening quotation, and therefore the most urgent to tackle? It seems to me these questions can be answered theoretically − in terms of an analysis of the social structure; qualitatively − by trying to see which one is "worst" − and practically − in estimating different struggles' chances of success.

I am not going to attempt a theoretical answer. To some extent "race" and racism have received some theoretical treatment in chapters 2 and 5, but the analysis of the links and connections between "race", sex and class and our social order is beyond the scope of this book. Class as we know it is obviously the product of our economic system. It is relatively easy to recognize that racism has its origins in the need to legitimate colonial expansion (and continued neo-colonial trading), to import and control cheap labour, and to divide the poorest sections of the population. It is not hard to provide a similar kind of analysis for the position of women; without arguing that capitalism invented sexism it certainly benefits from it and does a great deal to maintain it. But it is a lot easier to assert that these three structures conjoin and conflict than it is to tease out quite how.

If one is looking for a qualitative analysis, the student quoted at the beginning who said that the women's movement is still "either a pain or a joke" pointed out something important. In some company, most company, it is still entirely acceptable to make jokes about women. Indeed, people seldom seem to understand why they might be considered offensive. Racist comments and "wisecracks" still circulate fairly freely, of course, but their circulation is more restricted. It is still seen as funny to patronize women, and a joke can even be made of the fact that it is seen as objectionable. Thus a man can comment archly on women drivers or women CDT teachers to a woman, apparently mocking a sexist structure and yet supporting it. Consider women's intelligence and black people's intelligence. Both in the past have been held to be inferior to that of white men, but few people on meeting a new black deputy head would make a "joke" about the general unsuitability of black people for such jobs. Such "jokes", however, are not infrequently made to senior women educationalists.

A related example is one suggested at a seminar about sexism. To throw into sharp relief the way gender differentiation works in schools try substituting "black" and "white" for "girls" and "boys" in the way a school is organized. Separate lists in the registers, lining up separately for lunch, separate playgrounds (these still exist!), some subjects being dominated by either group without this being seen as problematic, the cane being used for one group but not the other, blacks being let out first from lessons! Why does this seem so striking? Why is it that we can do to girls what we would no longer dare to do to (male) black children? It is natural, it is accepted, it has nothing to do with inequality.... Now this could be taken to mean that sexism is actually a less serious problem. Because "we" can joke about it, it is therefore not full of tension and conflict, the whole issue can be looked at without everyone getting "upset". But many women would argue that that is precisely what is wrong, and until people start seeing that such "jokes" are offensive sexism will carry on, as strong as ever.

There is an interesting comparison to be made, too, in media representation. Women are overwhelmingly portrayed in advertisements as either sexually exciting or as mothers, sometimes as both, and in either case they are represented as servicing the needs of either men or families. (I will not devote space to justify this assertion since it is easily checked. A colleague set aside an evening recently to video a few examples of sexist adverts, but it only took him five minutes.) This is objected to by the women's movement and by many women who would not call themselves feminists because it is degrading on the one hand and partial on the other, and presents a set of powerful role models which shape people's lives.

Black people are also presented in a demeaning way, if they are represented at all, but there is more vocal objection made to it. Robertson's (the jam manufacturers) still use their golly, but it is hard to imagine them having a live golly on a TV advert. They continue to get away with using such an insulting image only by claiming it is not real and not meant to be (they also get away with it because spurred on by the publicity white people defiantly buy golly jam, defiant of the responsibility people like us in the "race" industry try to arouse in them). Women on TV are real, the advertisers and programme makers claim, how can they be offensive when they represent the ideal woman — firm, young, tanned bodies, drinking cocktails and pursued by men — is this not what all women want?

A recent film might illustrate this further. Our (white, male) hero swashbuckles his way through danger after incredible danger impeded by a dumb blonde who is more concerned about a broken fingernail than with people's lives (except her own), and assisted by a clearly subordinate and tirelessly loyal Chinese sidekick. This "Tonto" figure has useful skills like courage, car driving, and Tai Chi, but can be treated like a child because he *is* a child; the director has cast a child in the role. Ten years ago he could have cast an adult Chinese or some other "native", and the script and relationships would have been almost identical. In fact the woman has fewer "life skills" and is much more of a liability, but the film makers know their politics well. It is acceptable, even for the American market, to cast a woman as a simpleton but not to do the same for a non-white male. (The film makes up for this, however, by a full supporting cast of simple peasants and evil drinkers of sacrificed human blood.)

The advertisers have a point, too, when they claim that many women aspire to the image they, the advertisers, have constructed. (Not that they would concede that it is a construction, they are simply holding a mirror to society.) Many women are not offended by the dumb blonde image, or the less blatant images which are presented to us. Yet it is hard to imagine black people aspiring to the representations of them in Tarzan films, or the *Black and White Minstrel Show*, or as gollywogs, or really welcoming certain kinds of photos on page three. There is nothing in racism for black people. They may deny its existence or want to keep quiet about it, but that is motivated either by a wish that racism will gradually whither away if it is ignored, or by a (class) belief that some black people are their own worst enemies. It is seldom, if ever, the case that a black person has found a niche in Britain's racist structure and thereby benefits from it. Colonial racism convinced sections of native populations that it was the best thing for them, but metropolitan racism in Britain in the 1980s is shored up with no such illusions in its victims.

Sexism is. It works so well many women support it, indeed it could be seen as foolish for them not to. A 15 year old's face is her fortune, the man she will live with may be far more important to her lifetime standard of living than her GCSEs, so she wisely seeks her own sources of power; lipstick, sex, and emotions, and comes to defend the status quo.

It may also be said that racism is "worse" than sexism because of some of its more dramatic consequences. In the past few years there have been many clearly racist murders, people attacked and killed simply because they are black. Women are not beaten up in the street and sometimes killed because people are so hostile to them that they want them driven out of the country. In that respect at least, racism is harsher, or so it is often thought. If the preceding sentence is changed to "because their attackers have a hatred of all women" then the similarity is more obvious. Male violence against women is not to promote separatism it is true, it has more in common with colonial subservience, and women keep telling a fairly deaf male world that violence against women is all around us. At one level women are kept in their place by domestic violence, at another they are raped. It may be that "normal" men do not rape any more than they beat up Asians (though this is not to assume that all "true" rape has to conform to the "Straw Dogs" model), but rape and the murder which sometimes accompanies it are part of a continuum in the same way that young fascists' racial murder only makes sense in the context of a racist society. Sexism is really very little different in this respect, though for the reasons touched on earlier it may be harder to see.

I am inclined to think that however interesting a comparison of sexist and racist effects may be, it does not provide us with a guide for action. Far more productive is careful thought about which struggle will yield the most results (I have little doubt that we ought to concentrate on one). It is to this practical emphasis on tactics that I now want to turn.

Some of the quotations at the beginning of this chapter illustrate a problem for teachers that those outside of education (and even those inside education but outside classrooms) can scarcely appreciate. There are many forms of inequality, and mainstream education either ignores or maintains most of them. Can they all be opposed? In principle, from either a liberal position of conscience or a Marxist analysis of the indivisibility of oppression, there may be no question that all forms of oppression ought to be opposed, but practice often dictates otherwise.

Teachers are not employed to challenge the status quo. Many would want to claim, along with the DES,[1] that they are not supposed to support it uncritically either, but to actively question a lot of common assumptions is hard work. This applies as much to the resulting relationships with one's colleagues and the consequent conflicting emotions and stress as it does to the work involved in the extra reading, preparation, and meetings that seem to be inevitably required. Textbooks are written, syllabuses are laid down, schools are organized all with sets of often unspoken and unrealized assumptions about "race", sex, class and the rest. Since this was even more true in the 1940s and 1950s, the generation which now numerically dominates teaching has a job to do on themselves too, and that seldom comes easily or at the same pace with regard to the different "isms". (My own attitudes about disability lie largely unexamined, and the sexist assumptions of my 8 year old son demonstrate the influence of what I do rather than what I say. Feminists no longer expect left-wing men to have no need of anti-sexist challenges, any more than male factory activists are surprised at the class assumptions of some members of the women's movement.)

It is difficult to challenge the status quo. Most teachers know the outline of the argument about education being part of the "system" which reproduces workers both trained and socialized for their role in life. They know the argument because it was covered in their sociology of education course at college, but on the whole it is difficult to give it much credence because it is too undermining of a teacher's daily work. Our material position more or less obliges us to believe in some kind of gradualism, in compromises, in the possibility of doing something good in a system which, according to the strength of one's viewpoint, is either rotten to the core or has some unsatisfactory features.

That aside, it is an over-simplistic account of "the system" which argues that it is a monolith, without spaces to work in and without contradictions. An effective strategy seeks out the contradictions and the space to work on them. There is a kind of politico/moral terrorism which demands such a degree of purity that it seems to lead to paralysis on the part of its adherents, and either anxious inaction or deaf impatience on the part of those who have it inflicted upon them. That is not to say that the most practical thing in the world is not a good theory, or that doing something is always better than doing nothing, but it is to say that ideological purity is impossible when one is involved in the business of educational change.

Apart from personal work on ourselves there are at the same time the practical steps which need to be taken. To put Africa back into people's perception of world history requires more than a perspective, it requires study — even to make the step of adding something to the poor coverage of a textbook, or choosing a different textbook, takes some knowledge, and our own education has frequently given us no such knowledge. To add to this a questioning of the notion of history being made by a few great people, and men at that, amounts to revising the whole historical content of the curriculum from 5 to 18 and beyond. That is only one subject. I am not going to disagree that it has to be done, but it will not be done tomorrow and it will not be done by one person. To avoid being swamped, demoralized and defeated teachers have to choose. Part of the skill of bringing about change is devising an effective strategy with a realistic target, which is simply to say that given the scale of inequality one person will fail if she tries to do it all.

Another practical matter is colleagues' reactions and one's relationships with them. How much can individuals cope with being the "radical" in all aspects of staffroom conversation? How much is one's effectiveness diminished by being regarded as the automatic supporter of what many people see as just "causes" rather than just causes? Many teachers now find themselves ignored by their colleagues because they have made it clear that on virtually everything there is a considerable distance between them.

So this is a difficult arena of theoretical and practical conflicts. While many people see class, race and sex inequality as essentially similar, at least as regards the group of men who benefit from all three, most of those working against these inequalities, whether in their paid employment or not, speak of recognizing the links, the argument, the justice of the other two, for few people can equally commit their time and energy to more than one. Besides which, as already suggested, we do not tend to be equally free from all of them ourselves.

If this is a good practical basis for concentrating on one or the other of these inequalities, to do so at least seems like a strategy worth examining. What might be the outcome of this strategy?

First, it recognizes some of the human facts already mentioned, namely the personal wear and tear from dealing with colleagues, the curriculum, school organization, and LEA structures on several fronts at once.

Second, it recognizes the fact that people, and especially institutions, cannot deal with too much change at once. To look at one kind of training for change, racism awareness training, this can take a day or it can take a week, but the preferred format of trainers is for an initial course to last for about three days. This would be a very intensive three days, and many participants find that it gives them something to think about, to say the least, and usually something to do. A key part of the training is to identify realistic action plans and existing blockages, both personal and institutional, which prevent progress being made. Although class and sex are often raised in racism awareness they usually have to be set aside (not ignored) because of constraints of time and the constraint of how much challenging of world views it is realistic to attempt at once. Teachers have a full-time job without in-service training, especially in-service which challenges everyday practices. The work involved in significant restructuring is considerable, and realism dictates that we have to recognize that on the whole change will come about through the work teachers put in in their own free time.

Third, this strategy of attacking one main issue at a time recognizes the effect and significance of individuals in certain schools and in key positions. There is certainly a structural reason why racism, on the whole, has been more the subject of government funding and LEA policy than sexism, namely the "riots", but this does not preclude the fact that the circumstances may be far more favourable in particular places for attacking sexism. If individuals in key positions or simply in significant numbers are more personally concerned about sexism they will be more effective in working against it than in working against racism.

If the concentration on one aspect of inequality seems reasonable, we are still left with the choice of which one. This will often, inevitably, be a product of people's biography, and there is nothing wrong with that, but I would argue there are some grounds for attacking racism first. Not because it is "worse" than sexism or classism, though some will experience it as such and it is hardly for me to argue with them, but for reasons I suggested earlier sexism is "harder" to get on the serious agenda than racism, even in white schools where, naturally enough, half the pupils and maybe half the staff are female.

Given the scale of the enterprise, my strategy has been to make racism non-negotiable and then start on other forms of oppression. Racism is subtle and deep-rooted and takes a good deal of digging out, and once it is on the agenda the "ratchet principle" has to be applied to keep it there. But despite the comment earlier about our different paces of self-education with respect to the various "isms", learning about racism does teach about other things. It throws up questions and ways of thinking about the world which can be applied elsewhere, later perhaps, but applied nevertheless.

It does seem to be a fact of institutional life that one issue is focused on at a time. It can be the result of individual people or it can be outside pressures, but in the end (where will this ever end?) there is spin-off on to the others.

This is not a contradiction of the argument employed earlier against hoping pupils' studies about "prejudice" would lead to a general diminution of hostility about all "out groups", because we are not discussing "prejudice" as an all embracing psychological phenomenon. The analysis of, for example, racism, highlights structures, thought patterns, institutional procedures, and power distributions in ways which the vague examination of generalized "prejudice" does not. Once racism is made non-negotiable, there is a chink in the armour of a whole set of inequalities which people take for granted.

It may be that although it raises the temperature very quickly racism is easier for the "white highlands" to deal with because it is not so threatening to everyday arrangements as a challenge about sexism or class. On the other hand Rushdie's quote in chapter 2 (see p.35) is worth recalling: he suggests that our attitudes to race are symptomatic of a crisis in our whole culture. As I argued in chapter 5, to be explicitly racist is formally unacceptable, and as I have suggested above casual sexism is still the norm. As for class, although the state long ago stopped formally recommending separate schools for separate classes, until recently that is what actually happened, and in the case of the small class served by the private schools still does happen. It is rare for this to be publicly defended in such bald terms, however, the rhetoric is one of choice, excellence, saving up, and so on. This is only a defence with regard to opportunity, it is not the inequalities of class which the Conservatives deny supporting but the inequality of access to the inequalities. If people have different positions in life stemming from "race" or gender then it is unwise for anyone in public life to defend this, largely because of the unacceptable injustice of an entirely ascribed status. Class is defended as an aspect of social structure, usually on the presumption that it is achieved and not ascribed, and is therefore a mainspring of "our" way of life. One therefore appears as much more of a radical if one questions class structures (even if one's point is simply that there is a good deal of ascription rather than achievement). Racism cannot be respectably defended in public, though it is maintained by calling it other things. (Class is defended by theories of political economy, sexism by biology, and racism by hints about "national character" and "swamping").[2]

A final reason for giving priority to anti-racism is that racism is getting worse, not solely in terms of physical attacks, but in terms of the state's position. The Nationality Act goes as far as it is possible to go in limiting the right to British citizenship to white people without explicitly saying so. Yet at the same time it is common public dogma that racism is unacceptable. In terms of action for change this ought to be a fruitful contradiction, more fruitful, at any rate, than action against class and gender structures which carry far greater legitimacy.

I thus return to my question about which is the most productive way for teachers to work against inequality. It is not, I would suggest, to adopt a catch-all "prejudice" approach, because this becomes too general to have any effect, it spreads the energy too thinly, and because it wrongly equates prejudice with structured oppression. Equally, however, it can be ineffective to try and act upon a political analysis which demands opposition to all forms of oppression at all times. Teachers' jobs are just not like that, and institutions do not seem to change that way.

This book has been about "race" in education, in areas where the issues are considerably less sharply defined than they are in the large conurbations. Teachers are actually in the position of having to decide in a relatively abstract way about the sort of choices I have outlined here because there are no black pupils who are going to put the matter on the agenda for them, and gays dare not show their faces, and the nearest women's group is the Women's Institute.

Hard and fast conclusions are not possible. It may be that some will see a clear course of action implied for them in these reflections, which after all are only reflections on what I think I have learned through struggling against one particular oppression. We still have a lot to learn, and it is certainly not for a white man to make prescriptions about the only correct course of action. It is for us to listen to the perspectives and demands of those at the sharp end of the struggles, and if some think "struggle" is too strong a word, they are not listening. We do not know where the shoes of oppression pinch because we do not wear them, only those who do can say where it hurts the most, and without asking them it is not a bit of good designing new shoes.

References

1   *The Curriculum 11-16,* DES 1981.
2   Those whose sexual orientation is not staightforwardly heterosexual form another "minority group" who are included in some equal opportunity policies, though we are probably a long way from schools wishing to or being allowed to address themselves to the issue. Some feminists have offered an analysis

which sees the dominant definition of gender roles as imposing entirely artificial and restricting norms of sexual orientation. There are existing alliances on the left between gay groups and others, but presumably because of people's socialized disgust about homosexuality and the corresponding but unwarranted assumption that gay = paedophile, the gay movement is making little headway in schools. In principle one might have thought there is potential support, many estimates suggest that between 5 per cent and 10 per cent of secondary pupils are gay, bisexual, or would like to be. But to start looking for such support is not to know schools, and to invite the sack. Sixty years ago a teacher was a dangerous radical if he or she opposed separate schools for separate social classes, twenty years ago (s)he attracted the same label for recognized the racism of the DES bussing blacks policy. Less than ten years ago most schools quite explicitly offered different curricula to boys and girls. Seven years ago Warnock recommended the desegregation of many handicapped pupils. It will be another ten, at least, before challenges of conventional sexual orientation get overtly inside the school gates. In these circumstances, the productive arena for change seems likely to be in the areas legitimized by law and policy, at least in theory, at some time in the past.

Appendix 1   Where to look next: materials and resources

Contents

It is essential that any book about racial education has a section on resources. This is because the field is, if not new, only newly recognized.

I have tried to restrict the resources section in this book to materials for teachers, except in the section on teaching about "race". (Even here I have excluded works of fiction. This is because, although they are a potentially rich source of classroom work, I did not use them in my own teaching, so it would be unwise to recommend particular titles.)

Some will find this teacher emphasis frustrating and will want to have information on useable classroom resources. It should be recognized that good materials which attempt to be anti-racist do not exist in any quantity, and that the most likely way forward here is for teachers to develop their own perspectives and either produce or encourage better classroom materials.

It should also be pointed out that the emphasis in this section, as in many other places in the book, is on secondary schools. This is because my teaching experience is of secondary schools, and I doubt if primary teachers would thank me for pretending it was otherwise.

The most comprehensive guide to resources (over 600 entries) is probably C. Brooking, M. Foster and S. Smith, *Teaching for Equality*, Runnymede Trust 1987, 0 902397 69 9. Another very full guide is Gillian Klein's *Resources for Multi-cultural Education, an Introduction* published by Longmans for the Schools Council, and available from Longmans Resources Unit, 33–35 Tanner Row, York.

General works on race and education

ALTARF, *Challenging Racism,* 1984, 09509673 0 0. Available from Unit 216, Panther House, 38 Mount Pleasant, London WC1X 0AP.

Ranjit Arora and Carlton Duncan (eds.) *Multicultural Education, Towards Good Practice*, RKP, 1986, 0 7102 0229 6.
Not about white areas, though of course some points apply in any area. I have referred to some chapters under the subject headings which follow.

Assistant Masters and Mistresses Association, *Our Multicultural Society, the Educational Response*, available free from the Assistant Masters and Mistresses Association, 29 Gordon Square, London WC1H OPX.
Covers most of the main issues from the point of view of what teachers ought to do, but since it is published by a teachers' union it avoids sounding too idealistic or threateningly critical.

G. Brandt, *The Realization of Anti-Racist Teaching*, Falmer, 1986, 1 85000 127 8.
Traces the debate about anti-racist teaching and has some observations of particular lessons.

A. Craft and G. Bardell (eds.), *Curriculum Opportunities in a Multicultural Society*, Harper Education, 1984, 0 06 318285 8.
Largely the texts of the Schools Council series on examining in a multicultural society, so it focuses on secondary schooling in history, geography, social science, RE, English, PE, dance and outdoor pursuits, modern languages, maths, chemistry, biology, art and design and home economics.

Maurice Craft (ed.), *Education and Cultural Pluralism*, Falmer, 1984, 0 85000 000 X.
As with everything from Craft it is rooted in the cultural diversity model outlined in chapter 2.

Education for All (The Swann Report), HMSO, 1985, Cmnd 9453, 0 10 194530 2.
At £24 few teachers will be able to afford this, but it would be a mistake to read Lord Swann's *Guide* as a substitute, since it was written without any contribution from the rest of the Committee and has been disowned by several of them. A real summary has been published by the Runnymede Trust at 50p, a third of the price of Swann's *Guide*, and is available from Runnymede Trust, 178 North Gower Street, London NW1 2NB. See also NAME on Swann, a critical commentary from the National Anti-racist Movement in Education, available from NAME, PO Box 9, Walsall, W. Midlands, WS1 3SF.

Education in a Multi-Ethnic Society, an aide-memoire for the Inspectorate, ILEA Learning Materials Service, Highbury Station Road, London N1 1SB.
Thought out for a multiracial context, rather than a largely white one, but brief.

Chris Gaine and Louise Pearce (eds.), *Anti-Racist Education in White Areas*, 1987 NAME Conference Report, NAME, 1988.
Practical sections on in-service, classroom strategies, support and policy development.

Ideas Into Action, World Studies Project, 1980, 0 905 4434 41. Available from One World Trust, 24 Palace Chambers, Bridge Street, London SW1A 2JT.

A. James and R. Jeffcoate (eds.) *The School in the Multicultural Society*, Harper and Row, 1981, 0 06 318196 7.
A very practical book, covering curriculum objectives, language, teaching about race, stereotyping, and some black perspectives on the whole enterprise.

R. Jeffcoate, *Positive Image*, Readers and Writers/Chameleon, 1979, 0 906495 03 2.
This is disliked by many as liberally evasive, but has some interesting classroom accounts and some very clear statements of his position.

R. Jeffcoate, *Ethnic Minorities and Education*, Harper Education, 1984, 0
06 318 284 X.
Aims to be as comprehensive as the title suggests, but has to be seen as
part of a backlash against the kind of anti-racism supported in this
book.

James Lynch, *The Multicultural Curriculum*, Batsford, 1983, 07134 4510
6.

Jon Nixon, *A Teacher's Guide to Multicultural Education*, Blackwell, 1984,
0 631 13983.
Written by a teacher originally involved in Stenhouse's research into
teaching about "race", then seconded into teacher training.

Open University, *Ethnic Minorities and Education*, Course E354, Units
13–14 (Block 4).
The rest of this course is mentioned under teaching about "race",
because it is carefully designed to meet the needs of people like
teachers; it gives a sound and comprehensive overview.

A. Page and K. Thomas, *Multicultural Education and the 'All-White'
School,* University of Nottingham School of Education, 1984, 0 85359
098 2.
Well worded for tactful use in white areas, and well referenced, but I
find it inexplicit about the issue of racism.

M. Phillips-Bell, *Issues and Resources*, AFFOR, 1983, 0 907127 10 X.
No detailed arguments in this short book but a clear perspective on
education. It can be read in about two hours!

M. Straker-Welds (ed.), *Education for a Multicultural Society, Case studies
in ILEA Schools,* Bell & Hyman, 1984, 0 7135 2381 9.

B. Troyna and Jenny Williams, *Racism, Education and the State*, Croom
Helm, 1986, 0 7099 4316 4.
A useful and up to date sociological perspective on policies on racial
education.

J. Twitchin and C. Demuth, *Multicultural Education*. BBC, 1981, 0 563
16443 3, (now in a 1985 edn).
Entirely grounded in the practices of real schools, it is clearly thought
out as well as practical.

R. Willey, *Teaching in Multicultural Britain,* Schools Council, 1982. (Available from Longmans, address above).
Not detailed by any means, two hours' reading at most, but it covers the main issues with lots of quotes from ministers and other respectable sources.

Journals

Contemporary Issues in Geography and Education, from Frances Slater, Geography Dept, Institute of Education. 20 Bedford Way, London WC1H 0AL.

Multicultural Teaching, Trentham Books, 30 Wenger Crescent, Trentham, Stoke on Trent ST4 8LE.
This is certainly the best for practising teachers. I would highly recommend taking out a subscription.

NAME Journal, some back copies are available from A. Dorn, Commission for Racial Equality, Elliot House, Allington St, London. At the time of writing publication has been suspended because of financial difficulties.

Wasafiri, Caribbean, African, Asian and associated literature in English, 3rd World Publications (Co-op) Ltd, 151 Stratford Rd, Birmingham, B11 1RD.

World Studies Journal, World Studies Teacher Training Centre, University of York, Heslington, York YO1 5DD.

Books about children's attitudes, stereotyping, etc.

Sara Goodman Zimet, *Print and Prejudice,* Hodder and Stoughton, 1976, 0 340 21026 5.

G. Klein, *Reading into Racism,* RKP, 1985, 0 7102 0160 5.

David Milner, *Children and Race, 10 Years On,* Ward Lock, 1983, 0 7062 4268 8.
Readable and well researched, useful background for anyone concerned about pupils' attitudes.

Beverley Naidoo, *Censoring Reality,* ILEA and BDAF, 1985. (Available from IDAF, Canon Collins House, 64 Essex Road, London N1 8LR.)
An excellent study of the way school books try to make South Africa uncontroversial. Can be used with older pupils.

Racism and Sexism Resource Center Catalogue, Council for Interracial Books for Children, 1841 Broadway, New York, 10023-7648.
A lot of the material listed is probably not directly useable in Britain, but it makes interesting reading.

Roy Prieswerk (ed.), *The Slant of the Pen, Racism in Children's Books,* World Council of Churches, 1980, 0 28254 0620 1.
Very comprehensive, but set in a very international context, perhaps a bit much to take in at the same time as coming to terms with British material.

Judith Stinton (ed.), *Racism and Sexism in Children's Books,* Writers and Readers, 1981, 0 906495 18 0.

English teachers

Things to think about
Choice of texts.
a black literature in English,
b books about multiracial Britain,
c books about race relations elsewhere.

2   Exam syllabuses.
3   Mass media/communications "literacy".
4   Dealing with pupils' racism via literature, discussions, creative writing, drama.
5   Understanding issues of creoles and dialects.
6   Understanding of mother tongue and ESL issues.
7   Avoidance of or creative use of stereotypes in books.
8   Choice of school play.
9   Library policy.

Some sources
Books to Break Barriers, A Review of Multicultural Fiction 4–18, Oxford

Development Education Centre, 1987, 0 9510049 13. Available from Worldwide, 72 Cowley Rd, Oxford.

Bob Dixon, *Catching Them Young,* vol. 1, *Sex, Race and Class in Children's Fiction,* Pluto, 1977, 0 904383 50 4.
Other books on stereotyping are listed above, but this one is quite short and obviously of most relevance to English specialists.

D. K. Dunn, 'Multicultural literature in the classroom, some reactions by white teachers', *Multicultural Teaching,* **1** no. 3.

Education for a Multicultural Society (listed under general) has three chapters which may be useful, one on drama, a case study of responses to a short story, and a case study about TV.

The English Curriculum: Race.
Another product of ILEA's English Centre, virtually an in-service course in itself for an English department, with enough discussion points and classroom examples to keep people going for months.

Laurie Fallows, *Assessment in a Multicultural Society, English at 16+,* for the Schools Council, available from Longmans Resources.
This is an important booklet to be acquainted with as the GCSE takes shape. Also to be found in Chapter 5 in *Curriculum Opportunities*, see p.194.

Liz Gunner, *Teaching African Literature,* Heinemann, 1984, 0 435 92260 2.
The first book aimed at teachers enabling this vast source to be tapped a little.

Prabhu Guptara, *British Black Literature, an Annotated Bibliography,* Dangaroo Press, 1986, 87 88 213 14 5.
Comprehensive, with a useful final section on "Finding out and keeping up" and a long list of small publishers.

Eric Hawkins, *Awareness of Language, an Introduction,* Cambridge Educational, 1985, 0 521 28853 3.
A teachers' book by Eric Hawkins, complemented by a series of six thin books and an audio cassette for classroom use. It is really linguistics for beginners, and very useable.

An Introduction to Indo-British and South-Asian Literature for teachers in Secondary Schools and Colleges, Carla Contractor, Avon Multicultural Education Centre, Bishop Rd, Bishopston, Bristol BS7 8LS. 1987.

Chapters 3, 4, 5 of Jeffcoate's *Postive Image*, see p.195

G. Klein, *The School Library for Multicultural Awareness*, Trentham Books, 1985, 0 948 0800 35.

The Languages Book, ILEA English Centre, Sutherland Street, London SW1.
This arose from a survey of language and dialect in London schools; it makes interesting reading, is not too long, and is immensely practical.

A Motherland (video). Available for hire (outside ILEA) from Central Film Library, Chalfont St Giles, Gerrards Cross, Bucks. (Tel: 02407 4111) price £20. This is included because it is a particularly impressive piece of drama, moving and powerful, useful for teachers to see as well as to use.

Also on drama are chapters 15-20 in *Teaching About Race Relations, Problems and Effects*. Details under "Teaching about Race", and M. Wootton (ed.), *New Directions in Drama Teaching, Studies in Secondary School Practice*, Heinemann, 1982, 0 435 189271.

The West Indian Novel in English. A brief introduction and some recommendations for teachers and librarians. Mary Smith, Avon Multicultural Education Centre, address above.

White Lies, Links No 21, published by Third World First, 232 Cowley Rd, Oxford.
About media representation.

The most useful organization for English literature specialists to belong to is the Association for the Teaching of Caribbean and African Literature (ATCAL), which runs excellent conferences and has a good supply of useful speakers, workshop leaders, etc. and also publishes a journal, Wasafiri, listed above. They also produce annotated bibliographies of Afro-Caribbean and Indian literature for use in secondary schools, and one on 'A' Level texts. Contact via David Dabydeen, University of Warwick.

Specialist bookshops are listed at the end of this appendix.

History teachers

Things to think about

1 Caution over the values implied in "civilization", "culture", and "race".
2 Does "not European" mean "backward" or at an earlier "stage"?
3 Does the history of other societies begin with European contact?
4 Do historical accounts have the effect of legitimizing European actions?
5 Is it appropriate to transfer some judgements across time and space?
6 Awareness of stereotyping in textbooks.
7 "Until the lions have their historians tales of hunting will always glorify the hunter" – African proverb.

Some sources

Assessment in a Multicultural Society, History at 16+, Schools Council. Available from Longmans Resources Unit, 33-35 Tanner Row, York. Extended version in chapter 1 of *Curriculum Opportunities....,* above.

British History, Racist History?, Conference Report, Association for Curriculum Development, 1987. PO Box 563, London N16 8SD.

Sylvia Collicott, 'Approaches to Multicultural Curriculum', Chapter 7 of of Arora and Duncan's book, mentioned in General works, p.194 above.

David Edginton, *The Role of History in Multicultural Education,* School of Oriental and African Studies, 1982, 0261 5428.
A useful introduction to some arguments and a survey of some syllabuses.

'Ethnicity and Culture', edition of the ILEA *History and Social Science Teachers' Centre Review,* 6 no. 4, Spring 1986.
Written by teachers for teachers, with examples of classroom applications.

Peter Fryer, *Staying Power*, Pluto Press, 1984, 0 391 03167 8.
A very readable scholarly book about the history of black people in Britain. Individual chapters could be read by teachers to add an extra dimension to many of the periods studied in school.

A History of West Africa 1965, 0 582 60340 4.
A History of Southern Africa 1978, 0 582 60349 8.
A History of Central Africa 1974, 0 582 60298 X.
A History of East Africa 1977, 582 60886 4.
Caribbean History in Maps, P. Ashdown, 1979, 0 582 76541 2.
African History in Maps, M. Kwamena-Poh, J. Tosh, R. Waller, M. Tidy, 1982, 0 582 60331 5.
All published by Longman as textbooks, mentioned here just to indicate that some published material does exist in a form useable in school. Similarly there is also:

Lennox Honeychurch, *The Caribbean People* books 1,2 & 3. Nelson, 1981, 017 566236 3, 017 566241 X, 017 566242 8.

India, World History Outlines, ILEA, 1978. (Also available on China.) Excellent resource materials.

D. Killingray, *The Transatlantic Slave Trade*, Batsford 1987, 07134 5469 5.

London Strategic Policy Unit, *A History of the Black Presence in London*, 1986, 187 001 308 5.

R. Mascey (ed.), *All India*, Apple Press, 1986. 293 Gray's Inn Rd, London WC1 8QF.

E. O'Callaghan, *The Earliest Patriots*, Karia Press, 0 946918 538.

Avril Powell, *The Struggle for Freedom in India*, Macdonald, 1986, 0 356 1128 4.

Roy Prieswerk and Dominique Perrot, *Ethnocentrism and History*, NOK (New York and Nigeria), 1978, 0 88357 072 6.
An academic book, but potentially useful against racists who try to pull intellectual rank.

Roots of Racism, Patterns of Racism, How Racism came to Britain and *The Fight Against Racism,* Institute of Race Relations, 0850 01 0233, 0850 01 0241 (1982), 0850 01 0292 (1984), 0850 01 0314 (1986). 247 Pentonville Road, London N1.
Four excellent brief books, relating racism firmly to the economic forces which gave rise to it and sustain it. Well produced, and useable with older pupils.

Sneh Shah, *The Contribution of History to Development Education,* The Historical Association, 59a Kennington Park Road, London SE11 4JH.

Marika Sherwood, *Many Struggles, Black People in Britain in the Second World War,* Karia Press, 1984, 0 946 918 007.

M. Straker-Welds (ed.), *Education for a Multicultural Society,* chapter 9 by N. File and C. Power. Details under general.

Unlearning "Indian" Stereotypes, Racism and Sexism Resources Center, address under "attitudes and stereotyping", above p.198.
Worth the trouble of sending to the USA for if American "Indians" are studied, since the stereotypes (through Westerns) are so universal. Only $3.95 for the booklet, but it is worth getting the excellent tape/slide pack too.

James Walvin, *Passage to Britain*, Penguin, 014 02 2572 2.
Accompanies the TV series mentioned under Teaching about "race". There is also a teaching pack on the series.

Whose World Is the World?, Poster Film Collective, BCM PFC, London WC1N 3XX.
A really excellent and provocative set of 12 posters giving a black perpective on colonialism. Can be used with anyone from first years to heads.

See also the video series *Africa* listed under videos, and many books by the author of this series, Basil Davidson.

Maths and science teachers

Understandably enough the response of many teachers in these fields is that racism, culture, and inequality have few or no implications for their teaching. The Association for Science Education said as much to the Swann Committee: "Science is an international study, with no particular national bias, and with its own neutral terminology which is also culture free." The following items suggest that things might not be quite so straightforward, and some give classroom suggestions.

Some issues and possibilities

1 History of symbols/mathematical development.
2 Reference to other cultures' computational systems, number bases, notation, number words, symmetrical patterns, scientific developments, etc.
3 "Imperialism" of western mathematics.
4 Pictures/people used in textbook illustration.
5 Examples and problems which have a "content" illustrative of racism/anti-racism.
6 Concern of Afro-Caribbean parents over underachievement.
7 Stereotyping of Asian and Chinese pupils.
8 Consequences and impact of science — whose progress?
9 "Non-scientific" = primitive?
10 Racial myths and biology.
11 Language issues.

Some sources
Anti-Racist Mathematics.
A teaching package from Association for Curriculum Change in Mathematics, a draft version is in limited circulation, contact ACCM, PO Box 563, London N16 8SD for further details. They have some other papers, too, such as *Maths, Culture and Racism*, E. Singh, and *Maths and Political Indoctrination*, D. Gill.

'Anti-Racist Maths', *Race and Class*, **XXVIII** no. 3, Winter 1987.

R. Arora and C. Duncan, *Multicultural Education, Towards Good Practice*, Chapter 11, 'Science education for a multicultural society', RKP, 1986, 0 7102 0229 6.

Birmingham LEA Maths Resource Centre, *Maths in a Multicultural Environment*, 1986.

Black Pioneers of Science and Invention. Harcourt Brace Jovanovich, 1978.

Anne Bovett, 'Mathematics, a universal language', *Multicultural Teaching*, **1** no. 3, Summer 1983.

Alan Brine and Derek Bunyard, *Islamic Art: Vedic Square*, King Alfred's College, Winchester.
A booklet with a floppy disk for BBC Bs, using LOGO to generate complex geometric patterns like Islamic ones, derived from mathematical patterns.

A. Craft and G. Bardell (eds.), *Curriculum Opportunities in a Multicultural Society*, especially Chapter 7 by Ray Hemmings, Chapter 8 (chemistry), and Chapter 9 (biology), Harper Education, 1984, 0 06 318285 8.

Derek Dyson, 'Multicultural approach to mathematics', Chapter 10 or Arora and Duncan's book, mentioned in General works, p.194.

G. Flegg, *Numbers, their History and Meaning*, Andre Deutsch, 1983, 0 233 97516 0.

Dawn Gill and Les Levidow (eds.), *Anti-Racist Science Teaching*, Free Association Books, 1987, 0 946960 64 X.

Ray Hemmings, 'Multi-ethnic mathematics', two useful articles in the journal of NAME (at that time National Association for Multiracial Education), **8** no. 3 and **9** no. 1 (1980).

Martin Hollins (ed.), *Science Teaching in a Multiethnic Society*, ILEA Science Centre, 1984.

Pauline Hoyle, 'Language and anti-racist science', *ILEA Multi-ethnic Education Review*, **5** no. 1, winter/spring 1986.

George Joseph, 'A non-Eurocentric approach to school mathematics', *Multicultural Teaching*, **4**, no. 2, Spring 1986.

Marina C. Krause, *Multicultural Mathematics Materials*, National Council of Teachers of Mathematics, 1906 Association Drive, Reston, Virginia, 22091, 0 87353 206 6.

Liz Lindsay, *Racism science education and the politics of food*, ALTARF occasional paper no. 1, 1985.

Mathematics for All, Wiltshire ESG Project, Wilton Middle School, Salisbury SP2 0JE 1987.

'Maths teaching in a multicultural society', *Times Educational Supplement*, 11 May 1983, p. 41.

Multicultural Aspects of Science, A Record of an In-Service Course. Coventry LEA, 1986.

Seyyed Hossein Nasr, *Islamic Science, an Illustrated Study*, World of Islam Publishing Co., 1976, 09 05035 02 X.

Jenni Newman and Sue Watts, *Developing a Multicultural Science Curriculum*, Bell and Hyman, 1984, 7135 2371 9.

Nicholas, Pickles and Williams, *Introductory Lectures on Vedic Mathematics*, Vedic Maths Research Group, 106 Mercers Road, London N19. 869932 005.

Racism and Pseudo Science, UNESCO, 1983. 92 3 101993 7.

A. Ross, *The Story of Mathematics*, Black, 1984, 0 7136 2424 8.

Science Education for a Multicultural Society, Science Curriculum Review, Leicestershire LEA, 1985.

Ivan van Sermita (ed.), *Blacks in Science*, Transaction Books, 1983, 0 87855 941 8.

M. Straker-Welds (ed.), *Education for a Multicultural Society*, Chapter 11, 'Multicultural mathematics', by David Gilbert, Chapter 10.

Third World Science, University College of Wales, 1983. (Available from CWDE, address under geography p.207.

Sue Watts, 'Science education for a multicultural society', Chapter 11 of Arora and Duncan, see p.194.

Bryan Wilson, *Cultural Contexts of Science and Mathematics Education. A Bibliographic Guide*. Centre for Studies in Science Education, University of Leeds, 1981, 0 904421 10 4.

In a way I hesitate to recommend this, since it is quite expensive and is really a collection of abstracts. It is an invaluable source, however, for anyone really wanting to have a good look at this field with regard to science and maths. It has sections on, for instance, the context of language, the implications of different world-views for science teaching, and curriculum projects. Essential for advisers, teachers' centres, and teacher trainers.

'World Studies in the Science and Maths Classroom', *World Studies Journal*, **5** no. 4, 1985, University of York.

Claudia Zaslavsky, *Africa Counts*. Lawrence Hill and Co, Westport, Connecticut, 1979, 0 88208 104 7. (Available in Britain from Third world Publications, 151 Stretford Road, Birmingham B11 1AH.)
The sub-title is "number and pattern in African culture" which is really what it is about. It traces the development of different number systems and the cultural assumptions behind them, and lots more besides. Very readable.

Geography teachers

Things to think about
1   What message is given when, for example, South Africa or urban distribution in Britain is not treated as controversial?
2   Stereotyping in textbooks.
3   Images of the "third world", i.e. black peoples.
4   Colonial background to underdevelopment.

Some sources
Catalogue of CWDE, available from Regents College, Inner Circle, Regent's Park, London NW1 4NS.

'Curriculum opportunities in a multicultural society', Chapter 2, Craft and Bardell (eds.), Harper, 1984, 0 06 318285 8.

Dhaka to Dundee, Bangladesh and Britain in an unequal world. War on Want, 1987, 0 905990 12 7.

Disasters in the Classroom. Oxfam, 1986.
A teaching pack about the underlying causes of disasters in the third world.

Dawn Gill, 'Geography and education for a multicultural society'. The report the Schools Council commissioned as part of their series preparing for the 16+, but refused to publish. Available free from the Commission for Racial Equality, Elliot House, 10−12 Allington Street, London WC1E 5EH.

Dawn Gill, *Geography for the young school leaver/secondary school geography in London, an assessment of its contribution to multicultural education*, working paper no. 2, from Centre for Multicultural Education, above, 0 85473 138 5.

David Hicks, *Bias in geography textbooks*. A longer version of working paper no. 1, from Centre for Multicultural Education, listed below 0 85473 138 5.

David Hicks, *Images of the world, an introduction to bias in teaching materials*, occasional paper no. 2, Centre for Multicultural Education, University of London Institute of Education, 0 854473 102 4 (20 Bedford Way, London WC1H OAL).

Learning for Change in World Society, World Studies Project, 1979, 0 900581 034.

T. Mebrahtu, *Swann and the Global Dimension*. Youth Education Service, 1987. 14 Frederick Place, Clifton, Bristol, BS8 1AS.

Beverley Naidoo, *Censoring Reality*, ILEA and BDAF, 1985. Available from IDAF, Canon Collins House, 64 Essex Road, London N1 8LR. An excellent study of the way school books try to make South Africa uncontroversial.

Racist society − geography curriculum, Conference report, available from Centre for Multicultural Education, above.

Robin Richardson, *Fighting for Freedom; World Conflict; Caring for the Planet; Progress and Poverty* (4 different books), Nelson/Schools Council, 1978, 0 17 438174 3.
These are classroom books, included because I think they are unusual and especially good.

M. Straker-Welds (ed.), *Education for a Multicultural Society*, Chapters 6 and 8. Details under general works.

Teaching About Migration, (leaflet) Centre for World Development Education (for address see p.207).

Teaching Development Issues, Development Education Project, 1986. Manchester Polytechnic, Manchester M20 8RG
Seven books with detailed teacher's notes, aiming to deal with anti-racist (and other) issues.

Western Europe's Migrant Workers, Minority Rights Group, Report no. 28, Benjamin Franklin House, 36 Craven Stret, London WC2N 5NG, 0305 6252.

Whose Development?, Development Education Centre, 1987, 0 9506619 7 X. Selly Oak Colleges, Bristol Road, Birmingham, B29 6LE.

David Wright, 'A portrait of racism in geography', Commission for Racial Equality Education Newsletter, 1983. Address above.

D. Wright, *In Black and White*, Association for Curriculum Development/ILEA, 1985.

Religious education teachers

Things to think about
1   Understanding and appreciation of world's faiths.
2   Avoidance of "Christianity ...and the rest" approach.
3   Sensitive use of children and community as resources.
4   Facing children's racism in the classroom and in the syllabus.
5   Working for changes in the agreed syllabus.
6   Assemblies.
7   Sensitivity to withdrawal from RE and assemblies.

Some sources
A. Brine and D. Bunyard, *Islamic Art: Vedic Square*, King Alfred's College, Winchester.
A booklet which bridges Art, maths and RE in some ways. It comes with a computer disk which enables pupils to generate (with LOGO) patterns from Vedic Squares. An RE teacher tells me a pupil came to appreciate something of the infinite when realizing that a pattern would repeat itself for ever. . . .

E. Cashmore, *Rastaman*, Allen and Unwin, 1979, 0 04 301116 0.

The Changing World and RE, Centre for World Development Education (for address see p.207), 1979.

W. O. Cole (ed.), *World Faiths in Education*, Allen and Unwin, 1978, 004 371055 7.

W. O. Cole, *Religion in the Multifaith School*, Hulton Educational, 1983, 07175 1159 6.

W. O. Cole, *World Religions, a Handbook*, Commission for Racial Equality, 1984, 0 902355 69 4.

'Curriculum opportunities in a multicultural society', Chapter 4, Craft and Bardell (eds.), Harper, 1984, 0 06 318285 8.

R. Jackson (ed.), *Approaching World Religions*, John Murray, 1982.

C. Lawton, *Shap Calendar of Religious Festivals*, CRE, annually.

'Religious Festivals'. Wallchart from Mobile Education Project, 62 Chandos St, Leicester, LE2 1BU.

Art and music teachers

Things to think about

1   Implications of ideas of "civilized" and "primitive" art and music.
2   Criteria of selection of forms, techniques and examples, for example,

  a   to illuminate the relationship between art and society?
  b   to reflect what some would identify as "British culture"?
  c   to reflect the range of cultures and artistic traditions actually present in Britain?
  d   to show the arts as a world-wide enterprise, with a vast range of traditions?
  e   to concentrate on the arts of northern Europe but show the influence of and contact with non-European arts?
  f   to include anything which seems interesting?

These are not all mutually exclusive, though some are. Some are rather ambitious, but all except the second could claim to have a "multicultural" emphasis. If the aim is to reduce racism, which of the above stances would be more effective?

Some sources
Music
'Curriculum opportunities in a multicultural society', Chapter 11 (music), Craft and Bardell (eds.), Harper, 1984, 0 06 318285 8.
This chapter covers music so well that the best thing I can do is refer readers to it. Its resources list includes books for teachers, for classrooms, sources of instruments, performers, records, and specialist books.

Art
Alan Brine and Derek Bunyard, *Islamic Art: Vedic Square*, King Alfred's College, Winchester.
A booklet with a floppy disk for BBC Bs, generating complex geometric patterns like Islamic ones, derived from mathematical patterns.

'Curriculum opportunities in a multicultural society', Chapter 12 (art and design), Craft and Bardell (eds.), Harper, 1984, 0 06 318285 8.

CRE, *Britain's New Arts*, 1980. 0 902355 589.

Naseem Khan, *The Arts Britain Ignores*, CRE, 1976.

Horace Lashley, 'Arts education as an element of multicultural education', Chapter 8 of Arora and Duncan, see p.194.

Minority Arts Advisory Service, Beauchamp Lodge, 2 Warwick Crescent, London W2.

'World Studies Art in Action'. *World Studies Journal*, **5** no. 1, 1985, University of York, YO1 5DD.

PE teachers
Things to think about
1   Avoidance of "natural black talent myth".
2   Caution about "compensatory role" of PE.

3   Response to racial abuse in sport.
4   Sensitivity to religious/cultural factors in attitudes to PE.
5   Using team games etc. from other societies.

Some sources

E. Cashmore, *Black Sportsmen*, Routledge & Kegan Paul, 1982, 0 7100 9054 4.

'Curriculum opportunities in a multicultural society', Chapter 13, Craft and Bardell (eds.), Harper, 1984, 0 06 318285 8.

M. Willis, *Physical Education in a Multicultural Society*, Coventry LEA, Elm Bank Teachers' Centre, 1980.

Modern languages teachers

Things to think about

1   The "mother tongue" debate.
2   Use of introductory general "languages" course.
3   Recognition, as linguists, of the bilingualism or trilingualism of many pupils.
4   Knowing something of names and distribution of minority languages in the UK.
5   Racism in France, Germany etc.
6   Avoidance of stereotyping in books.
7   Awareness of colonial context of French (in particular), Francophone countries etc.

Some sources

'Curriculum opportunities in a multicultural society', Chapter 6, Craft and Bardell (eds.), Harper, 1984, 0 06 318285 8.

David Houlton and Richard Willey, *Supporting Children's Bilingualism*, Schools Council, 1983.

Linguistic Minorities Project, *Linguistic Minorities in England*, University of London Institute of Education, 1983, 0 85473 165 2.

Linguistic Minorities Project, *The Other Languages of England*, Routledge & Kegan Paul, 1985, 0 7102 0417 5.

M. Marland, *Multilingual Britain*, CILT, 1987, 0 948003 76 6.
Puts a coherent case for a curriculum policy for a multilingual world.

Jane Miller, *Many Voices, Bilingualism, Culture and Education*, Routledge & Kegan Paul, 1983, 07100 9341 1.

Euan Reid (ed.), *Minority Community Languages in School*, CILT, 1984, 0 903 466 70 8, 20 Carlton House Terrace, London SW1Y 5AP.

For introductory language courses, see the books edited by Eric Hawkins listed under English.

Language and Culture Guides, on Urdu, Hindi, Gujerati, Bengali, Punjabi etc., CILT, 20 Carlton House Terrace, London SW1Y 5AP.

For information on Caribbean dialects:
Viv Edwards, *The West Indian Language Issue in British Schools*, Routledge & Kegan Paul, 0 7100 0173 8.

D. Sutcliffe and A. Wong, *The Language of the Black Experience*, Blackwell, 1986, 0 631 148167.

For information on South Asian languages:
M. Mobbs, *Britain's South Asian Languages*, CILT, 1985. 0 948003 10 3.

Ralph Russell, *A New Course in Hindustani*, SOAS, 1980. Publications Dept, School of Oriental and African Studies, University of London, Malet St, WC1E 7HP.

C. Shackle, *South Asian Languages, A Handbook*, SOAS, 1985, 0261 5428.

Classroom materials

These are mentioned since they are the only French teaching materials I am aware of which have taken the issue of racism on board.

Richard Aplin, Ann Miller and Hugh Starkey, *Orientations*, Hodder and Stoughton, 1985, 0 340 24375 9 (pupils); 0 340 24373 2 (teachers).

Bibliobus, Mary Glasgow Publications, 140 Kensington Church St, London W8 4BN. (Free sample pack available.)

For anti-racist authentic materials in French for classroom use: *Okapi*, monthly magazine published by Bayard Press (contains strip cartoons, quizzes, articles etc.)

For introductory language courses, see the books edited by Eric Hawkins listed on p.199.

Teaching about "race": teachers' books

J. Bulmer (ed.), *Guide to Teaching of Anthropology in Schools and Colleges*, Extramural Division, School of Oriental and African Studies, University of London, Malet St, London WC1E 7HP.

Centre for Contemporary Studies, *Nazis in the Playground*, Ingersoll House, 202 New North Road, London N1 7BL.

'Curriculum Opportunities in a Multicultural Society', Chapter 3, Craft and Bardell (eds.), Harper, 1984, 0 06 318285 8.

Education for a Multi-Racial Society: Curriculum and Context 5—13, Schools Council pamphlet.

Education For All (The Swann Report), Chapter 5, Annexes C and D, and Chapter 6, HMSO, Cmnd 9453, 0 10 194530 2.

Simon Fisher and David Hicks, *World Studies 8—13, A Teacher's Handbook*, Longman, 1985, 0 05 003845 1.
Not solely about "race", but provides a wider educational context in which such teaching can take place.

Simon Fisher, (ed.), with Francis Magee and James Wetz, *Ideas Into Action, Curriculum for a Changing World*, World Studies Project, 0 9504434 4 1, c/o One World Trust, 24 Palace Chambers, Bridge St, London SW1A 2JT .

Stuart Hall, 'Teaching race', in James and Jeffcoate (eds.), listed under General.

David Hicks, *Minorities, a Teachers' Resource Book*, Heinemann, 1981, 0435 80416 2.

Gil Isaacson and Georgeanne Lamont, *Introductory Manual for Peace Education*, Manchester Peace Education Group, Manchester Polytechnic, Manchester M20 8RG.
Again not solely about "race", but it has useful classroom ideas about promoting empathy and about conflict resolution.

R. Jeffcoate, *Positive Image*, Readers and Writers/Chameleon, 1979, 0 906495 03 2.

V. S. Khan, *Minority Families in Britain*, Macmillan, 1979, 0 333 26190 9.

Gillian Klein, *Race Relations in the School Curriculum*, Centre for Contemporary Studies, 1983, Ingersoll House, 202 New North Rd, London N1 7BL.
This leaflet refers to many of the same items as this list, often with accompanying comments.

National Union of Teachers, *Combatting Racism in Schools*, 1981.

Lawrence Stenhouse et al., *Teaching About Race Relations*. Routledge & Kegan Paul, 1982, 07100 9036 6.

M. Straker-Welds (ed.), *Education for a Multicultural Society*, Chapter 24, A course on racism. Details under General works.

J. Tierney, (ed.), *Race, Migration and Schooling*, Holt Education, 1982, 0 03 910362 5.
The chapter by Dickinson is a guide to all the myths about race and immigration.

J. Watson, *Between Two Cultures*, Basil Blackwell, 1977, 0 631 18710 3.

Classroom materials

AFFOR, *Talking Chalk*, 173 Lozells Road, Birmingham, 1982.

Russell Ash, *Talking About Race*, Wayland, 1980, 85340 356 2.

Britain and India, an Uncommon Journey, Sandwell Department of Education, 1987. Pipes Lane, Oldbury, Warley, Sandwell.

Cartoon Stories on Immigration, National Extension College, 1978.

Different Worlds, Runnymede Trust/Borough of Lewisham, 1983.

Nigel File and Chris Power, *Black Settlers in Britain*. Heinemann, 1981, 0435 31173 5.

Tessa Hosking, *Black People in Britain 1650–1850*, Macmillan, 1984, 0 333 350 782.

Immigration, Batsford, 1976.
Its title shows the book's age and focus, and its last two chapters on Commonwealth immigration and immigrants in Britain today need rewriting. Earlier chapters may be useful for older pupils doing project work.

Mercia Last, *Race Relations in Britain*, Longman, 1979, 0582 22155 2.

Nance Lui Fyson and Sally Greenhill, *Family Life*, Macmillan, 1979, 0 333 21686 5.

Nance Lui Fyson and Sally Greenhill, *New Commonwealth Immigrants*, Macmillan, 1979, 0 333 21684 9.

Peter Moss, *Prejudice and Discrimination*, Counterpoint Series no. 4, Harrap, 1976, 0245 52819 9.

P. Page and H. Newman, *They Came to Britain*, Edward Arnold, 1985, 0 7131 7380 7.

Robin Richardson, *Fighting for Freedom*; *World in Conflict*; *Caring for the Planet*; *Progress and Poverty* (4 different books), Nelson/Schools Council, 1978, 0 17 438174 3.

David Ruddell and Mal Phillips-Bell, *The Race Relations Teaching Pack*, AFFOR, 1982, 0 907127 08 8.

D. Saunders, *The West Indians in Britain*, A. Shang, *The Chinese in Britain*, I. Bild, *The Jews in Britain*, Batsford, 1984, 0 71344 4 274, 0 71344 2360, 0 71344 2174.

All of these use a case study approach focusing on three real families, but I am not sure that the one on West Indians avoids some stereotyping. A headmaster who is quoted extensively speaks of "my West Indians" and says "It would be wrong to say that all West Indians are the same, yet they are ebullient." Though black parents are quoted there is nothing to balance this comment. For similar reasons I would not recommend *Multi-Ethnic Britain*, by Nance Lui Fyson, which in addition has some cultural/religious simply wrong.

E. Totten and T. Willard, *In The News — Race*, Wayland, 0 850 782945.

Rozina Visram, *Indians in Britain*, Batsford, 1987, 0 7134 5481 4.

Richard Whitburn, *Talking to People*, Macmillan, 1979, 0 333 26366 9.

Amrit Wilson, *Asian Women Speak Out*, National Extension College, Cambridge, 1979, 086082 152 8.

Some items under **history**, especially:

D. Killingray, *The Transatlantic Slave Trade*, Batsford, 1987, 07134 5469 5.

Roots of Racism, *Patterns of Racism*, *How Racism Came to Britain* and *The Fight Against Racism*, Institute of Race Relations, 1982, 1984 and 1986. Four excellent brief books, relating racism firmly to the economic forces which gave rise to it and sustain it. Well produced, and useable with older pupils.

Unlearning "Indian" Stereotypes, Racism and Sexism Resources Center, see p.198 for addresses

Whose World Is the World?, Poster Film Collective, BCM PFC, London WC1N 3XX.

I have kept almost entirely to Britain in this list, largely because I am suspicious of the tendency to look at racism everywhere except in Britain. At the same time it is worth mentioning that there are many good recent publications about South Africa, and a guide to resources can be obtained from the International Defence and Aid Fund, Canon Collins House, 64 Essex Rd, London N1 8LR (Tel 01 359 9181).

The Anti-Apartheid Movement can also provide up to date information on campaigns and useful background information, 13 Mandela St, London NW1 0DW (Tel 01 387 7966). Both of these organizations would welcome donations, however small.

Simulations

'BaFa BaFa', originated by Christian Aid, and reprinted in D. Hicks, *Minorities*, pp. 82—5, Heinemann, 1981, 0435 80416 2.

'Hassle', Community Service Volunteers, 237 Pentonville Road, London N20.

'Passport'   The simulation game described in chapter 4. Regrettably no longer available from Coventry Council for Racial Equality, who invented it.

Videos

Africa   A series on the forgotten history of black Africa hosted by Basil Davidson on Channel 4, and available from the Commonwealth Institute, Kensington High St, London W8.

Being White. Albany Video Distribution, 1987. The title is self-explanatory. Available from above at The Albany, Douglas Way, London SE8 4AG.

Black   Shown on BBC in August 1983. A comprehensive and very well made film about current British racism and its history. Available from BBC Enterprises, Woodlands, 80 Wood Lane, London W12 0TT (at a cost of £140!).

The Black & White Media Show, two BBC programmes in their Continuing Education series (which means it is legal to videotape it), of which the first is the most suitable, about media stereotyping. Too difficult for younger pupils.

Did You Know NAME Video, designed for use with youth in a variety of settings, with lots of fancy editing to keep their attention. 1987–8. NAME, PO Box 9, Walsall, W. Midlands.

The Eye of the Storm, the famous film about a teacher generating prejudice in a primary school classroom on the basis of eye colour. Available from Concord Films, 201 Felixstowe Rd, Ipswich, Suffolk.

Facing South 9.1.87, a documentary about racial harassment in two largely white areas in the South East. TVS.

Getting to Grips with Racism. BBC 1988. A series of five programmes produced for schools, and aiming to involve pupils. Accompanying booklet of same title, BBC Books, 1987, 0 563 34032 0.

It Ain't Half Racist Mum, made in the BBC *Open Door* series by the Campaign Against Racism in the Media. 14–15 year olds seem more able to spot the racism in the representation in this one. Available from Concord Films, 201 Felixstowe Rd, Ipswich, Suffolk or from The Other Cinema, 79 Wardour Street, London W1V 3TH who also stock some other anti-racist videos.

Motherland Available for hire (outside ILEA) from Central Film Library, Chalfont St Giles, Gerrards Cross, Bucks (Tel 02407 4111), £20.

Our People The original series was shown in 1979, and most of it re-broadcast at least three times in the schools' "English Programme" series. There is one on immigration myths, another on discrimination, and one on the colonial background. For sale or for hire from Guild Sound and Vision Ltd, 6 Royce Road, Peterborough PE1 5YB.

Passage to Britain Channel 4 series on immigration, possibly too detailed for school use. Note accompanying book and teaching pack listed in History section.

The Politics of Racial Hatred, in the ITV schools series *Politics, What's it all about?* This is about the Ku Klux Klan, and is essential viewing when doing any work on British racist organizations. Repeated fairly regularly.

Racism, the 4th R, again, made by school students, and conveys well to students in white areas how different life can be in a multiracial school. ALTARF, c/o Lambeth Teachers' Centre, Santley St, London SW4.

Scene, Every night we close the shutters, made by a group of young Asians in the East End, about racial harassment. Devastating.

Scene, Why Prejudice?, made by a group of school students, and speaks well to their contemporaries. Part of a BBC series but they do not know if this one will be repeated. Many teachers' centres apparently have it.

16 UP   One of a BBC series about various topics. Not, as far as I know, available for hire, but pupils liked it.

Teaching About Prejudice, BBC, produced by John Twitchin. Available from Concord Films, 201 Felixstowe Rd, Ipswich, Suffolk.

Tomorrow's People   Yorkshire TV, 1982, Television Centre, Kirkstall Road, Leeds LS3 1JS. Made for 9–13 year olds, but suitable for older students too.

The Whites of Their Eyes, made by Thames in 1981, as part of their *Viewpoint* series on media representation. Arguably too sophisticated. Address as above. CUP published an accompanying book for classroom use. For sale or hire from Guild Sound and Vision Ltd, 6 Royce Road, Peterborough PE1 5YB.

Filmstrips/tapeslides

The Enemy Within, Catholic Commission for Racial Justice, 1981. Available from the British Council of Churches, 2 Eaton Gate, London SW1. Much of this is aimed at adults, but the opening frames can effectively be used with teenagers.

Racism and Immigration, Mary Glasgow Publications, 140 Kensington Church St, London W8 4BN. Both well structured with reasonable accompanying teacher's booklets.

The Testimony of Chief Seattle, this goes well with the materials listed under history on native Americans. Published by the United Society for the Propagation of the Gospel.

Photopacks

On Bangladesh, India, Jamaica, and Botswana from OXFAM, 274 Banbury Rd, Oxford.

On Tanzania and Kenya, on urban/rural contrasts in India from Voluntary Committee on Overseas Aid and Development (VCOAD), International Development Centre, 25 Wilton Rd, London SW1 1JS.

Specialist bookshops

Independent Publishing Company, 38 Kennington Lane, London SE11.

Shakti Bookhouse, 46 High St, Southall, Middlesex.

Soma Books, Commonwealth Institute, Kensington High St, London W8.

Walter Rodney Publications, 5A Chigwel Place, Ealing, London W13 (has full catalogue).

Rachel Evans, Kiln Cottage, Culham, Abingdon, Oxford (has full catalogue).

Appendix 2   What do we call people?

Many white people are uncertain about what to call people who are not white — but "white" itself as a concept is by no means unproblematic. In common parlance it seems to mean "people of European ancestry", or even "people of northern European ancestry". Comparison of "white" skin with this piece of paper indicates that it is not meant to be taken literally. When did these people start using the term to describe themselves? According to the *Oxford English Dictionary*, first usages of "white" as a "racial" adjective were related to colonialism and British adventures abroad. We find reference in 1680 to non-whites as "of the blood of Cain"; another in 1876 distinguishing "whites" from a "Spanish Moor"; in 1726 "white" was used in Virginia to distinguish non-slaves and slaves, and in 1777 as an official classification in a census in Tobago.

This usage should not be taken for granted. Why was "pink" not used, since as a literal description it would be more accurate? A definitive answer lies in the preconceptions and assumptions of sixteenth- and seventeenth-century English (men) about the darker skinned people they were encountering and, one way or another, dominating, and in the nature of things these attitudes were not directly available to us. But it is clear that initial contacts and their developments did not proceed on a basis of equality. "Black" already carried all sorts of negative connotations in our language (and still does, arguably more so?) and thus its application to Africans served to symbolize for "whites" many of the things they feared or disliked or disapproved of. Current with this development were usages like "I meant to act white by you", meaning properly, honourably; and "there isn't a whiter man in the area" meaning more honourable, decent and the like. Partly from this colonial context and partly from before it, we now have a clear and striking contrast between the connotations of the words "white" and "black". Is it any wonder that

*Reprinted by permission from *Multicultural Teaching*, III, no. 1, 1984.

people sometimes hesitate about calling other people (or themselves) black?

Twenty years ago "coloured" was polite common currency for describing non-whites in Britain and the USA, except for "orientals" and American Indians, though I should say that the later may ask nowadays to be described as "Native Americans". It was also, of course, a legal category in South Africa, and still is. People of African descent in the USA adpoted the slogan "Black is Beautiful" in the 1960s, to rid themselves of the negative connotations of the word "black"; for them "coloured" is a euphemism, an apology for a skin colour which is linguistically and socially defined as undesirable.

There is little doubt that this was a matter which went very deep at the time. Though they should not be taken too simply, there are convincing studies which show many black children devaluing their own colour to the extent of denying it (Milner, 1975, 1983; Stone 1981); colour/status graduations were widely accepted among "coloured" people in the USA and the Caribbean; skin lightening creams were on the market; as were hair straightening devices and European hair wigs (have a look at an early Supremes LP cover). As a youth says at the beginning of the film documentary *Black*:

No black person who can truly say he is proud to be black can do so without having gone through a struggle, and a struggle of the hardest and most violent kind—within himself.

Thus the acceptability of the word "black" has grown *among those to whom it is applied* at the same time as the decline in acceptability of the word "coloured". As a rejection of the euphemistic resonances of "coloured", "black" was never intended as a literal adjective, it is a *political and social* term. In fact, of course, it always was such a term. People who perjoratively referred to "the blacks" made no distinctions about the actual skin tone; they were delineating a social category. As many people knew to their cost, one black great-great grandparent among fifteen white ones was enough to make you "a nigger", as in Nazi Germany one Jewish grandparent made you a Jew.

Being unable to ignore or sweep away the social distinction *white* people had created, black people went for redefining its significance in American social consciousness. The same process can be identified in a modified way in Britain.

"Black" is not yet a word which whites in Britain deal with easily. One can often sense circumlocutions, evasions or hesitations, sentences away from its possible use. So before going into the maze of different groupings in Britain, let me suggest that the word "black" has a certain limited applicability in the same sense as it has in the USA, namely a group of people socially defined not by themselves intially but by the majority (dominant, white) group. "Blacks" are socially defined by derogatory terms by the discrimination in, for instance, employment which we know takes place; by the conditions of the Race Relations Acts which were designed almost entirely with them in mind; and by the operation of the Nationality Act. Thus "black" in Britain is a socio/political term; it defines a group of people who have in common certain relationships with society, i.e. experience of racism, and it is widely recognized as such by "black" people themselves. Used in this sense, it is unlikely to cause offence, and there is a consistency in meaning even when referring to groups as diverse as Ismaili Muslims from the Gujerat via Kenya and British born children of a Welsh mother and a Trinidian father.

White people who nevertheless find *that* difficult might perhaps look at their own anxieties about the word "black" and its connotations for them, rather than possible offensiveness to others. It is increasingly more acceptable to black people than the word "coloured". (An exception that has been suggested to me may be East African Asians who were used to an important social and economic distinction between themselves and Africans, and who therefore may not welcome being included in a catch-all term.)

There are lots of other words and phrases used to refer to Britain's black population. In identifying and commenting on them, I am not making suggestions to other whites about what "we" should call "them"; that would be racist arrogance. The following list is a cumulation of the views of black people — written and spoken — and has itself been discussed among black people.

Immigrants

No longer an accurate term for the 43 per cent of black people born in Britain, nor particularly helpful in describing a population the majority of whom have lived in Britain for fifteen years or more. The term also technically includes white immigrants, though it is seldom used that way . . . same applies to "*people from overseas*". The thinking behind these terms becomes most blatantly absurd when press and people speak of *second generation immigrants*.

Other races/minority races

The problem with the word "race" is that there is no such thing. Scientifically or biologically speaking, the significance of skin colour and certain physical features is entirely social, so "race" is really a social evaluation of a cluster of physical characteristics. For this reason some people always put the word in quotes to signify that it is really one kind of term masquerading as another. Thus "race" relations or racism refer to the consequence of placing *social* significance on some *biological* facts which have no inherent social meaning in themselves. In principle then, to refer to black people in Britain by one of the above terms carries with it some pernicious assumptions.

Half-caste

The term is widely disliked in the USA, and increasingly in Britain (But why "caste"?). I am told that "mixed race" is preferred, not in the (non) sense of being biologically half one "race" and half another, but in the social sense. I am not aware of any other term for people of black and white parents, though some would choose to describe *themselves* as "black".

Non-whites

Not generally found offensive and having the advantage of clearly indentifying who the speaker means. But why not call "whites" "non-blacks"? Because it's our country? Its very clarity tells us something about our assumptions; "non-Europeans" is a very accepted term in South Africa — among whites!

Coloured (s)

As mentioned earlier, declining in acceptability to black people themselves; seen as a euphemism.

Black and brown people

A catch-all term that is unlikely to offend, but there are times when it fits very uncomfortably into a sentence!

People of colour

Growing in popularity among . . . people of colour. Maybe it will include the Chinese, who are not included in any other term.

Blacks and black people

The former can be used perjoratively; otherwise the most acceptable term in current use. The justification for its use is outlined earlier but, alas, nothing is simple. Are the Chinese politically "black"? The Arabs in Britain? The Irish? (Obviously at some stage we have to accept there is not likely to be a single neat word which sums up the complex social relations we are dealing with.) Many Black people prefer the word to have a capital letter when used in the political rather than simple adjectival sense.

Ethnic group

Means (fairly imprecisely) a largely endogamous group of people sharing some cultural features, typically language and religion. In the western world they are quite likely to be immigrants or their descendents and so are likely to have some distinguishing physical features in common. This logically includes the "English" and the Welsh, so it is fairly imprecise to say "ethnic groups" when one means "black", and it is euphemistic.

Ethnic (s)

Meaningless in this context, used as a euphemism.

Ethnic minority groups (s)

Technically accurate and can be used for all such groups or a particular one. Sometimes a bit of a mouthful, sometimes comes out like a euphemism. Minority ethnic groups is preferred.

Minority group

Tends to have a wider implications than simply numbers, so it usually carries connotations of disadvantage. It does not make a lot of sense when applied to blacks in South Africa, or to women. It can include other groups like the disabled, gays, etc.

Cultural minorities

Technically exact, but CMs tend not to be socially significant unless they are somehow tied up with the notion of "race". Racists categorize cultures according to ideas of "race", and if they use "culture" it's beware of speaking as if cultures were the real basis for inequalities. be aware of speaking as if cultures were the real basis for inequalities. On the other hand there are occasions (and there ought to be more) where being aware of cultural differences within black groups is vital. It's a code word, and is generally understood as referring to certain groups, but why not the British aristocracy — are not they a cultural minority?

Black British

Fairly generally acceptable depending on the context it is used in. It has the advantage of stressing that the people concerned are British; some people would see it as only including those of African or Caribbean descent.

Negro/Negroid/Negress

Not welcomed, it's too close to "nigger". Originally of course it was meant to be neutral, but even if it was, uses change.

West Indian

A term still acceptable to many, but inaccurate in respect of people born in Britain, and can be a sign of ignorance if the many differences between the islands are relevant to the particular context.

People of West Indian background

Unlikely to sound offensive, unless the user is obviously trying to avoid saying "Black". But it can be a long phrase to fit in.

African

Fine if you know the person/people concerned *are* African. Just like calling "us" "European".

Jamaican

Fine if you know the person/people concerned *are* Jamaican. Can be taken as ignorant and insulting otherwise.

Afro-Caribbean

Widely used and acceptable to almost anyone of that background. Somehow implies roots without denying Britishness.

Asian

Geographically confusing since it ought to include the Chinese, but does not. Usually taken to mean those originating in the Indian sub-continent, who in fact come from several distinct regions in India, Pakistan and Bangladesh. Generally acceptable to the people concerned *unless* it is used in a context where the many differences between "Asian" groups ought to be recognized, in which case it will be taken for ignorance at least.

People of Asian background

A term which is deliberately general amd makes no pretence at distinguishing different Asian groups; it has the advantage of including their British born children.

British Asians

As with black British, states an important fact, therefore a better term than simply "Asian".

Pakistani/Indian

As with "Jamaican" etc. fine if it's accurate, and note that Bangladeshis are often forgotten.

East African Asians

A small but important distinction; people whose relatives earlier this century went to Kenya, Uganda or Tanzania from some of the areas in India and Pakistan which later sent immigrants to Britain.

Index